GO

**A Payden Beck
Crime Thriller
by
MICHAEL GOLVACH**

GO
Payden Beck Crime Thriller – Book 4
Copyright © 2023 by Michael Golvach

All rights reserved. No part of this book may be used or reproduced in any manner whatsoever, without written permission, except in the case of brief quotations embedded in articles and reviews. For more information, please contact publisher at Publisher@EvolvedPub.com.

FIRST EDITION SOFTCOVER
ISBN: 1622532619
ISBN-13: 978-1-62253-261-2

Editor: Becky Stephens
Cover Artist: Richard Tran
Interior Designer: Lane Diamond

EVOLVED PUBLISHING™
www.EvolvedPub.com
Evolved Publishing LLC
Butler, Wisconsin, USA

Go is a work of fiction. All names, characters, places, and incidents are the product of the author's imagination, or are used fictitiously. Any resemblance to actual events or persons, living or dead, is entirely coincidental.

Printed in Book Antiqua font.

BOOKS BY MICHAEL GOLVACH

PAYDEN BECK CRIME THRILLER
Book 1: *10-30*
Book 2 (Book Omega): *Dormir*
Book 3: *Bad*
Book 4: *Go*

OTHER BOOKS/NOVELS
Bloody Gullets
Fix
Home
Jenny
Missing Pieces
Transmissions

mikegolvach.net

DEDICATION

For Ian Michael,

For being a good son and my best friend. For all the hours we've spent talking and watching movies. For everything you have been, are, and will be. And for reading this book without judgment.

I love you.

Prologue

READY, SET

Welcome back, Mr. Beck. It seems such a long time since you knuckled under, yet it's only been two years. Two years since you moved away from the town in which you insist on continuing to work. Two years since you started trying to trick us into believing you'd become obedient. We know why, but you don't own 'you' anymore. When will the fight in you finally die? How many more lives do we have to destroy before you truly submit?

Valarie Dooley née Jude—hopefully, the last woman you'll ever care for—has a family of her own now. With a child to take care of who isn't you. And, one merciful day, you'll forget her. She no longer wants, nor needs, you. She may as well be gone. If you'd have trusted her, she'd be with you still. Loyal. At your side. No matter what you'd done, what you're doing or what you've yet to do. And we wouldn't be able to stomach that kind of blind devotion. Pure weakness.

You still have your pet. Though you should let her go, too. Permanently. You know what we mean.

Have fun, Mr. Beck. Accept your place. What hasn't been taken from you already is slowly being ripped away. Embrace the sensation. Emptiness is bliss.

Now, get back to it. You've got a job to live and our life to work.

Don't beg. You're better than that.
Do as you're told.
Punish. Obey.
Your name is Payden Beck and you are a puppet. Dance.
Do as you're told.
Go.

I

A figure, dressed in black from shoes to hooded sweatshirt—its back to the wall—waits in an alley two blocks down from the local pub. Standing as close to the corner as possible and listening. Glancing left and right, checking for witnesses.

"Fifty," a dealer's voice whispers from around the corner.

The figure pulls out a revolver, cocking it.

"Fifty or you go to the projects," the dealer continues. "Trust me. They'll send you home with nothing. Not even the cash you brought."

"But," a much younger-sounding voice pleads, "we only have forty."

There wouldn't be a sale made. No crime, no punishment. No harm.

Not good enough. Not anymore.

The figure walks calmly around the corner, staying in the shadows.

The dealer hears footsteps and turns to look.

The two youths begin to run.

"Stop," the figure calls out, its voice low, guttural.

The two boys slow their gait and turn around as the dealer pockets what he's peddling.

"Please," the first of the boys says. "We didn't do anything, I swear."

The figure shakes its head. "You. The other idiot. Truth or else."

The second boy opens his mouth. Too frightened to form words.

"Okay," the first boy continues. "We were trying to buy—"

The dealer pushes himself off the wall he's rested his back against. "Already paid." He motions for the boys to come back to him, shaking his head and waving the figure off. "Pigs." He turns to face the boys. "Forty. Deal?"

The figure moves forward. "What do you think is happening here?"

"Look." The dealer puts his right hand over his eyes, squinting. Unable to make out the figure's face. "I not pay you to cost me. Fuck off."

The figure rushes the dealer, grabbing his shoulder and spinning him around. Twisting the dealer's arm behind his back, pushing up and pressing its gun against the dealer's opposite temple. Hiding its face from the boys, who back away.

The dealer stifles a howl of pain.

"Don't move," the figure barks.

The boys stop, looking on, addled, as the figure releases its grip on the dealer's arm.

The dealer turns to face the figure quickly, a look of recognition in his eyes. "*Puta*. I'll see you—"

The figure presses its gun's barrel's tip under the dealer's chin and fires, sending a bullet up and to the right. Covering its face with its other hand to keep the boys from seeing during the brief muzzle flash. Growling at them afterward. "This life ain't got no future. Understand?"

The boys nod, then turn and run.

The figure wipes the gun clean and pockets it. Making sure not to step in the mess the gunshot has made of the dealer's head and staying out of range of the weakening spray of blood.

The sound of the boys' feet furiously pounding the pavement trails off into silence.

The figure fades back into the shadows.

***

Two other near-identical incidents occurred that night. Only one noise complaint was called in. After the killing was done.

II

Payden Beck walked into the office he shared with his long-time partner—Bryan Verrill—fresh from his weekly Monday-morning reprimand. Judging by the look on Payden's face and the time on the clock, relations weren't getting any better between him and the captain. Judging by the look on Bryan's face, that wasn't a surprise.

Payden hung his jacket next to Bryan's on the door's coat hook and took a seat on his side of their facing desks.

Bryan opened his mouth to speak and Payden held up a hand. "Whatever answer you want to hear, you stone-faced prick."

Bryan looked down, almost smiling. "Good morning, Beck."

"Good?" Payden asked. "For who?"

"Us. What were you and the captain arguing about? I figured it was the dealers who got killed last night."

"Nothing about that. But we'll catch the case soon enough."

Bryan nodded, then shook his head, his expression lifeless.

"What's got you all giddy, Verrill? Can't be your woman. You been seeing too much of her lately." Payden looked at the ceiling. "You two finally tying the noose—I mean, knot?"

Bryan tapped his fingers on his desk. "We're—"

"Still at someday?"

"I am so done with you." Bryan looked to his right. "And your bullshit."

"Your life."

"You don't understand. It's complicated."

"No it's not." Payden picked up his desk's phone to check for a dial tone. Hearing it, he hung up. "It's simple. She said yes two years ago and she's been putting off the big day ever since. Why is that, you think?"

"It doesn't—"

Payden shook his head. "Look at the facts. Pretend you're a detective. She started seeing some other guy two odd years ago. He's still on her chain. She ain't ready to give up her options yet."

"I know for a fact she hasn't been cheating on me." Bryan leant forward, staring Payden in the eyes. "Never has. Anyway—" Bryan looked away again. "Forget it."

"I could," Payden said. "But you got to do something about your situation. It's unreasonable."

"As I was saying, it doesn't matter. Mindy and me? We're through."

"When?" Payden smiled. "This weekend? You gave Mindy the boot?"

"That's not what I—But, no. She broke it off. I don't want to talk about it."

"Of course you don't. But I need to have words with your woman."

"She's not my—What for?"

"You saying you don't want me to see if I can turn her around?"

"There's nothing to turn around." Bryan leant back in his chair.

Payden stood and grabbed his jacket from the door, slipping it on. "You kids have been going at this too long to just split."

Bryan stood and moved to grab his jacket. "Leave it alone. That window's closed."

"So, you're saying you wouldn't fly into it now? Under no circumstance?" Payden scoffed. "Bullshit."

Bryan shook his head. "We've got jobs to do."

"Helping the patrolling officers out?"

"No. Investigating last night's murders."

"That's what we do for a living. We're talking about your life. And the captain didn't say nothing about us catching the case, yet. We'll go see her together, yeah?"

"No, we won't." Bryan put on his jacket. "Why do you care? I thought you hated her. You should be happy for me."

"Sentimental, I guess."

Bryan opened their office's door. "Let it go. I have. Why am I talking you down?"

Payden threw his hands in the air. "Fine. I'll just chalk it up to some partnerships don't last forever."

Detective Lester Mansfield entered the station, wearing a smart suit and a smile, as Payden and Bryan approached the front door. "Did you hear?" Lester asked.

Payden looked Lester up and down, detecting a blush through the dark skin of Lester's cheeks before turning away. "Congratulations are in order, I understand."

Bryan patted Lester on the shoulder. "Way to go, Les. You paid your dues. Welcome to detective division."

"Thank you," Lester said, giving Bryan a quick handshake and looking at Payden, who stared at the front door.

"Of course." Bryan gave Payden a nudge.

Payden snapped out of his daze. "We good to go?"

Bryan motioned with his eyes toward Lester.

Payden looked at Lester, whose smile had begun to crack, and nodded. "Something you wanted?"

"No," Lester said, forcing himself to smile wider. "Here to see the captain about assignment."

"Fascinating. Maybe you and whoever they stuck you with—"

Lester puffed out his chest. "Captain says he wants to see me and Verrill."

Bryan looked at Lester and nodded, then at Payden, something resembling satisfaction in his features.

Payden patted Bryan on the back, moving to the door and cracking it open. "I'm heading out. Taking the car." His gaze floated from Bryan to Lester. "You okay with that, Sam—"

Lester put his hands on his hips. "My name isn't—"

"Yet another thing that don't mean shit to me." Payden opened the front door, letting it close behind him as he exited the station.

Lester opened the front door wide as Payden ignored him. "My name is Lester. Detective Mansfield to you. I passed the writtens."

"Despite the colour of your skin?" Payden yawned, looking back. "Bilford, too?"

Lester clenched his fists, shaking his head.

"Who'd have guessed you were the smarter monkey?"

Bryan pulled Lester back when he saw his right fist cock. "You said the captain wants to see us." He gave Payden a nod. "Don't worry about Beck. If you can't take what he's dishing out, you're no good to any of us."

"Fuck him, anyway," Lester said, releasing his hold on the door and turning to walk with Bryan to the captain's office.

Payden bobbed his eyebrows. "Give Bilford my love, black superman. Or throw him that fuck you owe me."

Before the door finished closing behind Payden again, Bryan called out, "Remember, Beck. My life. Stay out of it."

Payden yelled back. "Just get us the case."

III

Payden pulled his unmarked car to the kerb beside Mindy Hayden's home. Wondering what Lester, Bryan and the captain had to discuss Lester's first day as a working detective. Fearing the captain was going to do the right thing and partner Bryan up with the new fish. Though it would give Payden the freedom to work on his own, he and Bryan had spent years together, from the academy on. They had secrets. They held a trust — with regard to the job and what they'd done to get things done — that couldn't be shared freely. Not with anyone they didn't know wasn't a rat.

What bothered him most was that Mindy had kicked Bryan out of her life. Though Mindy didn't exist in his vision of a tolerable world, what she'd done upset the natural order of things. One less way to maintain control.

He exited his car and rolled his eyes as he marched to her home's door. Knocking for reasons he didn't understand and didn't care to.

The door opened a few moments later and Mindy backed up, beckoning him. Dressed in a pair of grey cotton shorts and a matching grey cotton T-shirt. Braless, as usual, to remind everyone small breasts flattered the female form. Her slender frame still nothing but soft, white fat, but perfectly sculpted, as her diet and modicum of exercise kept it.

Payden walked inside, closing the door behind him. She turned, walking away and waving for him to follow as he watched her bottom sway and wondered if she'd bothered wearing any underwear at all.

"Why are you here at this hour?" Mindy asked. "You're getting sloppy."

Payden shook his head and raced to catch Mindy by the arm, spinning her around to face him before she could reach the kitchen.

"Something urgent?" She looked at him, her lips trembling as she tried to smile and turned her head to the side, wincing.

Payden released his grip on her arm. "You finally got home security? I guess you ain't fucking around no more."

Mindy looked disturbed. "What are you talking about?"

"The echo. Very faint. They did a shit job." He looked around the room. "No video yet?"

"I'm sorry?" she asked, putting her hand to her ear.

"Where's the tape?"

The weak smile disappeared from Mindy's lips as she fussed with her hair. "What tape? You think—"

"Where?" Payden barked.

"Kitchen cupboard. Top right corner."

Payden stormed into the kitchen, rifling through the cupboard until he found the tape unit, wired, recording to local micro-cassettes. "What's this I hear about you dumping Verrill?" he asked as he approached her. "You think dumping him means you can talk? Gets you free of me?"

Mindy smirked, standing in the kitchen doorway, barely keeping herself from wincing again as she unconsciously nodded. "Why? You know I would never say anything to anyone about us, with or without him in my life. I'm not stupid and I'm not a masochist. I know the rules."

"I want you to set a date." He pointed to the phone in the kitchen. "Call Verrill before he gets off work. Apologise. No more fucking him around. The wedding's happening."

"No. We're over, and—"

Payden cracked her across the mouth, nearly dropping her, and dragged her by the elbow to the kitchen counter beside the sink.

Mindy flinched involuntarily when Payden released her, squaring her jaw as her body shook and she got her hair back in order. "Go ahead. I dare you to—"

Payden gave her another punishing smack, bumping her against the counter. Shaking her up harder. Taking her by surprise even when she was expecting punishment.

Mindy glanced away, then fixed Payden's gaze as she fought to keep from raising her hands to defend her face. "Please, go."

He grabbed her by the hair, picking a hand towel up from beside the sink and covering her face with it. "You ain't ruining Verrill's life. Promise me or you're dead. You know there's at least a hundred ways I can make your end look like an accident."

Mindy squirmed.

"And you know I will if you press it." Payden pushed her head, face up, into the sink's basin.

"No," Mindy screamed, her body shaking and fighting. Her panicked breath ensuring the hand towel stuck to her face, curbing her respiration.

Payden turned on the sink's tap, holding Mindy in place with all his strength. Feeling the terror that owned every inch of her body.

"I'll take Bryan back," she said, fighting for breath. Anticipating the water beginning to pour through the hand towel and nearly drowning her, over and over again. "I promise."

Payden released her and she dropped to the floor along with the hand towel.

Payden pulled Mindy to her feet. "You always got to make things difficult." He let go of her and turned off the tap. "You're taking Verrill back. Never letting him go. Did you lie to me?"

She shook her head, her eyes going wide, and Payden grabbed her by the chin.

"No? Say it. Tell me, you two-faced bitch."

Mindy shook her head more violently when Payden released his grip. "No, I swear."

"How he can love you, I don't understand." He knocked her back a step with another vicious slap. "You'll always be a worthless piece of shit. Alive or dead."

"Okay." She grabbed the counter to keep her balance, feeling the pain spread from her mouth through her entire body, and watched Payden open the cupboard, remove the micro-cassette from the tape unit, pocket it, walk toward the door and give her a wink.

"Do what you promised me. As soon as possible. Make it stick or you're my pet forever." Payden made a gun of his free hand as his other grabbed the front door's knob. "And forever don't last long. Not when I get sick and tired of ruining you. You're free. Don't fuck it up." He sneered. "Go for the life you think you deserve. Verrill will take you back. We both know that. Don't forget to put another tape in."

Payden closed the door behind him and Mindy rushed to lock it. Dropping to the floor with her back against it, listening to Payden whistling as he walked away. Letting the tears flow as she shook with horror and held herself. Just as psychologically disoriented as

Payden had ensured she'd always be. Having taken more punishment from her abuser and feeling powerless to do anything to stop it. Considering she could finally marry Bryan and feeling lost. The blessing of her desired life given to her by Payden, and her deep feeling of thankfulness for his kindness and generosity. Completely relieved, filled with dread, and utterly confused. Weeping like an infant and wishing she could stop imagining Payden had only stopped by to beat and rape her that morning, for reasons she couldn't admit even to herself.

IV

Payden walked into the town grocery. Considering whether Mindy was done playing games, and still concerned about the previous evening's events. The dealers under the department's protection who'd been ended. Hoping the force wouldn't put too many resources behind finding their killers since, though the corruption in his precinct had become so openly accepted they may as well have been running ads in the local paper, if Internal Affairs got involved, they'd ask too many people questions. And not everyone, including Payden, was on board with the pay-to-play model the police department had begun employing to keep a cap on drug-related violence.

Michael Dooley greeted him, from his place bagging groceries, as Payden walked past the registers. Waving him over. "Got a second?"

Payden nodded and walked to Michael. "What's the news, Mickey?"

"Ask you a favour?" He motioned with his eyes and Payden looked to see the manager watching them.

Payden flashed his badge and the manager looked away. "What's up?"

"It's Val. Only been a year since she gave birth—while we're on the subject, when are you coming by to see the kid?—and she's already talking about going back to work."

Payden shrugged, not answering Michael's question. "Valarie does what she wants. If you can't convince her not to get a job, I don't think I'm going to be able to."

"Not that," Michael said, chuckling. "I just can't leave right now. Don't want to lose the job I got, you know?"

"Not entirely. What's up? She here?"

Michael nodded.

"Who's watching the little one?"

"Val's a wreck, but she won't barely let our out-of-town guest do a thing to help, except hang at our home."

"Guest?" Payden asked, quickly changing the subject. "Back on Valarie. She's a wreck. And?"

"She's all fucked-out from walking here. The kid still keeps us up all hours." Michael cleared his throat. "You mind giving her a lift home? She's asking me, but I'm stuck, like I said."

Payden nodded. "Yeah, no worries. I'm just here to pick up a sandwich at the deli counter."

Michael looked past Payden and made a quick motion with his free hand.

By the time Payden could look over his shoulder, whomever Michael had signalled was out of sight. "If it makes you feel better, I'll stop in and see the kid. She ain't going to remember me, though."

Michael gave him a puzzled look.

"Your question. The reason I ain't stopped by to visit yet. Figured you two want your privacy, and the kid ain't going to remember me at her age."

"According to Val, kids remember tones of voices. Some shit like that. You stop by early, before they start forming memories that last, they'll put you together with your voice later. They'll know you better, see?

Maybe. Val reads all the books. She'll tell you if you ask. So, I'm warning you. Don't ask."

Payden nodded. "I'll steer clear of the subject." Payden pointed behind him with his thumb. "Just let me go grab my sandwich."

Michael began loading bagged groceries into a customer's empty shopping cart. "Got you."

"Cool. Catch you in a few. Just take me a second to grab—" Payden felt a pair of arms wrap gently around his waist. Looking down, he smiled.

"A roast beef sandwich?" Valarie Dooley asked, rubbing the wrapped sandwich against his stomach. "You're welcome."

Payden turned around as Valarie loosed her hold, not letting go. "You didn't give me a chance to thank—"

"You would have?" Valarie shook her head, looking trim in a white T-shirt with no bra beneath and a pair of loose-fitting light-blue jeans. Her face still as beautiful as he'd ever seen. Perhaps more so, with her hair pulled back in a ponytail held in place with rubber bands. Becoming more appetising with age.

Payden gave her a kiss on the forehead. "I was considering it."

Valarie released her hold. "You'll never change." She bobbed her eyebrows at Michael, motioning with her head toward the sliding front doors.

Payden put his left arm around Valarie's shoulders, realising she hadn't purchased anything but his sandwich, if she'd paid for that. "Why don't I give you a ride home? Save Mickey some grief from the boss and give us a chance to catch up?"

Valarie nodded, handing Payden the sandwich and wrapping her right arm around his waist, winking at Michael. "It's a bit early in my marriage to be stepping out with another man, but what the hell."

Michael laughed. "Have fun, kids." He gave Payden a nod and lowered his voice. "Thanks, buddy."

Payden nodded in reply as he turned himself and Valarie toward the front doors. Feeling like he was cheating with her, as she'd subtly suggested. Wishing that were true.

V

Valarie and Payden made it to his car five minutes after they exited the grocery. Valarie not speaking a word as they'd walked, only watching Payden's face and fixing his gaze when he looked to her, saw she was checking to see if he was going to take in her form, and turned his face forward again. She laughed softly every time their eyes briefly met, giving his waist a squeeze. Letting out an almost imperceptible sigh each time she felt how solid and muscular his stomach had become over the past few years.

When he opened the car door for her, she hunched over slightly and he moved to help her take a seat.

She smacked his hands. "I'm not dying, Payden. I'm just tired. You'll understand when you have kids."

Payden nodded and walked to the driver's side of the car, letting Valarie seat herself and close her own door. By the time he got to his door, she'd already unlocked it from the inside.

Payden took his seat and closed his door. "You'll never change, either."

He pulled out of the parking space and headed toward her home. In the once-bad part of town the increase in crime over the years had managed to turn into the best part.

"Meaning?" she asked, not wearing her seatbelt and turning her body to face him.

"Meaning, you always did that before. Opened my door for me. It's a good thing. Any girl don't do that ain't worth keeping."

"Am I a keeper?" Valarie asked. "If you say so. Your almost-niece disagrees, I think."

Payden glanced at Valarie. "You want me to stop by? I got a few minutes before I got to get back to work."

"Of course." Valarie yawned, not closing her eyes completely as she stretched. "As long as you can keep from ogling me."

"I wasn't—"

Valarie rubbed Payden's right thigh, giving his body a thorough inspection with her eyes. "If you apologise for finding me attractive right now, I swear to God I'll make your death look like an accident."

Payden chuckled, giving her a look and losing himself for a moment. "I fucked up when I let you go. You're perfect." He cleared his throat. "For me, anyway."

Payden pulled his car to the kerb a house down from Valarie's.

Valarie leant her head toward him. "Why are we stopping here?"

"I just figured, since Mickey said—"

"Don't blame him for what you choose to do," Valarie said, her voice huskier. "You still have serious trust issues. If you're letting me out to walk a few feet because you don't want to meet my child, you can tell me." She paused. "So tell me. Take that step. You have to grow up sometime, no?"

"It's not that," Payden replied, relaxing.

"What then?" Valarie pulled her knees to her chest, holding them loosely and resting her feet on the seat cushion. "What's the issue? Tell me." She glanced away.

"Tell me, or my daughter disappears from your life just like I did."

"Threatening me?"

Valarie nodded, rubbing her nose.

"I really did fuck up."

Valarie chuckled. "That's established. Why aren't you going to come inside and see my girl? The truth. Tell me."

"Mickey let me know you have a guest from out of town over, watching your kid and, to be honest, I don't want to make any new friends."

Valarie pulled her head back. "Who? My brother, Jimmy?"

"You got a brother? I never knew that." Payden looked at her, rubbing his ear.

"Our relationship never took that next step." Valarie switched to sitting normally, not moving to open her door, looking forward. "And I wish I was an only child. You'll understand if you meet him. He's a pain in the ass, but the best we can do for day care. Can't afford to pay for it on Mickey's wage. If I didn't own the house already...."

"What?"

"He's a bad guy, in both senses."

"That term has more than two senses."

"You know what I mean. He's an asshole and he doesn't have a regular job. Makes his money somehow. It's not legitimate. If we could find a halfway-decent sitter who'd work for free—or room and board, as is the case with my brother—I'd kick him out this second. He's not going to be a good influence on my daughter. It's bad enough she already knows his voice. And his temper." She looked at Payden, her eyes widening. "Did you know that when kids hear your voice before they begin to develop long-term memory, they can still—"

Payden held up a finger. "Let me stop you right there. Mickey warned me what would happen if I let you start going down that road."

Valarie squinted. "Really?" She grabbed Payden's right thigh with both hands, causing him to flinch. She looked down quickly, noting his trouser bulge. "Jesus, Payden. And, thank you for the compliment, even if you didn't voice it, but forget Mickey and his complete disinterest in child rearing." She released her hands. "Anyway, I should be going." She gave him a quick, soft kiss on the lips. "Get back to work. Go catch whoever snuffed those drug dealers last night. Read about it in the morning paper. And, when you catch him, though it will probably downgrade my neighbourhood and put an end to the gentrification, let him go."

"I have to," Payden said. "You know why."

Valarie opened her door and looked back into Payden's eyes. Seeing no deception in them—no hint of humour—and shaking her head. "Your secret's safe with me. You know that. And, thanks. For trusting me with that. It wasn't so hard, was it? And we're stronger now." She glanced away, looking lost. "I guess I met you, and Mickey, a little too soon. My whole life, I've been too eager. In a big rush to get to the end, I guess.... Promise you'll come see my daughter soon?"

"On a lunch break this week, if I can?"

Valarie nodded. "That would be great. You might have to meet Jimmy, but maybe he'll leave for a while when he hears a cop's coming over."

"I'll call you. But, first, I got to know."

"What?"

"The ponytail. Why rubber bands?"

"My new look?" She touched at her hair. "It's convenient. Cheap. Not very classy, I guess. Do you not like it?" She looked at him as she felt around the rubber bands, genuinely concerned.

"I love it."

Valarie gave him the finger. "I don't need my ass kissed."

"I would never—" Payden blushed. "I mean, figuratively."

"For God's sake, Payden." Valarie batted at air in his general direction. "Okay. I believe you."

"Keep wearing those. Seriously. They don't make you look like you live in a trailer." He smiled, a hint of mist in his eyes Valarie noted which made her heart skip a beat. "They're you. Adorable."

She put her hands between her breasts and tilted her head to the side.

"I'll call you. Or stop by, like I said. If I can't do a lunch break—Any time? You'll be home?"

Valarie nodded, blew Payden a kiss—which he returned—and exited the car, closing her door gently as she whispered on fragile breath. "Any time. I'll always be there for you—I mean, here."

Payden stayed in his car, devouring his roast beef sandwich, until he saw Valarie enter her home safely. Noting her looking back in his direction over and over as she did, a smile on her face. Giving him a wave goodbye as she opened her door. A wave he returned, though he was sure she couldn't see it.

Then he headed back to work. To find out where he stood in the new hierarchy in detective division. Hoping he'd be working solo soon, yet feeling strangely alone.

VI

Payden returned to the station to find Bryan gone. Most likely showing Lester how things worked when there was action. Lester would probably be a good detective, and he'd passed the tests, but the correct answers to those questions could get you killed if you took them too seriously.

As soon as he quit looking for Bryan and began walking to their room, officer Jonathon Bilford passed him, dressed in civilian clothes.

"Captain wants to see you," Bilford said as he walked toward the front door, not looking back.

"About?" Payden slowed his walk.

"I give a shit."

The door closed behind Bilford and Payden nodded, then walked through the bullpen to the captain's office, knocking on the door three times.

"Come in," the captain's voice called and Payden entered his office, closing the door behind him and moving to stand with his back a few inches from the wall, in front of the captain's desk.

Payden nodded. "You wanted to see me? Bilford said—"

"Forget about him," the captain snapped. "In his capacity as a messenger, he's still okay in my book, but he's out. You noticed he wasn't wearing a uniform, right?"

"What do you mean, he's out?"

"What do you think?" The captain got up from his seat and walked to Payden. "Wanted off nights. I gave him two options. He chose to walk."

"What was his other option?"

"Suck my dick." The captain got in Payden's face, making fists as he dropped his hands to his sides. "He requested transfer. He got it. Why do you care, now you've moved out of town? I'm still waiting for that shoe to drop. You here to request transfer too?"

"I'm here at your request. As I was saying—"

"Where the fuck you been all morning?" the captain snapped. "Verrill covered for you, but I know how tight you girls are. You weren't out working last night's homicides without orders, were you?"

"No, sir."

"Good," the captain roared, pacing. "Don't ever interrupt me again."

Payden glanced up, wondering how long it was going to take the captain to ask for his badge and gun, given his diatribe wasn't making any sense. Then thanking God the captain was on a rant, which meant Payden wouldn't have to explain where he'd been, or what he'd been doing, that morning. If the captain didn't ask, he wouldn't have to lie about visiting Mindy.

"The news. Verrill and Mansfield are partners now. Mansfield's taking your desk. I already had your shit boxed up. You're welcome."

Payden cleared his throat. "Sir?"

The captain unclenched his hands and motioned with them for Payden to continue speaking.

"Am I working alone?"

The captain looked deep into Payden's eyes, slowly shaking his head. "You'd love that, wouldn't you? No one to keep you from turning my town into the Wild West? That's your dream, ain't it? Don't lie to me."

Payden shrugged. "I'm not opposed to—"

"That shit ain't happening."

Payden nodded, keeping a straight face.

The captain smiled. "I love when that light in your eyes goes out. Every time."

"What happens to me, then?" Payden cleared his throat again. "Is one of my options 'suck your dick'?"

The captain chuckled. "Fuck no. I like you, Beck. You get shit done. Still, you piss me off. You know what's worse than losing your job?"

Payden shook his head.

"Working with a transfer from that swanky little town you relocated to." The captain rubbed his hands together. "Where you're either house-poor or on the take, like—let's face it—this entire department is. Except me, of course."

"Of course." Payden looked at the captain, confused. "What's so bad about working with a transfer?"

"Nothing in general. But I have a feeling you two ain't going to get along."

"Why's that?"

"She's got a college degree, she's put in the years and she just passed her writtens, like Mansfield."

"She?" Payden asked, squinting momentarily.

The captain laughed. "That's what I was going for. I couldn't pass her up, especially given the fact she just became available this morning and wants to move fast. Perfect timing, and you need someone to keep you in line. Bonus, we look better now, with the equality and shit. We got a skirt and a black guy in detective division. Let them tell me I'm racially or sexually prejudiced now."

Payden kept a stiff posture. "You're kidding, right? A woman? Tell me she ain't a little girl?"

"You ain't that old. Twenty-six don't put you in the home by a long shot." The captain walked to his desk and sat on the front edge, lowering his voice. "Just keep it in your pants. This girl's a looker, but she's five feet, two inches of ass-kicking dynamite. You can thank me for saving your balls irreparable damage later. Like you, she has a bad reputation. Not on the front page, of course. Big fan of excessive force. Likes to push it. Don't push it with her. I'm sure she knows how to fuck someone up so it don't show as good as you. Maybe better."

Payden glanced at the door. "So, when do I meet the eye candy?"

The captain turned around and picked up the receiver from his desk phone, punching a digit into its base. "Send her in." He hung up the phone and looked at Payden. "Any minute now."

A knock came on the door.

"Enter," the captain said, his voice loud and authoritative.

The door opened and a female officer, still dressed in blues, entered the room, closing the door behind her. Staring straight ahead as Payden scanned her from her polished shoes up. Shorter than advertised, slim but with curves. And her face, he hated to admit, was stunningly beautiful. Though she wore her hair somewhat short—pulled into a ponytail with a rubber band—no one would mistake her for a man. The skin connecting her neck to her chin—though sporting a nasty scar down the right side—looked strangely soft.

The captain pointed between her and Payden. "Detective Lisa Reid, Detective Payden Beck. I now pronounce you partner and partner. Make nice."

Lisa turned to face Payden, ninety degrees in one step, her shoes clacking on the floor. Looking directly at him before he could manage to turn to his left to meet her gaze. She saluted him immediately, professionally.

He returned the gesture half-heartedly, noting the disappointment in her eyes.

"Detective Beck," she said, extending her right hand. Again, in one swift motion, like she was prepared to go to war.

"Detective." Payden took her hand and shook it.

She released and snapped her hand back to her side.

"The captain pronounce that right? Ride?"

"Pronounced reed." She gave Payden a quick nod. Keeping her eyes locked with his. Making him feel the need to give her body a good inspection from the front more than he'd wanted to when he took in her profile. "It's a pleasure to make your acquaintance. I look forward to working with you. I hear good things."

Payden smirked, giving her a quick look anyway. Something her eyes told him she didn't appreciate. Something his eyes told her he couldn't care less about. "No shit? I hear good things too. If you got a problem being partnered with me, we'll work that out later."

"Detective? I wasn't suggesting — I was keeping my speech curt out of respect for your, and the captain's, time. I meant, in full, I've heard good things about you."

The captain took his seat behind his desk and leant back, clasping his hands and resting them on his stomach, smiling. "You two are perfect for each other."

Lisa kept her eyes locked with Payden's, making him increasingly uncomfortable. "If I may be so bold, captain?"

"Fire away," the captain said, still smiling. Enjoying the back-and-forth.

"May I ask where we'll be stationed? It's my understanding the two other detectives in this department are using the office Detective Beck shared with Detective Verrill."

Payden nodded. "Good question. Where you dumping me and the mascot?"

Lisa began to scowl, quickly forcing her lips into an emotionless line.

The captain grunted. "You and Beck don't have anywhere to hang your jackets yet. No room in the bullpen either."

"Sir?" Lisa asked, giving Payden's body a thorough examination the second he broke her gaze to look at the captain.

Payden shrugged, unaware he was being eyeballed. "So, we sit on our boxes? Where? Parking lot?"

"Close," the captain said.

Lisa looked to the captain, her body still facing Payden's, before he could glance back at her to catch her reaction.

"You'll be stationed in the car Verrill and Beck used to share." He bobbed his eyebrows. "That's right, Beck, you get to keep that rusty old boat. Put your boxes in the trunk. I requisitioned a nice, new four-door vehicle for your ex-partner and his fish. You already caught your first case, though Mansfield ain't happy about it. You're both aware of the triple murder last night? Some scumbag drug dealers? Mansfield and Verrill already identified and questioned the witnesses before I could tell them to back off. They left notes." The captain picked a stack of papers off his desk's top and offered them forth.

Lisa grabbed them after noticing Payden didn't appear eager to bulldog her.

"Read those. If you think they missed anything, go talk to the witnesses—all kids—again. To sum it up, a man, whose face they couldn't see, made them watch before he ended the victims, then sent them running with a warning. Something along the lines of crime don't pay. Same MO, all three." He looked at Lisa. "Thoughts, Reid?"

Lisa turned to face the captain, her right foot slamming down on the floor and her arms snapping to her sides. "It's this detective's opinion—"

"Beck?" the captain asked.

Payden turned to face the captain and patted Lisa on the right shoulder, noting her lack of startle reflex. "Talk about yourself in the first person. And we're all detectives in our little division, so you don't got to address any of us with full title. We'll return the favour."

She nodded without looking at Payden.

"Just say what you have to say."

"Is this a safe space?" Lisa asked, glancing in Payden's direction with something resembling disgust.

The captain laughed as Payden rolled his eyes.

Lisa continued. "My thoughts. From your summary, I believe the person, or persons—whom it seems presumptuous to assume were male—live in or around town. Possibly members of law enforcement. Definitely comfortable using deadly force to solve problems. No strangers to violence or lying. Pathological with regard to both. I have no reason to believe, from your summary, he, she or they will be here when the witnesses mature. They may well be transient. My money's on this happening again. Soon."

The captain nodded. "Well put." He looked at Payden. "Your thoughts? Pretend Reid's your ex-partner. Don't hold back." He looked at Lisa. "If you'll forgive me." He looked back at Payden.

Payden nodded. "Sarcasm noted."

The captain nodded and Lisa nodded immediately after.

"My thoughts? One person. Got no problem with violence, making a statement. On world tour or from town, he... or she" — Lisa cracked a tight smile, unaware Payden was watching her out of the corner of his eye — "capped those drug-dealing pieces of shit with purpose. Though I got to disagree with Reid on one point."

Lisa's smile didn't crack.

"This wasn't a cop. That being said, Reid's dead on with her final statement. This is beginning."

The captain nodded. "Sarcasm noted yet, once again, completely ignored." His gaze floated between Lisa and Payden. "Reid, allow me to apologise for Beck's language."

Lisa's expression turned serious as she shook her head. Almost unnoticeable. Her body language so tight, Payden assumed she'd been transferred because she'd been winding up long enough she was about to go off. "All due respect, sir. I've worked the streets. In uniform. Undercover. Beck's language neither shocks nor offends me. I appreciate his candour."

The captain shrugged. "Okay, then." He looked at Payden. "But, for God's sake, Beck. Okay?" He paused. "Anyway, after hearing your opinion of the... perpetrator, I'm not entirely sure you didn't do it."

Lisa spoke again. "All due respect, sir. We can't afford to assume anyone didn't do it. Especially not police. We're all capable of pulling when we must. It's my opinion most of us wouldn't be here if we couldn't."

The captain chuckled. "Noted, Reid. You can drop the 'all due respect, sir' stuff, too."

Lisa nodded.

"Since you're stuck with this joker and you've heard worse, get ready. Beck has a knack for making me lose my temper."

"Understood."

Payden gave Lisa a look she appeared to notice but didn't return. "He ain't kidding. Buy earplugs."

Lisa's lips curled up at the edges as she kept her speech even. "Thank you, Beck."

"On that note." The captain leant farther back in his chair, using his hands as a pillow. "Get out of my office. Figure out how you're going to attack this case. I'll give you the rest of the day to get used to not killing each other but, first thing tomorrow, I want this solved yesterday."

"So, today, then?" Payden asked.

The captain stood, pointing toward the door, his face turning red but his voice not raising. "What did I just say?"

Payden gave the captain a weak salute after seeing Lisa give him a proper one. Neither of them affected by the fact he didn't return it.

"One last thing," the captain said as Lisa cracked open the door.

She and Payden stopped and looked over their shoulders.

"Why are you two still here? Go."

VII

Payden and Lisa walked out of the station into the parking lot after checking to see if Bryan and Lester were back. They'd found Bryan sitting in the office he'd shared with Payden for years and made brief introductions. When they asked where Lester was, Bryan indicated he'd taken the afternoon off as he'd found a lead he was going to follow up on that evening. When they told Bryan that he and Lester didn't catch the case, Bryan pretended he wasn't already aware of that fact and said he'd try to get in touch with Lester, though he didn't seem too interested in making sure his new partner didn't solve the mystery before the detectives officially assigned to the case did.

When Payden walked outside, past the department's lot and down the sidewalk to the right, Lisa kept pace with him as she looked for what would now be their shared car.

"Any reason you don't park in the lot?" Lisa asked, moving to walk beside Payden, then moving behind him to allow opposing pedestrian traffic passage.

Payden looked over his shoulder as they approached their car, parked two blocks away on the street. "Yes."

Lisa raised her voice as she talked to Payden's back. "Shouldn't we be parking our official vehicle in the department's lot? It's my understanding—"

Payden motioned for her to walk by his side without looking back.

When she did — spotting pedestrians headed in the opposite direction — she moved to walk in front of him.

Payden looked down. "Where'd you come from?"

Lisa continued to face forward. "I transferred—"

"Apologies. Just meant I didn't see you there. Almost tripped."

Lisa flashed him an angry look over her shoulder, keeping her cool and continuing her thought. "We'd have more room to speak comfortably if you'd have parked in the lot." She paused. "And I'll thank you to stop inspecting my backside."

Payden scoffed as they reached their car and he opened the passenger door for her. "Rule number one, now you're a detective. Don't ever wear blues again. Except at funerals for fallen officers."

Lisa rolled her eyes. "I don't need you to open my door for me. I'm perfectly capable of—"

"Rule number two, since your body isn't repulsive, don't wear tight clothes. If you insist on doing so, spare me the manufactured grief over being looked at by a man with a pulse."

Payden closed Lisa's door after she took her seat, cutting off her complaint regarding her ability to close it on her own, and walked to his side of the car. When he got there, pulling on the door's handle and realising he'd have to unlock it for himself, he thought of Valarie.

Lisa put on her seatbelt tight as Payden slipped into the driver's seat. Looking at his wandering eyes again until she fixed them with hers. "I'll also thank you to not stare at my breasts."

Payden put the keys in the ignition, leaving the car off and turning his upper body to face Lisa, whose body faced forward. "You can quit thanking me, too. Being pleasant don't buy you nothing here."

Lisa let out an exasperated breath. "Tell me you got a good look, then."

"I got a good look."

"Curiosity satisfied?" she asked, looking adequately insulted.

"Not really. Free your hair from the fucking rubber band and we're good." He looked at her waist. "Or just beat me with your billy club. That would turn me off."

Lisa shook her head, bending her neck forward. Removing the rubber band from her hair, letting it hang free. Unfortunately, making her look even better. Shaking her head so her hair fell the way it was supposed to, behind the shoulders and reaching just below them on either side. Straight, with a slight, singular wave. "The scar doesn't?"

Payden cranked the ignition. "What scar?"

Lisa nodded, looking down and pocketing her rubber band. "Please. I know it's—"

"I'd hate to see the other guy." Payden looked over his left shoulder and pulled into traffic. "Don't go feeling sorry for yourself."

Lisa looked out her window, unsure how else to react. "Apologies. Just, it's not easy being a woman on the force."

Payden drummed the wheel with his fingertips as he stared ahead. "I get it. Lots of men on the force don't think you belong. What I did? What will probably continue happening, given your looks"—Lisa turned her face away, putting her fist to her mouth to smother her smile which she hated to admit was brought on by a compliment regarding the very thing she didn't wish to be judged by—"isn't right. But all of that shit? It don't matter to me. You're my partner. And I'm going to treat you like a woman, because you are one. That don't mean I don't consider you an equal. It just means I ain't going to treat you like one of the guys." He gave her a glance, noting she'd turned her head back to face him and was staring directly into his eyes. "I, and all the men in the world who catch a glimpse of you, will see a good-looking woman and treat you differently. You don't catch a break there. Not with me. Still, you're a cop. Sorry, a detective. And you have my respect. Least until you prove you don't deserve it. Get what I'm saying?"

Lisa nodded. "Yes. I won't treat you any way I don't want you to treat me. Same for you. Deal?"

Payden shook his head, looking at her out of the corner of his eye. "Deal."

"Then no complaints about the fact I'm taking a mental photograph of your package right now. You owe me. And you'll do me the favour of walking ahead of me when we exit our mobile office, so I can commit your ass to memory, too. Then we'll be square."

"Fair enough." Payden continued to clock Lisa as he took a right, noting she'd never stopped looking away from him. "We might just get along. And, if you don't mind my asking, why'd you request transfer? You fuck someone up who had it coming, or just someone who looked you up and down?"

"They had it coming." She looked out her window again. "They all have it coming."

"Could be that's true."

"By the way, where are we going? We have a case to solve."

"Tomorrow."

"Okay. Still, where are we going?"

"Your rubber band ponytail."

Lisa ran her fingers through her hair. "So, the hardware store?"

"No, a friend of mine. Maybe a lead. She invited me over. Your rubber band got me thinking. She does the same thing. A good enough time to stop by her place as any. We could get to know her brother, too."

"And the lead would be?"

"Like you said," Payden replied, patting Lisa on the left shoulder as she scowled. "Her brother may be transient. According to her, an outlaw. We should find out how long he's been in town, what his full name is, how he's acting. May be we got our guy already. He'll tell if we ask the right questions."

"That would be something." Lisa scratched the back of her neck. "Cracking our first case before we officially begin investigating."

"What I was thinking, Reid."

Lisa looked out her window as they drove, unsure what to say next. Waiting for Payden to continue their conversation. Wanting him to. Wondering why.

VIII

Payden pulled his car to the kerb in front of Valarie and Michael Dooley's home as he reassured Lisa it would be a short visit. Payden exited the vehicle and slammed his door shut as Lisa closed hers, stepped over the kerb onto the grass and waited. When Payden reached her, she let him pass and followed, her eyes drifting below his belt, as promised.

"This girl is just a friend?" Lisa asked.

"No. We can't stand each other." As he walked up the steps to the front porch, he took in the overhang above the door. Still the same, never updated, never mended, though property values were going up. Perhaps because of that. Reminding him of a simpler, more fulfilling time which had actually been much more complex and frustrating. "Why does that matter?"

"It doesn't."

"Our relationship's complicated." Payden looked at her like he wasn't quite as stupid as her response suggested. "Ask me how we met?"

"How—"

"We got partnered in the captain's office. Less than an hour ago. You were there."

"Hilarious." Lisa faked a cough. "I was just having fun. At your expense, of course. Curious what her name—"

"Valarie." Payden knocked on the door, looking back, moving to the right and nodding slightly. "We'll work on our 'fun cop, bad cop' routine later, when we meet her brother for the first time. And wouldn't that be something? Meeting her, and her husband Mickey's, firstborn? Giving her a little coo and a cuddle while we break her uncle's arms putting him in braces?"

Lisa slammed her hands together behind her back when the door swung open.

An imposing, ugly man stood in the doorway. His knuckles bruised, with a face that looked like he rented it out as a speed bag at the local gym. Valarie's brother, James Jude. "Help you?" He watched as Lisa moved to Payden's front left, out of his shadow. "Shorty?"

"Who is it?" Valarie's voice called, followed by the sounds of her shushing her daughter with a soothing voice, then her footsteps growing nearer. "Who's at the door?" she asked in a goofy voice, cradling her daughter. "Who's your silly uncle Jimmy talking to?" Before she came into Payden's view, her tone changed and her eyes widened. "What did you do this time?" She nudged James until he moved out of the way. "Look, Officer. I'm not sure why you were called here, but I can—Payden?"

"You said any time," Payden replied, smiling and tilting his head slightly toward Lisa. "I'm going to have my hands full pretty soon, if I don't already."

Valarie glanced at Lisa, her cheeks pinking.

Lisa looked away.

Payden fixed Valarie's gaze. "We caught the triple murder last night. And, where are my manners? May I introduce—"

Lisa looked back at Valarie and extended her right hand.

Valarie offered her daughter to Payden as she pretended not to notice the look on Lisa's face as Lisa dropped her hand to her side. "Not before you take this little angel and give her a great big hug. Say hi to your uncle Payden, Charity."

"Hey, cutie." Payden took the baby girl in his arms, being careful not to drop her as Valarie absently smoothed her clothes and brushed back her hair. "Aren't we priceless."

Valarie chuckled weakly as she moved James farther away from the door. "Didn't think I'd see the day you showed anyone that side, Payden. Especially not...." She looked at Lisa. "Are you here on a separate matter?" She glanced over her shoulder at James, who backed up another step. "What did he do?"

"No. Nothing like that." Lisa smiled. "I'm—"

Valarie took her baby from Payden and he stopped making embarrassing noises. "That's right," she said, looking like she wanted to smack herself on the forehead, if only she had a free hand. "Payden was just saying."

Payden cleared his throat. "Short, but sweet, backstory. Verrill's partnered with Mansfield now and I'm stuck with this pistol, Detective Reid. Valarie, Lisa. Lisa, Valarie."

Lisa moved forward slightly and extended her hand again.

Valarie nodded to Lisa, gesturing with her eyes for James to take Charity.

Lisa pulled her hand away as soon as James took Charity, keeping it dropped to her side as James carried Charity back to her crib in the living room beside the couch, directly in view from the opened door.

Payden walked in through the doorway, giving Valarie a hug.

She gave him a soft, slow kiss on the cheek in return as she registered Lisa's reaction. "Pleasure to meet you,

Lisa." Valarie pulled away, took Payden by the hand and walked him farther inside, motioning for Lisa to follow. "Good luck with this one." She rolled her eyes, then smiled at Payden and punched him in the shoulder with a little too much force.

"Thank you." Lisa entered the house, closing the door behind her. "It's nice to meet you too." She looked at James. "And this is Jimmy?" She extended her hand again.

Payden chuckled. "She just started today. All done licking boots. She'll dress like a human tomorrow."

"Keep the outfit," James said, walking into the kitchen and grabbing a beer from the refrigerator. Opening it, taking a chug, then letting rip with an obnoxious burp. "Make you money on the side."

Lisa looked down, her anger appearing as shame. "I'm sorry?"

"Why?" James walked to the living room couch, taking a seat and looking around for the remote. "I'd pay."

Valarie turned away from Lisa to face James, rubbing Payden's stomach, her voice low. "Not funny, Jimmy." Then she turned to face Lisa, moving her hand from Payden's stomach and scratching her left inner thigh quickly. "You'll have to excuse him... Lisa?"

Lisa nodded, looking pleasant.

"He's a character." She looked back to Payden, putting her hand on his arm. "Did you want to stay for supper?" She didn't look to Lisa for affirmation.

Lisa walked toward James, keeping her eye on Valarie. "Isn't it a little early? I mean, we'd love to stay, but—"

James chuckled, looking Lisa up and down. "Customers?"

"As was noted, the lewd remarks are not appreciated." Lisa turned and smiled at Valarie, faking it. "He's your brother?"

Valarie nodded, glancing at Charity's crib, moving toward it and in front of Payden.

"He's new in town?"

James stared at Lisa's ass. "Tight. I'd pay extra."

Lisa remained calm, facing James once more. "I apologise. We really must go. Detective Beck threw me a bit of a curve." She looked over her shoulder, glancing to see if Valarie would put more of her body between her and Payden. Nodding when she wasn't disappointed. "Tell your husband we said hello?"

James stood and began to move toward the kitchen. "Don't go, working girl. Tell me a story. Make the ending happy."

Lisa moved into James's path, putting her body perpendicular to his, with her left shoulder facing his chest. Noting he stood at least a foot taller than her. "Why don't you start?" she asked as she waved to Charity who, to her surprise, waved back and smiled.

"Start what?"

Lisa replied, facing him and not looking up. "Telling stories." She gestured with her head toward the front door, then gazed up. "We can speak more freely outside. I mean"—she batted her lashes—"if it's something you'd like. Give these two some time alone before the old man catches them. Who knows? Maybe we can be... friends?"

"Doubt it. Your knees are too clean."

"I just meant. Well, you know." Lisa patted his left wrist playfully.

James swatted Lisa's hand and, before he could pull his own away, she had his wrist bent up and back, walking him to the front door like he was a school child.

"Open the door, Jimmy," Lisa said, her breathing even. Glancing over her shoulder to note Valarie was attempting to shield Payden from view, though apparently not conscious of it. Then Lisa whispered. "This can be a lot more painful, if that's what you need."

James opened the door, backing up to get out of its way, unable to wriggle free of Lisa's grip.

"We'll be back in a second," she called to Valarie and Payden. "All's well."

James closed the door behind himself and Lisa a moment later and Payden gave Valarie a shrug. "She was a lot friendlier on the drive over."

"I'll bet." Valarie took Payden's right hand in her left, then released it. "You two aren't...?"

Payden shook his head, almost chuckling. "I told you, I just met her today. Got put with her so the captain gets a pretty woman in detective division. Crumbling under some politically correct pressure. Don't really know her." He shook his head. "Captain said she has a history of excessive force. She had me convinced otherwise until a few seconds ago."

Valarie crossed her arms and stared at the front door. "You think she's pretty? I mean, I guess."

Payden watched Valarie as her eyes focussed squarely on the front door.

"Why did you come by with her?"

"Captain gave us an afternoon off before we chase the street cleaner. Figured I might not get to see you for a while. Time would pass. We'd forget—"

"I never forgot. And she's not that good-looking." Valarie shook her head. "So, you're not?"

Payden cleared his throat. "Why would it matter if we were?"

"It wouldn't," Valarie responded immediately, not looking at him. "Just, I'm getting my old job back as soon as the manager clears it. And, when I saw you today, I thought of this girl I worked with. She's gorgeous. And she's real. I thought you two... you know?"

"Can't say I do."

Valarie elbowed Payden in the stomach softly. "Shut up, jerk. I'm just saying, it would be nice. If you two got together, then I'd see you more often. You know what I—"

The picture hanging on the wall to the right of the door shook as a thud sounded outside, followed by another, louder one.

"That didn't sound good."

"Maybe it was a bird."

Valarie gave Payden a confused look. "That's a wall, not a window."

The door shook as a heavy blow landed directly against it from outside.

"Seriously. Your partner could be in trouble."

Payden put his hand to his ear. "Don't hear nothing. You?"

"Christ, Payden," Valarie snapped, looking somewhat upset. "I mean, I get us, but this bitch—girl hasn't done anything to deserve—"

Valarie swung the door open to take in Lisa sitting on James's back at the waist, his hands twisted up.

"Please exercise caution, ma'am," Lisa said, inadvertently putting more pressure on James and nearly breaking his right arm. "This situation is under control. Detective Beck?"

Payden rushed to the door, glancing back to see Charity asleep in her crib. "What happened?"

Lisa looked down and to the right, at her utility belt, nodding to Payden. Licking blood from her lower lip and swallowing as Payden reached to grab her cuffs.

As Payden handed Lisa her cuffs, Valarie looked up and down the street. Thankful no one was outside to see. Noting Lisa's scarred neck and feeling a fleeting sense of security. Like Payden was still hers, though she could never be with him again unless life put them back together in a way she didn't want to imagine.

Lisa motioned for Valarie to step outside and close the door.

Valarie did so, after Payden stepped outside and she made sure she had the keys to her home in her jeans pocket.

"I asked, he didn't answer," Lisa said. "He's only been in town a while. He fits the description."

"For what happened last night?" Valarie asked, shaken. "He was home until we went to bed."

"At what time?"

James looked to Valarie and Payden. "Get this reeking muff off me."

Lisa slapped the cuffs on James and cranked them extra-tight.

"Ain't right."

Lisa struggled to stand James up. "I'm afraid further questioning is necessary."

"She tried to—" James began.

Lisa whispered into James's ear, from behind, on the side of his head neither Valarie nor Payden could see and, when she pulled her mouth away, James nodded violently.

"No problems. My word."

"You understand I'm charging you with assault, yes?" Lisa asked.

James shook his head. "Okay."

Payden gave Valarie a hug as she stared forward in a daze, whispering into her ear. "Sorry I brought her by.

But it was good to see you. Your daughter's beautiful. And I'll see you again soon. I promise."

Valarie returned his hug as he finished speaking, talking at regular volume. "Okay, sweetie."

Lisa glanced at Valarie when she heard her term of endearment.

"And stay for a while, at least. The next time. Promise?"

Payden nodded.

Valarie kissed his cheek. "Be careful."

"I will," Payden replied, speaking normally. "And I'll be back." Payden kissed Valarie on the forehead, releasing his hold, and she waved goodbye as she smiled, enjoying the way Payden hurried to his car to open the back door while his new partner fought to move James along. Watching her struggle, imagining the scar on Lisa's neck ran the length of her face and uniformed body. Deforming it beyond measure. Confused as to why that thought gave her no comfort. Feeling ugly, lesser, insecure beyond any reason.

Valarie opened her door and waved goodbye again as Payden's car pulled away and Lisa smiled at her, waving in return. Feeling a chill run up her spine when she realised the smile Lisa had given her was genuine, polite, without malice. Charming, even.

She walked back inside her home when their car was out of view. Not wanting to imagine a life with Lisa in it. Nor a life without Payden. Inside, she felt she'd have to accept one or the other soon.

IX

Payden opened the station's front door for Lisa, who marched James inside, giving Payden a nod. Holding the cuffs tight, though whatever fight might have existed in James had died on the ride over. The fact he'd been made to lie face down across the rear seats, his hands in cuffs behind his back, with nothing to keep him from falling onto the floor had done the trick. A trick Payden had never considered before. And, as they'd made their way back to the station, Payden considered maybe having a new partner was a good thing. It was time for a change. Still, he smiled and felt a wash of relief — obliterating stress he hadn't realised he'd been carrying — the moment he saw Bryan walk out of their old office.

Lisa walked James past Bryan, giving Bryan a nod which he returned.

Payden opened the door to the interrogation room, closing it behind Lisa while assuring her he'd be with her again directly.

Bryan's eyes floated up to meet Payden's.

Payden bobbed his eyebrows. "Not bad, yeah?"

Bryan adjusted his jacket. "Are you asking if she's good-looking? Objectively, I'd have to say yes."

Payden chuckled. "Interesting you think I was asking that."

They stood, feeling awkward in each other's company for the first time either could remember. Like two homosexual school kids on their first date.

"So." Payden cleared his throat, looking at the door to his old office. "Where's your trainee?"

"Are you going deaf, old man?"

In the still of the moment after Bryan asked the question, Payden heard the captain's voice. Dulled from past the bullpen.

"He's getting chewed out for pushing it."

Payden scratched the back of his head. "His lead on the dead triplets? You told?"

Bryan gave him the finger. "Kiss my ass, you all-day prick."

Payden put his hands together in prayer. "Did she call?"

"Who?"

"The fuck who. Did she come to her senses?"

"Mindy?"

"Mindy?" Payden repeated, mocking. "Who else? Are you two good again?"

"Your guess. She's been leaving messages all day. Says she wants to talk about Friday night. I'm going to head over there later. Though, for once, I'm thinking maybe you're right."

"How so?"

"Other fish," Bryan said. "The seas full of them. I'm going to listen to what she has to say. But if it isn't a solid, workable, measurable plan that gets us to the altar, I'm done."

"Couldn't ask for more, birdy. Give her another chance. While the window's open."

"Don't ever call me birdy again." Bryan moved toward the interrogation room. "You didn't have anything to do with her change of mind, right?"

Payden followed, looking over his shoulder as they reached the interrogation room's door. "When, birdy?"

Payden chuckled. "Sorry. Last time, I promise. But, seriously, I've been busy all—"

"Your day's unaccounted for," Bryan snapped, regaining his cool immediately. "The captain doesn't know, because I covered for you, but you had plenty of time to call her. Maybe stop by and visit. Did you?"

"You got me. I finally fucked her." Payden pulled a long face and shook his head. "Of course not. I remember what you said. Your life, your business. Stay out of it. Message received." He pointed at the interrogation room door, moving past Bryan. "Want to say hi to one other fish before you go back to yesterday's?"

X

Payden entered the interrogation room with Bryan, to find Lisa sitting across the table from James, staring him down. Payden slammed the door closed as soon as Bryan passed him, but neither Lisa nor James broke their eye lock.

James blinked, pulling at his cuffs, which tied his wrists to the back right leg of his chair.

"Detective Lisa Reid," Payden said, causing her to look at him as he pointed to Bryan. "Meet one half of the other pair of detectives in our little home. Detective Bryan Verrill." He pointed his hands between them. "Bryan, Lisa. Lisa, Bryan." Payden coughed into his fist. "And, remember, Reid, once introductions are over, he's just Verrill."

Lisa looked at Bryan—who extended his hand—and gave him a firm, yet gentle shake. Her smile made her squint. "You used to work with this one?" She pointed at Payden with her thumb, not looking in his direction.

Bryan nodded and smiled in return.

"God bless you. I look forward to working with you and Detective...?"

"Mansfield," Bryan said. "He's talking with the captain at the moment."

Payden chuckled. "He's getting his ass reamed by the captain is what stone-face meant to say."

"Beck." Lisa gave Payden a pout, then looked back at Bryan. "How you put up with him, I guess I'm going to find out. Can't say I'm looking forward to it, but he seems decent."

Payden nodded. "And he's a damned good detective."

"Also very good at tooting his own horn. Anyway, I'm sùre that will be me in there with the captain someday."

Bryan shook his head. "I doubt it. At least not in that way." He cleared his throat. "By which I didn't mean to say—I mean, what I meant to say was—"

Lisa shook her head, keeping her gaze fixed on Bryan, batting her eyelashes, as Payden looked at James. "You're sweet. And thank you."

Bryan nodded, trying not to look at the scar on Lisa's neck, waving at the interrogation room's wall-mounted video camera for someone to open the door for him from the outside. "I have some personal business to take care of."

Payden grinned. "Can't wait until you get home? Careful no one catches you."

Bryan eyed Payden with embarrassment and anger as a shift officer opened the door for him. "That's not—"

Lisa called after Bryan. "I appreciate your show of respect. Truly."

Bryan nodded and exited the room, leaving the door open—with no crack to allow outsiders to peek in—behind him.

"Remember," Payden said. "The world can hear us now if they listen closely enough, so feel free to cry rape, Jimmy."

"You'd like that," James said. "Not your lucky day, homo."

Payden looked at James quickly, chuckling, then at Lisa. "Do all the boys fall in love with you that fast, Reid?"

"She's damaged." James grunted. "He just wants to fuck her. See what it's like."

"Shut your mouth." Payden pointed at James. "We'll get to you in a second."

James scanned Lisa from her tits to the tip of her nose. "You don't want inside that? Faggot."

Payden rolled his eyes. "Look, Reid. I'm not sure what your act got you on patrol, but—"

"I was just being polite," Lisa said. "And I don't need you to stand up for me."

"Apologies for existing, then." Payden scowled. "I take it back."

Lisa's eyes softened. "I didn't mean—" She shook her head. "As I noted, I was merely being—"

"That was more than polite. What happened to your stance on—"

Lisa held up a hand. "Just because I don't appreciate being treated like an object doesn't mean I can't use what I've got to make a good impression."

"I guess not," Payden muttered, then began speaking at normal volume. "Is that how you hope to get Jimmy to open up?"

Lisa stood, pushing her seat back with her legs, and walked around to James's side of the table as he looked at Payden and shook his head. "You don't believe in foreplay?" She gave James a wink. "I think Jimmy's just about ready to start talking, isn't he?"

Payden remained in place, watching his new partner show him how she took care of business.

"Sure." James looked into her eyes and spat in her face. "Lawyer."

Lisa didn't flinch, wiping the spit from her face with the sleeve of her uniform. "Your lawyer's coming, Jimmy. You don't want to have a nice talk first?"

James grunted. "You smell like day-olds."

Lisa moved behind James. "Where were you last night between the hours of —"

"Lawyer." James glanced at his crotch. "Sit on my lap. Maybe I'll talk."

Lisa looked to Payden. "What do you think? Viable strategy with the front desk watching?"

Payden shrugged. "Riding the masked pony? Never worked for me. Not even in private. If he ain't saying nothing else, press the assault charge."

Lisa removed James's cuffs as she shook her head. "He was never here."

James stood, looking at Payden. "Free to go now?"

Payden nodded. "As the lady wishes."

"No Miranda. No paperwork. I'll fill Val In. We're good." James looked down at Lisa. "You and me? Maybe not. Unless you want to give that mouth some real exercise."

Payden pushed open the slightly ajar interrogation room door and watched as James walked out and exited the station. Noting Bryan had left, and Lester was most likely gone, as well, based on the quiet and the time on the wall clocks. Just past five in the evening. When everyone regular walked and forgot they were cops.

Lisa gave Payden a wink and a smile as she walked out into the hallway past him and toward the front door. "No need to thank me. Your hunch was solid, but he isn't the guy."

"You keep it up and I'm going to miss that smile when it dies." Payden shook his head. "Need a ride home?"

Lisa opened the front door. "I appreciate the offer, but no thank you."

Payden nodded. "There's a pub down the way. A little welcome to the precinct drink on me?"

"Thank you again, but—"

"Sure? You got someone waiting at home, you're welcome to bring him, or her along."

She shook her head, squinting.

"You're positive?"

"Maybe tomorrow." Lisa gave him another wink and a more seductive smile. Confusing the hell out of him. "I'll be sure to dress less provocatively."

"Until then. Take care of yourself, which we've established you can."

Payden waited until Lisa exited the building, and then a few more minutes, before he made his way out to his car. For reasons he didn't understand—given how outwardly attractive she was, and how much her reputation fit the profile of his kind of woman—Payden didn't want to know anything more about Lisa than he already did.

XI

Bryan pulled his car alongside the kerb by Mindy's home and made his way to her front door. Not running, but not moving as slowly as he used to. There was still something wrong with them, as a couple. Possibly just with her. And if things were going to end as cleanly as possible, they may as well end as quickly.

She opened the door before he could knock, looking fresh, wearing a short white skirt, a sheer white crop top and nothing else. Neither fabric as white as her skin. Dressed to entice. Smiling.

"Hey," she said, opening the door wide and waving Bryan in, then closing the door behind him. He didn't return her greeting.

He looked around at the kitchen and living room, wondering why he thought anything might look different than it had before. "I got your messages," he said, as she walked up behind him and draped herself on his shoulders.

She rested her neck on his right shoulder and kissed his cheek, speaking into his ear, soft and smooth. "You had a busy day. It's okay."

"Is it?" Bryan didn't look back as her right arm wrapped around his waist.

"We need to talk." She let out a slow breath, kissing his ear's lobe. "About us."

Bryan shook his head, his eyes dead. "That's the line you use before you show a man the door. Not a few days after. What do we need to talk about?"

"Us," she said, beginning to smile, then looking serious, though Bryan still hadn't so much as glanced in her direction.

"I got that part. What about us requires further discussion? As I recall, you told me we were over. No reason why. The years together didn't matter. You decided. And I sucked it up, as you suggested, and took it like a man." He turned his head to face her, stopping before their eyes connected. "Was your first date not everything you'd hoped for?"

"Excuse me?" Mindy asked, doing her best to not look insulted. "There was never anyone else. There isn't."

"Did he disappoint?" Bryan asked, ignoring her response.

"I'm serious." She loosed her hold and turned him to face her. "I have never been unfaithful to you."

"That's not you talking."

"I don't—" she grabbed her hair with her right hand, exposing the soft flesh of the bottom of her freed right breast. "What are you saying?"

Bryan fixed her gaze. "I didn't come here to explain myself to you." Bryan eyed the front door. "I shouldn't have come at all."

Mindy stood firm as Bryan moved toward the door, not allowing him to displace her. "You don't understand. You never will. You just have to trust me. Friday night? I don't know. Something snapped. Maybe all of this time since you proposed, with our marriage looking like it might never happen, finally got to me and I—"

"Get out of my way, Mindy." Bryan looked past her. "Are you expecting me to believe you ousted me from our relationship because you got fed up with your unwillingness to follow through on accepting my proposal of marriage?"

"No," Mindy snapped, calming herself as she patted Bryan's arms, stepping backward slightly as he moved to the front door. "I didn't mean—I just, I don't know what I was thinking. I need you, can't you see that? Do I really mean that little to you? You're over me already?"

Bryan moved past Mindy and faced the door, his hand on the knob. "You froze me out over years. And your reigniting our sexual relationship, while satisfying, wasn't enough. The damage you did? I didn't ask for it, I didn't deserve it and I won't walk back into your trap. You've had your fun. More than you ever expected, I assume. If this was all we had to discuss, consider the matter closed. I need to get some sleep."

"I have a bed you could use." Mindy stood in place as Bryan cracked open the door. "I could let you do to me what you never believed I would."

Bryan glanced back when he heard Mindy's skirt and top fall to the floor. Looking at them and fearing, if he gazed upon her body, he might do something rash, like take her up on her offer.

He shook his head. "What did I never believe you'd let me do to you?"

"Treat me like the nickel whore I am."

Bryan closed the door and turned to face Mindy, directly, taking in her body in all its beauty and cursing the demon between his legs. "What did you say?"

"Tell me what to do," Mindy replied. "Hurt me if I don't. Make me submit. Humiliate me." She paused, looking down. "I can dress myself again so you can shred my clothes. You can treat me like your dog without intercourse. You can dominate me without penetrating me. Isn't that what you've always wanted? Total control?"

"For how long—I mean, why?"

"So you'll know what it feels like, and why I did what I did. This weekend and every day after you made me apologise to Payden."

Bryan waved her off. "Your suggestion, again, being he's had you under his thumb—he's been using you, sexually or otherwise—ever since the night he walked you home and didn't rape you. Yes?"

"Of course not."

"You're being ridiculous."

"Am I? You won't believe he ever hurt me and you won't believe he never did. Which of us is being ridiculous? If you want to punish me for acting foolishly, then do so. But don't make it the end of us. I said I was sorry. And if I didn't, I'm saying it now. Take me back. I'm begging you. I wasn't in my right mind."

"Don't blame the rag again."

"I'm only blaming myself," Mindy screamed. "How can you not forgive me?"

Bryan turned away. "I'm going to call Mansfield. Maybe just go back to the office. Or home. This was a mistake."

Mindy slipped into her skirt as she shook. Grabbing her crop top and wiping her face clean with it before putting it back on, as well. "Who's Mansfield?" she asked, rushing to him and hugging him around the waist from behind. "Please don't go?"

"My new partner," he said, turning to face her. "He's a little eager, but it's nice to finally be working with someone who takes the law seriously."

"New partner?" Mindy looked into Bryan's eyes, moving her hands to his chin. "You have a new partner?"

"As of today," Bryan said, staring into nothing. "The captain put me with a new detective. He put Beck with a transfer."

Mindy looked down, scowling.

"Thought that might lighten the mood."

"I guess it did." Mindy shivered. "Can we please talk now? It's—"

"Maybe." Bryan looked at Mindy, wishing he hadn't come to see her. Knowing he was about to take her back before she'd gone into her long-winded offer to repay him for her dismissal. Knowing they'd be moving to the bedroom if he didn't leave, so she could seal the deal. "But, no bullshit. Real talk."

Mindy nodded.

Bryan walked into the living room and took a seat on the couch, looking around for the television remote as he removed his jacket. Praying he wasn't being suckered again. By Payden or by Mindy. If it happened again, he wouldn't know who to blame. Though, ultimately, he knew the blame would lie with himself.

XII

James knocked on Valarie's front door softly. Looking up and down the street in the dark of night. Waiting for a few minutes, knocking lightly again, then figuring 'fuck it' and pounding on the door.

Valarie opened the door five minutes later, Charity crying in her crib in her bedroom.

James quit knocking. Pushing past her and into the kitchen, making straight for the refrigerator.

Valarie pulled on the cotton robe she wore over her day clothes, to hug her body tighter, and shivered, noting dirt marks on the door's front as she closed it softly but securely. Praying, when Michael returned from the pub later, he'd have the common decency to be quiet. Easy, since he had a key, but out of respect for their child's—and his wife's—well-being. No talking-tos had ever been necessary since they'd wed.

"Good to see you, too," Valarie said, watching James grab a beer from the refrigerator and open it, not looking back at her. "Thanks so much for waking my daughter. You realise you're a guest here, right?"

James walked out of the kitchen and sat on the couch, giving Valarie a sideways glance before looking around for the remote.

"It's not anywhere near you. Though it may not be obvious, it was Charity's bedtime. She was asleep minutes ago. Just got that way not much earlier. No television. No more noise."

James grunted and took a slug off his beer.

"So?" Valarie grabbed her robe tighter, her knuckles turning white.

"What?"

Valarie moved into the living room, blocking James's view of his reflection in the turned-off television's screen.

"I knock. You don't open, I make noise. What's the problem?"

Valarie shook her head. "When Mickey gets home, I'm going to have a talk with him. You're not welcome here anymore."

"Because you are a bitch, don't mean you got to be."

"What is that supposed to mean?" Valarie shouted and Charity's cries grew louder momentarily. "And how am I being a bitch? You don't have a job and you contribute almost nothing to helping with Charity—"

"Get a job." He took another drink.

"What did you say?"

"Get a job," James repeated. "Don't need me watching the kid. You're still home."

Valarie moved closer to the couch. "I don't trust you watching the kid, Jimmy. Of course I'm still home." Valarie stopped herself. "What happened outside while Payden was over today? At the police station? Why didn't you come home after? Did they charge you?"

"You want answers? What order?"

"I don't give a—What the hell was that outside our door earlier?"

"Little whore tried to tell me."

Valarie nodded, releasing her grip on her robe and raising her hands, gesturing for James to continue answering. "Tell you what?"

"What's what. Poked me."

"Poked you? With her tiny fingers?" Valarie glanced at the ceiling and shook her head. "What did she want to talk about that ended with you in cuffs?"

"Said I was the guy," James replied, his eyes going blank.

"Then, what? That pocket-sized policewoman made you throw a punch? I saw her bleeding from her mouth."

"She got lucky."

Valarie crossed her arms in front of her chest.

"She asked about the triple. Three dead. Dealers."

Valarie looked away. "Where does your money come from?"

"Off subject. Slut didn't know shit."

"So you hit her?"

James shook his head. "Told her to walk."

"Walk?"

"Fuck off."

"I will not be talked to like that in my own—"

"What I told her. Made her mad. She poked me. I gave her a slap."

Valarie rubbed her forehead, almost laughing at the absurdity of James's piecemeal recounting. "She poked you and you slapped her? So hard you made her bleed? Come on, Jimmy."

"She's soft."

"Soft?"

"Not weak. Got the scar to prove it. Soft. Like your queer friend. Payden." James grunted and took another sip of beer. "No. He's softer."

"Really?" Valarie's eyes misted as she recalled how brutal Payden could become. The way he'd been when they were a couple. The way she'd asked him to be for her, and he'd delivered on.

"Enough. Too many questions."

"Fine," Valarie said, hearing Charity cry for her again and ready to leave James for Michael to handle. "Last one, then. Why are your hands bruised?"

"Kiddie cop. Told you already."

"They weren't when you left. I saw. And you're filthy. That didn't happen outside my front door. I was there, remember?"

"They were. It did. Check your glasses."

Valarie clenched her hands into fists. "I don't wear glasses."

"Maybe you should."

"You know," Valarie said, stopping herself from yelling. "That's it. I want you out."

James chuckled, glancing at the ceiling, and Valarie moved swiftly to her bedroom, closing the door gently behind her and cooing to Charity.

As James inspected the rest of the room, trying to figure where Valarie hid the television's remote, he rubbed his sore knuckles, then the side of his neck.

Before he grabbed another beer, James went to the guest room and changed into a pair of jeans and a T-shirt. Stepping outside—making sure to leave the door open a crack—and taking a walk three houses down. Disposing of his dirtied clothes in a neighbour's outside garbage bin. Making it back in time to catch the nothing on the turned-off television and wait for Michael. Praying Valarie had her attention on Charity to the degree she hadn't noticed his brief exit. Wondering why he'd bothered to return.

XIII

Payden took his regular seat at the pub's bar. Ordering his new usual. Scotch. Neat. Triple it. Scanning the room and seeing lots of familiar folks. None of whom he'd spoken to before.

The bartender put Payden's drink in front of him and he paid without looking.

"Keep the change." He looked around the pub again to make sure the girls he thought looked good were actually good-looking.

"Thanks, Beck," the bartender said. "You just missed Mickey. And whatever happened to your cop buddy and his woman? I'll tell you what, when they stopped hanging here nightly, we lost more than a few customers."

"Mindy? She still brings them in?"

"The brunette with the body she can't show enough of? Oh, yeah."

"She hasn't changed." Payden downed his drink and motioned for another. "Just getting closer to married. Still can't be bothered with underwear. Still showing her future old man less than she shows everyone else. Poor bastard loves her, though. What you going to do?"

"Fuck her, right?" the bartender said, refilling Payden's drink. "I mean—"

"I get you." Payden downed his second drink, feeling the scotch wash around his brain, warm and dulling. "Who wouldn't fuck her?"

"You doing okay?" the bartender asked. "Looks like you came straight from the gym. Boxing? And you're drinking like you feel it."

Payden glanced at the bar and pulled his hands away when the bartender slammed down his third drink.

"Work-related?"

Payden took his drink and knocked it back, rapping on the bar three times and pulling his hand away again as he stood and quickly looked over his shoulder. "Unfortunately, it wasn't him. Or her. Or any of them. This town's gotten rough. Even if you ain't dressed like what you do, the streets can be mean."

"I hear you. Walk safe."

Payden nodded, backing away. "You have a good night, my man."

The bartender wished him a good night in return as Payden felt himself bump into someone he hadn't noticed when he'd plotted his course to the door.

"He's sorry," the bartender called out. "Just in for a quick three. Take it easy on him. He's a cop."

The pub fell silent for less than thirty seconds as Payden shot the bartender an admonishing glance.

"I'm sorry." Payden turned his body around to face the door. "My fault. I didn't see you...?"

"Layla," the girl he'd nearly stumbled backward over replied. Extending her right hand. Clearing her throat as Payden inspected her full, yet slim figure and cream-coloured skin. Half of her packed into a pair of jeans a size too small and the other half barely contained by the light pink silk chemise she'd managed to squeeze into her jeans along with her lower half. "Love the casual look."

"Sorry, again." Payden looked her in the eyes.

"You the good cop or something?" she asked, smiling.

He gave her a funny look.

"Too bad."

Payden shook his head. "Yeah. I guess."

Layla moved into Payden's space, tilting her head to the right and whispering into his ear. "If you were, you'd tell me your name."

Payden reflexively moved his hands away. "My name's Beck."

"First or last?" Layla chuckled, taking a seat at the bar.

"Depends who you ask."

"Many songs been written about my name."

Payden turned to face the bar as Layla guided him to sit to her right. "I think I've heard one or two. But I really got to—"

"Name one."

"Something about the Copa." Payden looked away.

"Her name was Lola," Layla said. "Close enough." She leant on the counter with her right arm, caressing the left side of Payden's face with her free hand. "Buy me a drink."

"I should really get going."

"Or maybe you should slow down. Enjoy the moment."

Payden chuckled. "I ain't—"

"Yeah, sure you ain't." Layla moved her body closer to Payden's and nudged his head with her nose. Breathing into his ear, warm and wet, as she spoke. "Can I ask you a question?" She grazed Payden's upper thigh with her left hand.

Payden nodded. "Only if you phrase it as a statement."

"Funny man. Do you want to fuck me?"

"That sounded an awful lot like a question."

She gave his inner thigh a lingering touch. "Tell me."

"No. I mean, not because—"

"You pass up this chance, there won't be another."

Payden nodded. "I really do appreciate — But I was leaving. Nothing personal."

"Hard to get," she said, kissing his ear's lobe, then pouting as he stood. "Love it." Layla got up from her stool, following Payden as he made his way toward the door.

She hurried ahead and backed into him, bumping his crotch with her ass and looking over her shoulder, giving him a wink. "You got no idea how good I can make a man feel."

Payden rolled his eyes, done with playing games. "Look. I'm not interested. And, a piece of advice, you'll catch more bees if you take a bath once in a blue moon. Now, please, get out of my way."

Layla turned and smacked him hard across the mouth, screaming, "Hands off, creep. Just because you carry a badge don't mean you can—"

Payden held up his hands. "Never touched her." He moved to walk past Layla, scanning the pub. "Just leaving."

Layla walked back to the bar, whispering, "Your loss, faggot."

Payden whispered back. "Say that louder. See what happens. Pray someone in here can stop it from happening before it's too late."

Layla stared back at Payden, unable to keep her lips from trembling. Real fear inside her, blooming the moment she heard Payden threaten her and felt, deep inside, he definitely would hurt her if he could. Kill her. "Buzz off." She looked to a few interested gentlemen surrounding her and began rubbing their arms, looking back at Payden and winking once more, selling her cool even weaker.

Payden shook himself off, straightening his top and walking out the door. Thanking God he had women like Valarie — and Lisa — to remind him his life was good, even if neither of them was his.

XIV

Lisa returned to her home late in the evening after a night out alone, running. She didn't have any friends where she lived and she hadn't made any where she now worked. Most women despised her, and most men just wanted a physical relationship with her. She'd never understood why other women held her looks against her. She didn't wear makeup and she didn't dress to evoke interest. Yet she'd also never gone out of her way to ensure she didn't look good. The job should have done that part for her. She'd taken plenty of punishment and she gave at least as good as she got but, even with the heavy, unconcealable scar on her neck, she was still attractive. A baby face with beautiful eyes no one had ever thought to put out a cigarette in. And she made no apologies for looking the way she did. It was genetically pre-determined. Ironically, her parents had been extremely difficult on the eyes.

As she closed her front door and locked it, she continued to jog in place. Her sweatpants dirtied and her sweatshirt soaked at the armpits and lower back. Perspiration which cooled quickly in the conditioned air of her home.

She turned to face away from the door, bringing her light jog to a slow halt, disrobing and bringing her dirty clothes with her to wash in the upstairs shower along with her body.

The dirt muddied the tub and she spent a half hour after cleaning herself ensuring every chunk went down the drain as her body dried naturally.

She threw on a bra and panties before grabbing a new garbage bag from the kitchen and throwing her night's clothes in them. Considering setting them on fire, but then figuring a quick walk around the block — dressed in fresh sweatpants and a fresh sweatshirt with a hood — was a better idea. She took a walk and, thirty minutes later, she was back home, her clothes disposed of in a far neighbour's half-full outside garbage bin.

When she returned, she went upstairs, stripped to her underwear and hopped onto her bed.

She turned on the television and, as she flipped through the channels to find something visually appealing yet easy to ignore, she thought about her first day at her new assignment. Partnered with a man named Payden Beck. A man who, to her limited knowledge, was a boor and a misogynist. A man who'd insisted she dress in a manner he preferred. A man who'd tested her and upset her on purpose, to take her temperature, possibly looking for weaknesses to exploit, possibly just figuring how to act around her if he wasn't who he seemed. A man whose butchery of the English language knew no bounds. A man who'd managed to enrage her and make her feel welcome within the span of a short afternoon. A man she'd wanted from the first, and a man whose only real friend she'd met — a woman named Valarie — didn't have to say a word to tell her she hungered for him too. A man she, essentially, wished to own for at least one night because he was desired by another woman she felt was more outwardly attractive than she could ever be.

The phone in the kitchen rang, snapping Lisa out of dreaming awake.

Her answering machine picked up on the fourth ring.

The message left for her was a dial tone.

XV

Lester Mansfield, dressed in black jeans, a black T-shirt and a black hooded sweatshirt, walked the back alleys where the previous evening's murders had taken place. His black skin and attire, with hood up, keeping him nearly invisible. As expected, all three corners were shut down, dressed in crime-scene tape. And, as expected, the three corners a few blocks away from each were in business. Lester waited until he reached the last to do more than give the dealer lurking in the shadows a nod. Each time, he found it more disturbing. Not the carrying on of business as usual, or the fact he knew half the force was taking money to look the other way, more the amount of real estate he had to cover to get from the first crime scene — two blocks from the local pub — to the last, nearly on the outskirts of town.

When Lester reached the last corner, he turned it and approached the dealer hanging in the shadows, giving him a slight nod, squinting to keep his eyes from drawing attention to his shrouded face. "Holding?" he asked.

The dealer waved him along, letting his hands do the talking. Nothing to see. Take a walk.

"Seriously, brother," Lester said, throwing in a faked slow-growing shake. The withdrawals and the need building inside him. What the dealers looked for in a customer. Repeat business, until death. "Hook me up, man. Just a baby balloon. To get me by."

"Looking to ride horsey? Outside grocery. Only cost you quarter."

"Just need a fix." Lester shuffled his feet, looking at the ground. "Please, man. Do me a solid."

Lester heard a click and the dealer looked down, showing he was armed. "Walk away, cop, or I put as many in you as it takes."

"Cop?" Lester asked, shaking for real. "Shit, I'm just a citizen, brother. Looking for the real deal."

"Maybe. Everyone know who did us last night. Tell me it not you. Lie to me, *negra*."

"Look. Okay. I know what you think, but—"

"Tell me, rubber chicken."

Lester slowly reached into his jeans pocket.

The dealer looked up and down the street for potential witnesses.

Lester pulled out his badge. "You got me, okay? I am a police officer. A detective. Believe it or not, I'm tasked with finding out who committed those murders last night. Make sure they don't happen again. Ever. If a cop, or cops, did it, I'll see they go down. But I need some questions answered."

The dealer nodded and Lester nodded in return.

"So, what's the news?" Lester asked. "You hear anything?"

"Lies. Maybe woman. Maybe man. I think man."

"That's good," Lester said. "It's all good."

"Is it?"

Lester nodded.

The dealer grunted. "Why you fuck with me?"

A stranger in what appeared to be a sweatsuit came from around the corner farthest from the street. "Holding?" The stranger appeared to look back around the corner. "What's this?"

Lester motioned with his hands for the dealer to put away his weapon, then flashed his badge. "Excuse me. I'm police, but I want you to know you aren't in trouble."

The stranger didn't move. "What would I be in trouble for? Saying a word in the form of a question?"

The dealer growled, whispering, "That's a man's voice. Maybe tonight's lucky."

"Stay cool," Lester whispered back, then began slowly advancing on the stranger. "Sir, I just want to ask you some questions. I don't need to see your face. If you want, I won't move any closer. Then I'll go and you can do whatever it is you were going to. Sound fair?"

The stranger moved into the shadows, still in sight. "Sounds like a setup. I'm just trying to pass. Get to the street. It a crime to walk the streets past dawn?"

The dealer moved swiftly behind Lester, pressing his gun's barrel into Lester's back. "That maybe the guy. Waste him."

Lester didn't turn back to look at the dealer as he replied in a whisper. "Could just be a customer. Someone hooked on the junk. You start killing all your clients, who are you going to sell to? You start murdering civilians, we can't take your money and look the other way. Think."

The stranger began to back up. "What you whispering for?"

Lester raised the volume of his voice, trying to sound like he knew what was going on and that—gun pressed into his back or not—he was in control of the situation. "We're just worried, man. Shouldn't we be? Three got taken down last night. You heard?"

The stranger appeared to nod.

"Then you know. This isn't a setup. No buy and bust. I already told you I'm police. Would I do that if I wanted to take you in?"

The stranger didn't move.

"I'm looking out for you. Okay?"

The stranger remained still. "You telling me you're providing on-location protection for drug dealers now? You telling me you're not only ignoring, but endorsing, illegal drug trafficking? Out of respect, one chance. Go."

"Sir?" Lester replied. "We're just—"

The dealer pulled the gun from Lester's back. "This ain't right," he whispered. "Nobody hide. It's the guy."

Lester whispered back. "Calm down, I said. Of course he's hiding. He doesn't want a cop to know he's using."

The stranger backed up a step, nearly out of the shadows. "Why you whispering again?"

Lester raised his voice. "Look. You have to understand—"

The stranger backed up quickly, turning the corner and disappearing, and Lester gave chase.

The dealer stuck to his spot, safely releasing the hammer of his gun and pocketing it, as he watched Lester race to the end of the alleyway and around the corner in the direction the stranger had vanished. Certain, more than ever, that whoever had run had been the man who'd taken out his fellow dealers. Certain—since he heard nothing but what sounded like running until he couldn't hear any noise from down the alleyway—that Lester had either caught the doer or was still chasing.

Fifteen minutes later, another stranger in a sweatsuit approached him from the street. Walking toward him and looking back, being careful not to be spotted, like a good junkie. Staggering and keeping their face hidden in the glare of the street light.

The dealer checked the ground and moved to pick up his bag. "What you looking for? Long night or short trip?"

When the dealer looked back up, the stranger was within a foot of him, hand extended. Revolver pointed directly in the dealer's face.

"It's safe," the dealer said, shaking. "There's cops everywhere tonight, looking. Trust me, you're not—"

The dealer was dead—minus one quarter of his skull and on the ground—before he could finish the thought he was in the middle of voicing.

The stranger wiped down the gun, pocketed it and jogged away, looking like a pedestrian out for a run.

Lester didn't return after the gunshot went off.

XVI

Payden finished cleaning and dressing himself, after waking an hour early, and called in to the station, requesting Detective Reid's contact details. When he'd procured her number and address, he called her on her home phone. The phone rang three times before she picked up.

"Put me on your no-call list, please," she said.

"Don't hang up. It's Beck."

"What couldn't wait until we spoke in person?"

"I'm picking you up. In our car. Don't want you to have to drive in all alone."

"I've heard some weak lines in my time," Lisa said. "But never anything so sad. Did you miss me last night? Was that you who called? Is this your way of insisting I go out for a welcome drink with you after work?"

"Maybe, I don't remember, and excuse me?"

"Pay — Beck," she stuttered, stopping to take a breath. "The fact you think you can insist in such a manner is not only offensive to me as a woman, it's offensive to me as a person. Please know this. When I'm working, I'm working. When I'm off the clock, I do what I want, with whom I want. I don't need you to guide me through the dangerous waters of social interaction and I don't want you to do me favours. When it comes to the job, we're solid. When it comes to real life, we don't know each other yet, so keep it professional, always. And I'll tell you another thing. I don't appreciate being interrupted outside of work hours for anything other than my job mandates I be available for. For future reference, if whatever you feel like calling me about—at any hour—has to do with anything other than the case, or cases, we're working on, it can wait. At the risk of offending you, know this as well. You are not to call my home phone number except with regard to police business. You are not to visit my home except with regard to the same. I don't wish to alienate you, but I feel you've made it necessary for me to define my boundaries. If I have offended you, I apologise. Do you understand the words I've spoken to you? I will not tolerate any form of harassment, no matter the intent. Am I understood? Beck?"

"Sure. Just, one question. For clarification?"

Lisa let out a disgruntled breath. "You may ask."

Payden's grin came through in his voice. "What are you wearing?"

Lisa let out an unexpected chuckle. "You are shameless, I swear."

"I guess. See you—"

"And to answer your question. Nothing."

Payden gulped.

Lisa let out another chuckle. "Pick me up in fifteen minutes. No later, please. Goodbye."

"Okay. See you—"

"Until then."

Lisa's end of the line clicked off and Payden stared at the phone for a moment, eating into his deadline. Then he rushed into the bathroom to check his teeth and hair. With ten minutes left on the clock, he was in his car, speeding to Lisa's home. Jamming a fat envelope into the glovebox. Eager to get to work for the first time in years. Telling himself it had everything to do with the slight dent in drug-related crime that weekend, and nothing to do with his new partner.

XVII

Payden arrived at Lisa's address to find her standing on the sidewalk, waiting, dressed in comfortable beige jeans and a loose-fitting white shirt with no indication of affiliation with any brand or organisation, except perhaps the company that manufactured her bra. As he pulled to the kerb and unlocked her door, he reminded himself she was just another officer and the fact he enjoyed looking at her face and body didn't make her an object. Repeating that in his head as she walked slowly to his car.

Lisa opened her door and slid into her seat, not looking at Payden as he compulsively inspected her, noting not a single inch of her body had been shaped by her tight dress blues. Also noting she had her hair pulled back in a ponytail again and a part of him wished the scar on her neck ran along its left side.

She fastened her seatbelt and Payden pulled their car away from the kerb.

"So," she said as they drove. "Did I nail it? I'm assuming so, since you didn't ask me to go back inside and change. Or are you taking things too far the other way and not seeing me at all?"

"Nailed it? You talking about your clothes?" Payden kept his eyes on the road.

"Yes, my appearance." She crossed her arms in front of her chest. "Should we go shopping? Is this going to be an issue with us?"

"Not at all." Payden glanced at the back of her head. "Lose the ponytail, though."

Lisa shook her head unconsciously. "I've found, over the years, people take me more seriously if I don't let my hair down."

"That was good." Payden grinned. "May be hope for you, after all."

Lisa gave him a hard sideways glance. Hiding the embarrassment she felt at not realising the play on words she'd let go until Payden pointed it out to her.

"You could go bald. Then people would really take you—"

"What must I do to stop you from having these fits?"

Payden shook his head, smiling. "Nothing about you is going to stop me from having fits." He paused. "But, I was curious...."

Lisa looked at her outfit, wondering if she'd perhaps gone with too relaxed a look. Hoping it didn't please Payden only slightly less than she hoped it did. "Yes?"

"Where you keep your gun?"

Lisa squinted. "In my locker at the station, though I don't require one to do my job. Did you not notice I wasn't carrying a firearm yesterday? And, offensive suggestion aside, where do you keep yours?"

"Up my water-tight ass. Where else?"

Lisa shook her head, the ugly look wiping itself from her face.

"Under the front seat, usually. Rather not carry, like Verrill. No reason to, really. Puts people off. Use my belt holster, mostly, to hold my flashlight. Also, only when I need it." Payden cleared his throat. "Sorry I asked you that. You're right, it wasn't... proper."

"Then, may I assume we're done discussing my look?"

"Yeah. Just lose the rubber bands. They're too precious."

"Precious?" Lisa scoffed. "What is that supposed to mean?"

"I mean, they make you look like a little girl."

Lisa smirked. "Because no man likes them young, right?"

"So, the line about being taken seriously? That wasn't intentional?"

Lisa pulled off her rubber bands and threw them in the back, ensuring her hair fell behind her shoulders as she leant forward, then rested in her seat. "Are you happy now?" She used her hands to showcase her head. "Do I look old enough? And how old is old enough?"

"Yeah," Payden said, not looking, which upset Lisa though she felt it shouldn't. "Your stock rose. And old enough for what?"

"Old enough for whom? Stop pretending and we'll get along better. Professionally and off the job. Tonight, for sure, when I have my borderline-coerced drink with you to welcome me to the force."

"Who's pretending?" Payden asked. "About what?"

Lisa looked out the window, touching at the right side of her neck and chewing on her lower lip. Glancing back at Payden's left hand as they drove and feeling the scar she'd noticed on the pad of his left index finger as if it were her own. Wondering if what she felt in his presence was a result of their individual disfigurements and, then, if that was a good or a bad thing.

XVIII

Payden and Lisa entered the station to the sounds of various catcalls from the few women in the bullpen. Lisa blatantly continued giving them all a thumbs up until they stopped. When he turned to see what she was doing behind his back, she dropped her hands to her sides and glanced away before fixing his gaze and giving him a baleful smile.

When the men in the bullpen followed up by praising Lisa's body aloud, Payden silenced them with a hand held high. No words spoken, just a gesture demanding they show his new partner the respect she deserved. Not looking back to see the self-satisfied smirk he assumed she was wearing, causing him to miss the awe in her eyes and the way her facial expression turned soft, nearly liquid, when he'd silenced the entire station with an action. A look he might have interpreted as sexual desire. The thought of which disturbed her almost as greatly as it turned her on.

When the din died down, the sound of the captain screaming from his office echoed through the halls. Payden looked back at Lisa and nodded, not seeing thanks in her expression—nor apology for the verbal dousing she'd set him up for at a point he couldn't figure—and not expecting it. He motioned to her and they walked to his old office, where he eased the door open to find it empty.

Lisa cleared her throat quickly. "And I remind you, I don't need—"

"Fuck me," he said, and Lisa stopped herself from agreeing to. "Yeah, I get it. And I'll try to keep it in check." He paused. "Verrill and Mansfield? You think?" He pointed toward the captain's office. "They haven't even caught a case yet."

Lisa shrugged, then followed Payden as they made their way to the captain's office.

Payden knocked, the noise in the captain's office ceased immediately, and Payden opened the door a crack. "Pardon me. May Reid and myself enter?"

The captain waved them in from his place, sitting behind his desk. "Reid doesn't know better than to interrupt, but 'yourself' may come in too." He looked at Lisa. "This is what the system produces. Garbage in, garbage out. Try to teach Beck how to speak English. And close the God damned door."

They saw Bryan standing at the far side of the room, opposite the captain's desk, looking hangdog and giving them a nod.

"Forgive me for asking, Captain," Payden said as Lisa closed the door behind them, "but why are you so angry—"

"I'm mad because Verrill let Mansfield try to grab your case." He looked at Payden hard. "What the fuck's wrong with you? You ain't pissed?" He looked at Lisa harder. "And you, half-pint? Got nothing to say about your first break, happening on your first day no less, and this fuck trying to steal it from you?"

Lisa clutched her hands behind her back and took a deep, calming breath before replying. "Of course that news upsets me. I'm just curious what's actually being discussed here."

The captain stood and marched to Lisa, getting in her face. "Let's set one thing straight, tits. The fact you're a woman don't pull no weight with me. So quit trying to use what you got to fuck me up. When it comes to the job, you're as worthless as everyone else. You do as you're told or you're out on your perfect little ass. Got me?"

Lisa's expression remained calm as her upper lip twitched slightly. "Yes, Captain. My question remains. What are we discussing here? I'm assuming we're invited, though our presence wasn't specifically requested."

"You're fucking right you're invited," the captain continued. "You're mandatory. And, as I was saying, for those of you paying attention—like Reid—Mansfield went off on his own last night. No paperwork, no nothing except some bullshit line he fed Verrill. We got another dead drug dealer and that mother fucker hasn't shown his face yet. He's late. And he ain't answering his phone or his pager. Tried him on the portable, too. I want his fucking ass in here now. I want an explanation. You're telling me we got a cop looking to keep the dealers in this town safe, roaming the streets at night, and not only did he fuck that up, he can't be bothered to justify his actions? What the hell is that?"

Payden cleared his throat and looked at Lisa.

Lisa faced the captain with her hands at her sides, her shoulders lolled forward to downplay the fact she had well-proportioned breasts. "Are you asking us to help find him?"

The captain switched his gaze to Payden. "If it wouldn't be too much trouble. I'd hate to inconvenience you."

"Verrill will be coming with us?" Payden asked.

The captain chuckled, looking at Bryan, then Lisa. "What do you think, tuna fish? You want to drag this mutt around all morning?"

"Sir," Lisa said, unable to keep her cheeks from flushing. "I'd greatly appreciate it if you stopped referring to me using—"

"What, Reid?" the captain snapped. "Tell me you ain't dressed for—"

"Sir," Lisa snapped back.

The captain looked at her in disbelief, anger in his eyes.

"All due respect—"

"Didn't I tell you to knock that shit off—"

Lisa continued, unfazed. "Just because you feel I'm worthless does not give you the right to—"

"Look, this is the way things are. And if you think—"

"I will not be talked to like I exist to please your eyes. If you wish to write me up, do so, but this will be the last time you speak to me in that manner. It's unprofessional, and it's conduct unbecoming an officer. I'll understand if you excuse me."

The captain moved behind his desk and took his seat, looking like he'd just been interrogated with a phone book. He spoke slowly and calmly. "You're right, Reid. I was out of line. I suppose working with men has desensitised me to a degree." He looked Lisa in the eyes. "But, if you ever speak to me like that in front of my men again, I will drum you out of the force. Don't let Beck's unprecedented streak of good luck poison you. Do we understand each other?"

Lisa nodded, holding back tears of rage she correctly assumed would be misinterpreted as tears of weakness.

"Excellent." The captain let out a heavy breath, defeated. "But I will not excuse you, Reid. I'm ordering you to bring Verrill along with you and Beck to investigate the scene of the murder last night—get the specifics from dispatch—canvass the area and bring Detective Mansfield back to this office. Am I understood?"

Lisa nodded, calming down. "Yes, sir."

"Good," the captain said as Bryan and Payden watched him, their expressions loose and dead. "Now, let's hope this whole Mansfield business is resolved before end of day and—"

The phone on the captain's desk rang and he picked it up immediately, like he was drowning and it was a lifeboat. "Yeah," he answered, the piss and vinegar back in his voice. "I'm in the middle of a very important meeting. What the fuck is—"

The captain nodded as the voice on the other end rattled. When it finished speaking, he grunted and hung up the phone, looking around the room at no one.

"It seems," the captain said, "Mansfield barked up the right tree." He nodded. "They found him half a block from the crime scene. Covered in dirt. Discovered in a brick-walled backyard by a landscaper. Skull crushed. Now we got five murders in two days, and one of the dead is our own." The captain snapped out of it, pounding his desktop and raising his voice, yelling at everyone in the room. "Our vigilante just moved to the top of the menu. Bring me that mother fucker, now. I want his ass. I want him dead. I don't care what order. He killed an officer. And—you'll love this, Beck, maybe even your thin-skinned new partner will—I don't care what you do to catch this prick. I don't want to know. Just do it. I hear any complaints, I'll have your back when you go up against IA." He pounded his desk with both hands. "Do it now." Then he looked Payden directly in the eyes. "And just so you know, you self-righteous cunt, if this goes bad again—if whoever's doing this walks away—I don't care who's responsible, it's your fucking badge. You got me?"

Payden nodded.

"And you're okay with keeping Verrill on? Think hard about this one. He don't owe you shit no more. You already got a partner with no experience to keep in line. You positive you want him on this case?"

"Yes, sir," Payden said, not looking at Bryan or Lisa. "As you ordered."

"Then why the fuck are you still here?" the captain yelled.

Lisa, Payden and, lastly, Bryan hurried out of the office.

Bryan got details on the location from dispatch and, within a few minutes, they were all piled in Lisa and Payden's shared car, headed to the scene of what the initial witness could only describe as the most horrible thing he or she had ever seen in his or her life.

XIX

Payden, Bryan and Lisa sped off to the crime scene, with Payden at the wheel. The news of Lester's death had come as a shock, and none of them found any measure of comfort in what they saw when they arrived. The back alley outside the brick-walled backyard had been sealed from the street in both directions between the facing buildings.

All three flashed their badges as they passed under the crime-scene tape, ignoring the crowd. The first thing on their list was to ensure the dead man was indeed Lester Mansfield.

Lisa walked into the backyard, exiting just as quickly as the lead CSI investigator snapped at her. She put up her hands, fussing with her hair to make it seem like she wasn't intimidated or flustered by how she'd been spoken to.

Payden and Lisa moved farther away and stood, hands in pockets, as Bryan took the lead and got close to the body, much to the evidence collection team's chagrin. Bryan put on light plastic gloves and brushed some of the dirt away from the body's head, not turning it any more than it already was. Even with Lester's skull obviously traumatised — misshapen with blood all around it — Bryan recognised him and confirmed his belief aloud.

One of the crime-scene collection team spoke. "Careful where you leave your footprints, Verrill. We haven't cleared the area yet."

Bryan inspected Lester's body more carefully, wondering if the previous night with Mindy had clouded his judgement and was causing him to allow emotion to overrule his common sense. "I'm sorry, guys," he said calmly. "I'll be just one second."

Payden whispered to Lisa. "What the fuck is up with this?" He shook his head. "You see whatever Verrill thinks he does?"

Lisa shook her head, stuffing her hands deeper into her jeans pockets, not noticing Payden doing the same in his own pants pockets.

Bryan finished his initial examination and assured CSI neither he, Payden nor Lisa would be entering the backyard until they'd been cleared to.

Bryan walked to Lisa and Payden, then whispered, "This is bad."

"No shit," Payden said. "Why you whispering?"

"Seriously," Lisa added. "Why you — I mean, why are you whispering? If it's something you can't say here, we should go elsewhere. Beck?"

"Jesus," Bryan said, calming down and bringing his voice to a whisper again. "This is new. And keep it down."

"Yeah, no bullet wounds," Payden said at normal volume.

"Why are you whispering about that?" Lisa asked Bryan.

"Seriously, Verrill, what's with the fucking whispering?" Payden walked past the scene to the far side, avoiding the line of officers guarding the near perimeter and more than a few spectators, some of whom claimed to be witnesses, though none had seen anything.

"That's h—" they heard a voice shout from the crowd. "I was in my apartment upstairs. Heard the whole thing."

Payden, Lisa and Bryan stared into the crowd, unable to make out whomever had been railing but seeing more than a few hands pointing in their direction, raised above the mob from somewhere in the middle.

"That's who I heard, I know it," the voice from the crowd screamed again.

The officers gave their official responses. "Remain calm. Please disperse."

Payden turned away from the crowd and Lisa followed suit.

Bryan gave Payden a hard look, which Payden returned.

"What's your problem?" Payden asked Bryan.

Bryan shook his head. "I don't know."

"If you're asking, I didn't do it."

Lisa grabbed Payden's forearm, releasing it quickly. Betraying a tenderness she feared the world might learn she possessed. The thing that once kept her down in a man's world.

Bryan didn't notice as he looked Payden in the eyes and nodded, revealing neither belief nor disbelief. "Not this time?"

"The fuck?" Payden gave Lisa a strange look she interpreted as admonishment for grabbing hold of him, though he hadn't noticed either. Unconsciously dismissing it as a bump. "We're in mixed company. By which I don't mean there's a lady present."

"Excuse me?" Lisa asked.

"You know what I mean," Payden replied to her, then fixed Bryan's gaze again. "Now's not the time to go there."

"No?" Bryan asked. "You want to make things right with me?"

Payden nodded, then shrugged. "When did I make things wrong with you?"

"Tell the captain I'm on this case until it's solved. Don't take an ounce of bullshit when he tells you I'm too close." Bryan locked eyes with Lisa. "The only person in detective division who isn't too close hasn't put in the hours."

Lisa returned Bryan's hard, steady look.

"Watch how you talk to her." Payden waved his hand between Lisa and Bryan, cutting through their staring match. "I'll ask the captain if you can work this case with us. Don't expect he'll care since you ain't got a partner no more. Funny how your prayers get answered sometimes."

"That wasn't funny," Lisa said. "A man is—"

"Dead. I know. Am I laughing?" Payden gave Lisa a glance and walked to the captain. After a few moments of heated argument neither Lisa nor Bryan could understand over the din of the growing crowd, Payden waved for Lisa to join him, calling back to Bryan. "It's official, stone-face. You're on the case."

Bryan waved to Payden. "Tonight. The pub. Eight o'clock. Bring your partner."

Lisa nodded to Bryan, squinting as he talked about her like she wasn't there, and walked to Payden. They returned to their car as Bryan began talking to the officers guarding the perimeter nearest the scene, who were taking random questions and statements from the crowd.

When they reached their car, Lisa stopped, looking down. "And, once more, Beck, please refrain from standing up for me. I'm perfectly capable of—"

"Jesus Christ, Reid. I remember fifteen minutes ago." Payden didn't look her in the eyes. "Things between us will go a lot easier if you just let me, or anyone, have your back. Partner. In the meantime, you'll pardon me for fucking breathing."

Lisa gulped as she got into the car, feeling truly weak and vulnerable. Afraid of losing something she was quickly coming to believe she'd always needed. And—for reasons which made no sense to her—going out of her way to ensure she lost it.

XX

Payden and Lisa pulled into the parking lot of the grocery, out of view of the sliding front glass doors. They'd left Bryan to begin his own investigation of the now-quadruple drug dealer homicides and the fresh kill of fellow officer, Lester Mansfield. A man Payden never held in high regard and now felt somewhat conflicted about thinking poorly of. Something his father had told him once. Some idiotic piece of philosophy. Don't ever speak ill of the dead. While it had never made sense to him, it had kept him from starting more than a few funeral home brawls. To his way of thinking, if he hated someone while they were living, it would be hypocritical to think the world of them just because they no longer existed, though he could fake that well enough—and had often—since the fact they no longer existed meant the world to him.

Lisa looked at the radio in their car, noting, for the first time, it didn't have a clock. Something she'd come to depend on at her old station, since she didn't wear a watch. "What time is it?" she asked. "It can't be lunch already, can it?"

"It's past lunch." Payden opened his car door. "Time flies when you're being accused of murdering a fellow officer."

Lisa exited the car with him after undoing her seatbelt. She slammed her door closed as Payden slammed his. "What? No one accused you of—"

"The fuck Verrill didn't." Payden marched toward the grocery. "Let him try to pin four dead scumbag drug-dealing pieces of shit on my ass, too. Never realised he had that bad a hard-on for me."

Lisa slowed her walk while Payden kept his pace. "What happened between you and—"

"Forget I opened my mouth," Payden said as he put six or seven feet between them. "The tabloids are more interesting, anyway."

"You've got a real mean side, you know that?" Lisa asked, keeping her distance. "I'm not your problem."

Payden saw Michael standing outside the grocery having a cigarette, and waved to him.

"Yo, Mickey," he called out. "What's the good news? Any specials on roast beef today?"

"Only ham." Michael chuckled, pushing himself off the wall. Meeting Payden as he strolled onto the sidewalk in front of the sliding glass doors, and shaking his hand. "Oh, and before I forget, Val wants you to come by the pub tonight. She's got this great girl she knows. Didn't catch her name. Says you two would be perfect for each—"

"Hi there," Lisa said, stopping to Payden's left, looking at him. "Payden, you didn't tell me you had friends."

Payden shook his head as his eyes rolled. "Mickey, I'd like you to meet—"

Michael extended his hand. "Pleasure." He looked Lisa up and down, speaking to Payden. "I guess I'll tell Val it's a hard no. Lucky bastard."

"Name's Lisa." She took Payden's left hand in her right. "And I'm not his girl. I'm his new partner. Detective Reid."

Michael saluted her. "No offence meant, Detective. Just, you're looking good."

Lisa smiled and gave Michael a light smack on the elbow. "Cutie."

Michael blushed and backed up a step. "And I'm taken. Wife, daughter." He looked at Payden. "Should I tell Val no, or—"

"I'll be there anyway," Payden said. "Be happy to meet her. Doubt she's my type, but you never know."

Lisa gripped Payden's hand harder.

"According to Val," Michael said, taking one last drag and putting out his cigarette on the sidewalk, "this girl is everyone's type."

"Kind of like Reid? Though she's a bit possessive."

Lisa let go of Payden's hand, keeping up her smile.

"Cool," Michael said. "We'll see you there tonight?"

"Eight good?" Lisa asked.

"Yeah," Michael replied, slightly shaken. "You coming, too?"

"Of course." Lisa winked. "Beck insisted."

Michael and Payden gave her awkward looks, creating an unsettling quiet.

"I'm sorry." Lisa looked at Payden. "Are we here for lunch? Or are we running down a lead?"

Michael broke in. "The only thing he ever runs down round these parts is a roast beef sandwich. And my wife, Val. She loves him. Can't blame her. He's a good guy. You're new, so I'm assuming you think he's a complete asshole. I get that."

Payden shook his head and gave Michael a look.

"But he's a good man."

Lisa smiled. "You must trust him, if he's visiting your wife while you're at work."

"Course I do," Michael said, smiling in return. "She'd kick his ass if he ever got out of line. He knows that." Michael gave Payden a wink. "Like she finally booted Jimmy last night, right?"

"Come again?" Payden asked.

Lisa's eyebrows cocked.

"Yeah," Michael continued. "You guys keep him at the station all night or something?"

Lisa shook her head. "We ran him through pretty fast. He wouldn't talk, if he had anything to say."

"That's odd. From what Val tells me, he showed later, while I was out. All dirty and fucked-up, like he'd gotten into it with someone. God bless him, he's my wife's brother and I love her to death, but he's got a serious attitude problem. By the time I got home from the pub, he'd already skipped."

"He don't live with you two no more?" Payden glanced at Lisa. "Like that?"

Lisa replied to Michael. "That doesn't sound like the Jimmy we brought in yesterday. By which I don't mean to imply he shouldn't be afraid of you, Mickey. You're just so darned cute." Lisa kicked at the ground with her right foot. "I can tell you one thing, he has no respect for women. But I'd think he'd at least try to turn things around. Seeing as you gave him a place to stay."

"Had me wondering, too," Michael said, nodding. "Maybe he took a good beating. Lord knows he could use one. Maybe he just wandered off and he'll be back. Who knows? Val's happy. That's all that matters."

Lisa gave Michael a wink. "Mickey's a keeper. As usual, I'm late to the party."

Michael blushed again. "My man. You got yourself a charmer. She's going to be a lot better for you than what's-his-fuck. You'll probably get more done faster. Definitely easier. Couldn't happen to a better guy." He looked at Lisa. "Did I tell you he saved me and Val when we almost didn't get married?"

"No." Lisa glanced at Payden and smiled. "But he's something of a cupid, isn't he?"

"That he is."

Michael's boss called out for him through the grocery's sliding front glass doors and Michael excused himself.

They all walked in together. Michael to get back to work. Payden and Lisa to visit the deli counter.

Payden and Lisa were back on their car's hood, eating, within fifteen minutes.

XXI

Payden finished scarfing down his roast beef sandwich and looked at the sky while Lisa ate hers slowly, finishing her can of pop before her sandwich. Asking Payden if she could finish his unopened drink after. Surprised he agreed without hesitation. They didn't chat while they ate. He'd told her, with his eyes and small gestures, work could wait a half hour. And she hadn't pushed it. Any man who looked as fit and muscular as he did and made waste of a foot-long roast beef sandwich like he was sucking a milkshake through a straw wasn't someone she wanted to upset for no reason. A man like that was focussed. In her experience, the way a man ate described the way he interpreted and dealt with the world. And, she assumed, to Payden, the world was the enemy. At least, folks outside his circle were. And she didn't want to be one of them unless it became necessary she took on that responsibility and assumed that risk.

As she finished her sandwich—having reminded Payden they weren't to talk while eating, with her eyes and small gestures—she watched him. Clocking his every tic, his every unique move and look. She already knew, from what little time she'd spent with him, he could tell a lie without giving any indication he was doing so. She'd also found, when he did lie, there was what most people would accept as a good reason for it. She'd learnt he'd easily confess to a lie if he felt he needed to or if doing so was of no consequence to him or anyone he cared about. In her estimation, given what she'd seen of him so far, and the way he reacted to surprises both planned — her razzing of him with his co-workers' cooperation — and unplanned — the death of a fellow officer — he was a solid detective. A good cop in the sense he could stomach whatever it took to see justice served. And she could tell, easily, his sense of justice wasn't what he'd read in books. His sense of justice was internal. She loved that. Because she was the same as him in that respect. If there was one level on which they could connect, it was that. They both believed in what they were doing and they would both do what had to be done to achieve their ends, no matter if doing so required them to act in hypocritical fashion.

But she also sensed he had a soft side. That a part of him hurt, more deeply than whatever had scarred his left index finger. That maybe that part of him allowed him to do what was necessary. And she felt she knew, were she to divulge any secrets to him, he'd take them to his grave before he gave her up. At the same time, she could sense he wouldn't be telling her any of his secrets. Not any time soon. The overt, verbal interrogation, of which part of their getting to know each other consisted, hadn't stopped yet. He was still taking her temperature. Clocking her as she was clocking him. Comfortable in her presence, but not content enough to really open up. To trust her with information that could mean his life or his career.

Mostly, she admired the fact that a woman's beauty didn't affect his judgement and that, when she was alone with him for long enough, she forgot the things about her body that made her feel unattractive, especially the scar she couldn't hide no matter how she wore her hair. If she were perfect, she couldn't turn him against himself, or anyone else, with a wink and a smile. A tender touch or a sensual breath. She assumed, were they to have just met and begun a physical relationship, rather than a work relationship, he'd be just as sturdy in that regard. She liked her men strong. And she loved them silent. Especially when she needed them to be.

And he could pretend he didn't notice he was being scrutinised and analysed with the best of them.

When she finished her sandwich and his pop, Lisa hopped off the hood without a word, motioning to the car doors and getting in.

Payden followed, giving her a nod, and entered the car through the driver's side at an easy pace.

"All settled?" Lisa asked as she put on her seatbelt. "Feeling better?"

"I suppose." Payden's eyes admired her midsection as she smoothed her shirt. "Where is this coming from?"

"Where is what coming from?"

"Every time you meet someone new, or maybe someone you want to keep at a distance, you're all smiles and winks and—I hate to admit—disarmingly attractive. With men, anyway. What's the deal with that? And, more importantly, why were you acting that way with me when we met Mickey?"

"I never—"

"You called me Payden."

She rubbed her forehead. "Must be getting used to you or something. No offence meant, I just slipped and—"

"Held my hand?"

Lisa absently placed her hands between her legs, slamming her thighs shut as she looked away, her cheeks pinking and her eyes floating. "I didn't—I mean, I was just—"

Payden nodded. "Did they put us together to bang me off the force with their politically correct bullshit?"

Lisa freed her hands, patting Payden's chest softly, giving it a quick rub and calming down. "Relax, you male chauvinist pig." She continued to look away, blushing. "I guess I got confused. In the moment."

"You never get confused."

"That's not true of anyone," she said, nodding. "But, before we waste any more time debating, I think your buddy, Mickey, just turned your weak lead into a pretty strong one."

Payden cranked the ignition and was careful to look both ways, as Lisa reminded him, while backing out of his parking space. Then he motored out of the grocery's lot, onto the street.

"So," Payden said. "Tell me what's got the hamsters rolling that wheel in your head extra-fast now? Was it the comment about Jimmy's appearance? The third-party hearsay evidence from Valarie?"

Lisa replied calmly. "Exactly. Mansfield was covered in dirt. Just like Jimmy. The borderline-psychotic, possibly criminal—"

"Definitely criminal, according to Valarie."

"You don't think he's someone we should be looking for?"

"Probably, he is."

"Then take us to the projects," Lisa said.

"What for?"

"Jimmy isn't at Mickey's house. We just learnt. Seems we shouldn't start where we know he isn't, yes?"

Payden gave her a sideways glance.

"He's running. Where else would he— Trust me on this one?" Lisa smiled, batting her eyelashes. "I mean, Verrill's doing all the crossing and dotting. I'll bet Jimmy isn't even on his radar."

Payden nodded, taking a left, headed toward the projects. The area where violent crime was normal. The area their town was slowly becoming. "Verrill doesn't talk to Valarie much. She and his woman, Mindy, don't have a great history."

"Then let's pray Verrill doesn't bring Mindy to the pub tonight, or my welcome drink is going to be even more awkward."

Payden chuckled, heading out of town. "Let's avoid that subject completely."

"Mindy? Or just your friend?"

Payden gave her a funny look, then re-focussed his attention on the road.

"I noticed her husband calls her Val. Jimmy does too. You call her by her full name when the people closest to her don't. Why?"

"Why not?"

"It's a simple question. Not a trap."

"We had a relationship before she got married. Serious. Mindy fucked it up. There's still feelings there. Okay?"

Lisa held up her hands, glancing out her window at the haunting state of the neighbourhood. "That explains a lot. The touching. And kissing."

"You're reading too much into things."

Lisa turned to stare at Payden, leaning toward him. "No I'm not. You remind each other of something you wanted. Maybe something you still want. Did she want something from you, back then? Something you weren't willing to give her?"

Payden pulled down an alleyway, slamming the car into park and pounding the dashboard with his right hand, causing Lisa to snap back into an upright seated position. "Look. My relationship with her—what she may or may not have wanted, back then—is immaterial. And it won't affect my judgement of her brother. If he did it, he'll go down hard—"

"Okay." Lisa shrunk into her seat slightly, her lower lip trembling against her will as she let out an even breath.

"Don't talk to me about anything that ain't our business. Your demand, if I recall."

"Understood, Pay — Beck."

"When it's just us, Payden's fine," Payden said, relaxing.

"Is it? I'm not someone with whom you've had a...."

Payden's lightening mood began to turn dark again.

"I'm sorry. Didn't mean to bring her up." She let out another breath, more hesitant, betraying her state of emotional discomfort.

"Do I have your permission to call you Lisa from now on, flirt? Outside the station?"

She nodded, giving Payden an ugly, yet sad, stare. "You're not nice, you know that?"

Payden nodded. "You run hot and cold like a broken washing machine, you know that?"

Lisa suppressed a laugh. "But you are a softie. What's your middle name?"

Payden shook his head. "While we're getting cosy, what's Lisa short for?"

She looked at him, dreams in her eyes, possibly nightmares. "What do you think?"

Payden shrugged. "Never pegged you for a Melissa."

Lisa considered lying before she realised her immediate pupil dilation had already given her away, opting to change the subject and forget her original question. "Can't fool you."

"Just keep batting those lashes, Lisa," Payden said, scoffing. "Someday, maybe they'll make me stupid too."

Lisa stopped herself from touching her face by clasping her hands together as she looked away. "And maybe someday you'll answer my question? Tell me?"

"If it ever matters." Payden shifted the car out of park.

XXII

Bryan turned away as Lisa and Payden walked from the crime scene, realising he didn't really know either of them. Lisa was easy to write off. She was a fresh transfer. When she wasn't doing what she was told, she was following her partner's lead. New precinct, same laws, but fresh rules. Payden wasn't so simple to dismiss. Though they'd worked together, and known each other, for many years, he still didn't know what went on inside Payden's head. Just as Bryan had what Payden referred to as a stone face, Payden wore a mask most of his time on the job and, from what he knew, most of his time off.

Bryan interviewed several witnesses. None of the people he talked to had much to say that helped. The sex of the offender was in question, since, from what little folks saw before and after the dealer was killed, all the players were dressed in shady clothes. Sweatsuits with hoods. Even Lester. Several witnesses claimed they'd seen Lester chasing the killer but, in the dark, the only things they could be sure of were the ensuing fight didn't last long and Lester had been handed his ass in brutal fashion.

The only thing anyone had to say that Bryan found interesting was that they were sure they'd heard the killer's voice. Not only on the night of the murder, but somewhere past the crime-scene tape that day. When he followed up immediately with questions that might help him narrow the police-only suspect pool, he was disappointed yet again. The killer had an even voice. Not deep. Not high-pitched. Still, they said, it was distinct. Like it belonged to someone who came from the streets. Or someone who'd become them.

And, through all the questioning and pouring out of contradictory answers, one thought flowed through Bryan's mind with consistency. Not a single one of the witnesses had bothered to call the police. Not after they'd witnessed a gunshot execution. Not during, or after, watching whomever take their time ensuring another citizen died in someone else's backyard. Not a one of them had thought to call.

Bryan left the scene after speaking with the captain, making a stop by Mindy's home to ensure she was okay. When she told him he was acting silly, he didn't laugh. Neither did she after that.

He spent most of the rest of his work day there, until three in the afternoon, happy enough to feel her lips on his flesh. Happier still when she showed him the progress she'd made with the wedding planning. And that made him think of Payden again.

Payden Beck. The man who'd gotten sick and tired of crime taking over his town while he said and did nothing. If anyone could get away with murder, Payden Beck could. If anyone could lie, cheat, steal, name your poison, and ultimately kill to get what he felt he deserved, Bryan knew from first-hand experience, Payden Beck could.

Though their relationship had been severed politically at the department to a degree, he was going to have to test the waters. And do so carefully, because if anyone could hold a grudge and pay off on it much later, his ex-partner, Payden Beck, could.

XXIII

"Where are we going?" Lisa asked, faking a smile, as Payden drove down what she could swear was the street where Valarie lived. Her and Michael. "Are we going to see if we can turn this afternoon into a win? Maybe catch Jimmy unawares? At Val's house?" She shook her head. "Or is this just another excuse to see her?"

"Maybe so, maybe no," Payden said. "We've got to do something."

Lisa's forced smile cracked slightly. "How do you mean? We've not been wasting time looking for him elsewhere."

"Never suggested we were." Payden grunted. "Your instincts were good. I just mean, we were bust at the crime scene. We walked away."

"And now we redeem ourselves? Okay. Be sure to park at least two houses away. We don't want Jimmy to see us coming, if he's there."

"Definitely don't want him to see you coming. He'll run, for sure."

Lisa nodded, glancing at Payden and touching the side of her neck he couldn't see.

Payden parked the car, pulling up to the kerb a few houses down from Valarie's. "But, before we go taking a truncheon to Jimmy's skull, open the glove box."

Lisa opened it, giving Payden a queer look as she grabbed the fat envelope that fell out. "What's this?"

Payden looked around. "That's your weekly."

"My weekly?"

"Yeah, you know." Payden gestured with his hands for Lisa to hurry. "You open the envelope, you take the money, you put it in your pocket and everything's cool."

Lisa shook her head, her smile gone. "You aren't serious."

"You ever had a heart attack?"

Lisa shook her head.

"Then you got no idea how serious I am."

Lisa glanced at the back seat, sweating cold. "You can't be on the take, Payden. You don't—"

"Got all fucking day?" Payden asked, his stare turning harsh. "That's true. And neither do you. What is it?" He looked deep into her eyes, feeling her fear rising. "Too good for dirty money? How do you think things work here? It's only your second day, but you see. You think this shit our town's become happened because we didn't let it?"

Lisa shook her head. "No." Her cheeks pinked as her expression went loose. "I mean, yeah. I don't know. Are you serious?"

"Ask me that one more time."

Lisa shook her head. Her lips trembling.

"I'll tell you what. If you don't feel comfortable yet, I'll hold it for you. Like a bank. When you come around, let me know. It'll all be there. Just don't take too long deciding or you'll make the wrong people nervous. On the bright side, if you choose incorrectly, no one will ever have your back again. That's something you say you want, yeah?"

Lisa didn't answer.

"I said, deal?"

Lisa turned to face Payden with her body as she backed away involuntarily. "Look. I don't want to—"

Payden slammed the roof of the car with an open hand and Lisa flinched.

"—upset you, but this isn't what I...." She looked at him, helplessness in her eyes.

He snatched the envelope from her hand, opened it to dump the wads of shredded newspaper onto her side of the car's floor, and let out a cackle. "Got you." He continued to chuckle as Lisa looked away, wiping the embarrassment and fear from her face.

"Really funny." She gave him a hard smack on the arm. "Your sense of humour is...." She shook her head and fussed with her hair. "Anyway, I knew you were pulling my leg."

"You're too proud." Payden opened his door. "And it wasn't a joke." He glanced at her. "If you'd taken the 'money', we'd be done already."

"I know," she said, another form of fear on her face she thanked God Payden wasn't able to see.

Payden stared down the street toward Valarie's house. "No backyards, but we stick to the greenery. Blend in, be cool, don't attract undue attention."

"I know how it works, Payden."

"Good to hear, Lisa."

Payden and Lisa exited their vehicle and began to walk slowly, holding hands at her suggestion to avoid seeming like they didn't belong in what was slowly becoming one of the safer family neighbourhoods. She, mostly doing so to grip Payden's hand hard. To shake the worry from her system while she prayed his test hadn't been a double bluff.

XXIV

Lisa and Payden slipped around the side of Valarie's house, undetected. Lisa kept her hold on his hand as they walked like they were entering their own backyard, having already passed another couple taking their children for a walk, and acting like a married couple. Pulling it off nicely. Ensuring themselves a place in the hall of fame for things nobody ever heard of or cared about.

When they neared the far corner of the house, they heard Valarie inside, soothing her daughter with a song. And, for a moment, Payden wished he were beside her. He'd never heard her sing before. Never imagined she could carry a tune, though she could weave words into some of the most beautiful music he'd ever heard. He put his index finger to his lips.

Lisa let go of his hand and put her middle finger to hers, looking at him like he might really believe she'd just graduated the academy. Wondering when the tests would end. Thinking, with a man like Payden, they never really did. No matter how much he liked, trusted or even loved you.

Payden's attention drifted to the foliage growing on the chain link fence demarcating the rear of Valarie's property as he picked up a large, yet probably harmless, rock and threw it at the fence. When the rock hit the fence, he heard Valarie's voice quiet.

Within a few moments Valarie opened the door to her wooden back patio and walked onto it, dressed in blue jeans and an extra-large sleeveless white top with arm holes that reached to her hips. Looking in the direction of the fence, the expression on her face one of relief.

Payden whispered to her. "Valarie."

Valarie's head turned down and to the right, stopping shy of looking in his direction.

"It's Payden. I'm not here."

She scratched the back of her neck and looked forward, nodding very slightly, very slowly.

"Nod once, more quickly, if Jimmy's in the house."

Valarie clasped her hands above her head and stretched.

"Nod once if he's anywhere near the house."

She continued to stretch, her right breast partially exposed.

"Shake your head if you don't know where he is."

Valarie relaxed her arms and adjusted her shirt, shaking her head as she looked at the wooden floor. "It's safe to talk," she said at a slightly muted volume. "Just not too loud. Charity's sleeping." She sniffed the air. "Make sure your new partner knows."

Payden and Lisa walked around the corner and Valarie moved to close her back door, leaving it open a crack so she could hear if her daughter woke.

"I should have seen this coming," Valarie said, her eyes avoiding Lisa and focussing on Payden. "Did Jimmy do something bad before or after he left last night?"

Lisa spoke, keeping her voice low. "We think he might have. Another drug dealer—"

"Heard," Valarie said, leaving dead air.

Lisa continued. "An officer was killed as well. Witnesses say both murders happened at the same time."

Valarie jerked her head forward in a nod. The news hadn't gotten out yet. "Jesus."

Payden walked to Valarie and took her right hand in his left, facing her. "Was there anything off about Jimmy last night?"

"What don't you know?" Valarie pulled Payden in for a hug, glancing at Lisa.

Lisa looked away, trying too hard to pretend she didn't care about what she was seeing.

"He came home dirty," Valarie continued. "It was dark, he was being an asshole. I didn't want to turn on the lights and keep Charity awake longer. We had words. He left." She kissed Payden on the neck softly, lost. "I didn't want to argue, but there's no other way to talk with him. He looked like he'd gotten into it with someone." She took in a breath. "What did he do?"

"That we know?" Payden asked. "Nothing. But, from what you say, maybe something really bad. The cop we found dead was Verrill's new partner."

Valarie began to chew on Payden's jacket's collar, fixing Lisa's gaze. Subtly shaking.

"His partner was there when the drug dealer got hit. Maybe tried to stop it. We don't know yet. All we know is he was beaten bad, then finished. Buried alive in the backyard he died in." Payden paused, putting his arms around Valarie's waist as she continued to stare at Lisa. "You say he got dirty? Literally?"

"I had to clean where he sat on the couch." Valarie looked away from Lisa. "Why did you bring her back here?"

Lisa turned away, noticing Payden's eyes drifting to inspect her ass when she did.

"Oh." Valarie said, clocking Lisa's awkward body language. "I see. I guess I can't blame you."

Lisa tugged at her shirt, trying to cover her behind.

"Anyway. I haven't seen or heard from him since he left." She tilted Payden's chin up and kissed him on the nose, watching Lisa out of the corner of her eye. "He might show at the pub tonight. Mickey and I are going out. We found a sitter, so my friend will be there too."

"Saw Mickey earlier. He said."

Valarie scanned Lisa's short, perfectly proportioned body from feet to hair. "It's not too late, is it? I mean —"

Lisa turned to face Payden and Valarie. Speaking low as she interrupted. "No, Mrs...?"

"Dooley." Valarie unconsciously moved to protect Payden from Lisa.

"Mrs. Dooley. There's no need to call off the blind date you've set up for everyone's favourite roguishly ugly pretty boy. I'm his partner, ma'am. I'm a detective. You have nothing to worry about with regard to me. Our relationship is strictly professional."

Valarie glanced away. "Why would I be worried about you?"

Lisa moved closer. "I didn't — I only meant —"

Valarie cradled Payden's head in her hands, looking him in the eyes. "You're a terrible liar, Lisa. And you're sweating. Oddly, it smells sweet."

Lisa shifted in her shoes. "I'm not sure what you're implying, but —"

"Does it matter?" Valarie held Payden closer. "What you two do together is none of my business. I figured maybe you both enjoyed your first chase and tackle today. Took down some scumbag who didn't want to answer questions. What did you think I meant?"

Lisa pulled her absently wandering hand away from her crotch and crossed her arms in front of her chest. "I thought you suggested that we'd slept together."

Valarie looked Payden in the eyes. "Why did I let you go?"

Payden chuckled softly. "Baby, you never let me go. Just booted me out."

Valarie looked down. "You made me." She paused. "Still, I'm sorry."

"I'm sorry, too." Payden released his hold on her. "But we really must go. Not only do we have a killer to track down, I don't know if I can take much more of you recommending another woman to me."

"Not even a good-looking one?" She nudged his chin, as she felt Lisa's unvoiced irritation. "I understand. But be careful. Jimmy's violent, you know that. And he's unbelievably stupid. I mean, like a bull. Hitting him in the head with a brick won't convince him he can feel pain. So, please, take him seriously." She paused again. "What I'm saying is—"

"He's dangerous," Lisa said. "We get it." She crossed her arms more tightly in front of her chest. "Are you two going to kiss goodbye yet? Or am I ruining the moment? I can give you time alone."

Valarie looked at Lisa, her body shaking slightly again. "No need. You're a big girl." She kissed Payden's cheek and gave his ass a smack. She startled, smiling, when Payden returned the gesture, giving her ass a squeeze. "Get back to work, Payden. Your puppy needs someone to let out her leash."

"What did you—" Lisa began, the volume of her voice raising, and Payden moved from Valarie swiftly, covering Lisa's mouth with his hand.

He looked back at Valarie and spoke softly. "We'll see you tonight. Thanks for the information."

Valarie nodded. "Anyone but you two know about Jimmy?"

"Just Verrill. He was there when we questioned him yesterday."

"But not about his state last night?"

"How could he?" Lisa asked through Payden's hand, her voice barely intelligible.

"I guess he couldn't, if you say so. But try to say so with a little less volume. And enunciate." Valarie smacked herself on the forehead. "Be at the pub tonight. Jimmy knows Mickey and I will be there. He also knows I'm bringing a guest. He's delusional enough to think she's for him. He may show. You should both come. Enter through the back. If you see him standing outside smoking, your new partner can take him away and we all win. If you don't, come on in, be cool and, if he's not there already, it's your best bet where he'll end up."

"Thanks, Valarie," Payden said.

"Yes." Lisa pushed Payden's hand from her mouth, exposing her neck. "Thank you very much, Val."

Valarie blew Payden a kiss, staring at Lisa's scar, which didn't ease the dulled pain inside her, as she felt it should have. Instead, making her feel less attractive and emptier. Then she turned away, scratching her back with her middle finger until she heard Lisa and Payden leave.

When they reached the front of the house, Payden took Lisa's hand again. Reminding her, when she pulled away, that they were still in Valarie's neighbourhood and, if they wanted to nab James as early as possible, they'd keep up pretences until they got back to their car.

Lisa reluctantly agreed, just in time to wave, say hello and smile at another couple walking down the block, kids in tow.

When they were far enough away, Lisa looked down, tucking in her chin. "Whatever that woman wanted from you, back when you two were together, you should have given it to her. She's beautiful. Doesn't like you being anywhere near me." Lisa growled. "And don't even think about taking this 'couple' act farther. If you ever put your hands on my ass like you did with her, I'll break them."

"That was just—"

"Keep pretending."

Payden scratched his head with his free hand. "It was complicated. And she did almost flat-out state she thinks you're better looking than her. In her own, backward way. Even though we're not... It hurts. I know how she feels."

"No. Or maybe. But she saw. She knows she won that battle."

"What battle?"

Lisa smacked Payden's arm and released her grip on his hand when they reached their car. "You can stop pretending now. Don't pity me."

"Why would I?" Payden asked, getting into the car as Lisa did.

Lisa rested her neck against her right hand after putting on her seatbelt. "If you're lying to me, I'll never forgive you."

"Okay. Against your sage advice, I'm going to pretend I know what you're talking about so we can do what's got to be done sometime today." Payden pulled away from the kerb. "Odds Verrill got less working the crime scene all afternoon than I got from an old flame in five minutes?"

"I doubt he got any."

Payden looked at Lisa, grinning. "Fresh. I'm starting to like you, kitty cat."

Lisa sat straight, smiling against her will. Feeling sexier than Valarie which, for some reason, now mattered to her. "Just Lisa." She winked at Payden. "For the time being."

"You're doing that thing with your eyes again." Payden grinned. "You prefer your men confused?"

Lisa chuckled. "Confused about what? And... did you just refer to yourself as my man?" She grinned when she noticed Payden's nose twitch. "To quote a wiseacre, 'maybe so, maybe no'."

"Keep pretending."

"Only if you promise to."

They drove to the station at regular speed. Accidentally holding hands several times, and reminding themselves—out loud—play time was over. Then they practised referring to each other by last name only. It took them the entire car ride's conversation to nail that trick.

XXV

Lisa entered the station in front of Payden, waving to Bryan down the hall, who looked to be coming back from the captain's office. Bryan waved in return, looking beaten down, possibly elated—it was impossible to tell from the expression on his face. His eyebrows cocked when he noticed Payden entering the building, which made Lisa feel like she was finally being taken seriously. An officer before a woman, which was how things should be. For the most part.

Bryan called out, waving Lisa and Payden into his office as he disappeared into it.

Lisa took that door first, as well, noting a woman dressed in a sheer white blouse and a pair of tight grey slacks—Mindy, she presumed—sitting at the desk opposite Bryan's.

Bryan sat at his desk and clasped his hands together on his stomach.

Payden entered and closed the door behind him, noticing Mindy as well, giving her a nod, then looking at Bryan. "Got yourself a new partner already?"

Bryan rolled his eyes. "The seat's free now. No longer yours."

Payden held up his hands as Lisa moved to stand closer to Bryan and put distance between herself and Payden.

"And how are we?" Payden asked Mindy, moving farther away from Lisa and to the side of his old desk. "Ready to hit the aisle running?"

Mindy looked halfway up at Payden, then turned her face back down.

Payden nodded and looked at Bryan. "So, you get any solid leads from the crime-scene rabble?"

"No," Bryan replied. "And you two? What happened after you left? Haven't seen you all day and it's quitting time."

"For who?" Payden asked.

Mindy shook her head, muttering. "For your new little friend, if she's not completely—"

"What was that?" Payden patted Mindy's desk. "Speak up. Believe it or not, sometimes people are interested in what you have to say."

Mindy looked away.

Payden shook his head. "We stumbled onto a good lead." He pointed to Lisa. "Sprouted from Reid, and my relations in the neighbourhood."

"What do you mean?" Bryan asked, looking defeated, having questioned witnesses until he wanted to deafen himself and coming away with nothing.

Payden cleared his throat. "You remember that fuck, Jimmy? The piece of shit Reid brought in yesterday?"

Mindy glanced at Payden. "There are ladies present."

Payden pointed to the door. "And there's work being done. You're free to wait outside just like you're free to take up space in here."

Bryan waved Payden down. "Easy, Beck, she's just...."

Lisa smirked.

Mindy looked at Lisa, slow and ugly. Seeming to focus on her neck.

Payden glanced at Mindy. "I know. She's a lady. Heard that somewhere once. Anyway, it turns out, this Jimmy ain't just a borderline-criminal asshole, he also don't get along well with others, including his own blood. Mickey and Valarie were set to evict him last night, but he beat them to it."

"Yes?" Bryan asked.

"Turns out, when he showed last night—much later than when he left here, late enough to be a possible, I'm thinking—he was dirty. From head to toe. Valarie said he looked like he'd been in a fight. We didn't get too into it with Valarie. Her kid was sleeping and we weren't there to make her life miserable."

"The dirt's interesting. But the rest. That could have been from earlier yesterday. You and Reid weren't looking good by end of shift either. Still don't."

"For good reason," Lisa said, and Bryan turned his head to look at her. "It wasn't easy getting that big guy here. Putting him in cuffs. He didn't go down soft."

Bryan nodded. "Doesn't explain Beck, though."

"Luckily for me," Lisa continued, lying with a straight face, "Beck was good enough to act as a punching bag while we got Jimmy settled. In interrogation. After you left, when we uncuffed him and had to put him in braces again almost immediately. But Jimmy may have bigger problems than we thought, it seems."

Bryan nodded again. "If you say so." He looked at Mindy. "We're going to head to the pub."

Payden moved to stand beside Lisa. "Now? You're starting to drink earlier."

"You're not?"

Mindy stood. "Enough, please. It's past six. We're going to stop by my home and drop off our things, then we may as well head out. Bryan was to have told you we'd meet at eight. That'll give us plenty of time to get comfortable if we arrive early, or make it on time if anything comes up."

Payden patted Lisa on the shoulder. "We'll see you there, then. And, from what Valarie told us—"

"Just, please," Mindy said as she opened the door, waving a finger in Lisa's direction. "Do something about that. It's off-putting. I'm sure it doesn't bother Payden. He probably loves it, but you really can't afford to—"

"I'm sorry?" Lisa brushed her hair forward over her shoulders. "To what are you referring?"

"You know," Mindy said. "The—On your—"

Bryan hurried Mindy into the hallway, as she looked back at Lisa. "And we'll see you both later." Bryan slammed the door shut behind them.

Lisa moved closer to Payden. "She's exactly what I expected."

"Yeah?" Payden shook his head. "How so?"

"I didn't do any homework on you before I started here, but news gets around when an officer is accused of—"

Payden looked down.

"I'm sorry. I shouldn't have brought that up." Lisa combed her hair with her hands. "Tell me again. You really don't see it?"

"Why is it so important I do? It's a scar. On your neck." He held up his left hand. "I got one too. And you wore yours loud and proud with a ponytail. Day we met, and this morning."

"You said you hadn't noticed." Lisa looked down and away. "Not less than an hour ago. What else have you lied to me—"

"No. I said I didn't know what battle you lost with Valarie."

"You knew full well what I meant."

"Honestly." Payden let out a heavy breath. "I didn't. Because we were on a completely different subject and you"—he brushed Lisa's hair to hang behind her back—"aren't like Mindy."

Lisa shook her head. "I don't respond well to presuppositions or loaded statements."

"I just meant to say, God forbid a minor blemish should upset the fragile world of Verrill's lonely, condescending shrew of a fiancée." He looked Lisa in the eyes. "And, if that was what you were asking, then I apologise. Yes, I noticed, but—and I hope this doesn't make you angrier—it wasn't something that made a big impression." Payden moved to touch the right side of Lisa's neck and she backed up a step quickly. "Relax. I'm not putting the moves on you."

"You don't think I'm aware of that? Believe me, if I thought you were trying to...." Lisa looked away, her cheeks pinking and her lips frowning. "I guess you can't win from the position I put you in. Neither of us can."

Mindy's voice sounded from the hallway, not meant to be heard. "Jesus, this is pathetic. If I have to listen to that little freak fish for compliments one more second, I'm going to beg Payden to do to her what he did to—"

Payden moved away from Lisa and swung open the door, catching Bryan and Mindy off guard, focussing his gaze on Mindy, which Lisa noticed before she looked away. "The fuck are you still doing here? And what was that you were saying?"

"Easy," Bryan said, as he and Mindy entered the room. "I insisted we come back before we exited the building. We left too soon. Before you finished telling us something about tonight I felt might be important."

"Yeah, true." Payden began to pace, his cheeks turning red. "I let your mouthpiece throw me off again."

"Apologies." Mindy smiled, waving to Lisa, her gaze floating between Lisa and Payden. "As for what I was saying. I was merely referring to—Don't you two make the attractive couple."

"Meaning?" Lisa asked.

"Just." Mindy sniggered. "You know."

"Knock it off," Payden barked, snapping his fingers, causing Mindy to flinch.

Lisa's internal temperature spiked as she considered mounting Payden, then and there, while she stared directly into Mindy's eyes.

"Mindy, baby," Payden continued, "you're gone. And you better believe I'm serious when I tell you, if you fuck tonight up for me—for every cop who puts his life on the line so you can shop the sales in safety—I will do everything in my power to see you're punished. You worthless clothes horse." Payden wound down, fixing his stare on Bryan. "And you, my friend—if I can still call you that—are better than this half-assed ambush. It couldn't wait, so you bided your time in the hallway?"

"Calm down, Beck," Bryan said. "And what the hell are you talking about?"

Mindy didn't reply, only kept her gaze fixed on Payden. Terror and helplessness in her eyes.

"You don't know?" Payden snapped. "I've got to get the fuck out of here." He looked to Lisa who nodded, also unsure how to react to Payden's increasingly violent energy. "We'll meet you at the pub. Valarie and Mickey will be there. And we need everyone cool, because, as I was about to say before you two left a few minutes ago, Valarie says Jimmy might show there tonight and, if he does, we need to bring him in clean."

Lisa followed Payden out of the room.

"That's not a plan," Bryan said, looking unaffected as Mindy attempted to look the same.

"We'll make it up as we go along. We're not robbing the mint. Just be there and don't go in until we talk again."

Lisa stopped and turned, taking up the space in the doorway—barely containing her rage—keeping Payden in the hall. "Mindy. If you aren't comfortable playing this by ear, stay home."

Bryan looked at Lisa in disbelief. "I'll not have you talk to my—"

"Verrill. You made sure the streets will be patrolled heavily tonight? You spoke to the captain? Tell me yes or tell me no, so I can do so myself if necessary."

"Yes," Bryan said, nonplussed. "Patrols are doubled from now until we get the guy, or girl. Or the brass give up."

"Exactly what I wanted to hear."

Payden yelled as Lisa closed the door on Bryan and Mindy. "We'll see you outside the pub later."

Lisa turned and walked toward the front door, not looking back at Payden. "Too much excitement. I need to eat something."

"In case you're looking for a head to bite off, I won't take that the wrong way." Payden followed her out the door. "And, apologies. Didn't mean to stand up for you in there—"

"Why?" The front door slammed closed behind them and Lisa walked out onto the street, Payden hot on her tail while his eyes adored it. She glanced over her shoulder and shook her head when he looked up to meet her gaze a fraction of a second too late. Clearing her throat to mask the look she assumed was painted on her face when she realised she hadn't noticed Payden had stepped to her aid once more, against her express wishes. And that she hadn't minded. "There's no law against it."

"And the mixed signals are back. You're making me like you again."

She looked at him as they neared their car. "I'd better use that while it lasts. Let me drive?"

Payden chuckled and pulled the keys out of his pants pocket, tossing them to Lisa, who snatched them out of the air almost before they left his hand. "You're something else, Reid."

She looked at him, pouting, as she got into the car.

Payden hopped into the passenger seat.

Lisa closed her door, put on her seatbelt and cranked the engine.

Payden cleared his throat. "I mean, you're something else, Lisa."

"Thanks, Payden. But, seriously, would it kill you to wear your seatbelt?"

Payden looked to his right, shrugging and putting on his seatbelt. "I don't want to find out the hard way." He paused. "Why'd you lie for me back there?"

Lisa didn't answer, only nodded.

"You haven't been curious about my appearance at all today?"

"It looks like you took a good slap, which doesn't surprise me at this point. Maybe from the part of last night you claimed you couldn't remember with regard to possibly calling me, when we talked on the phone before work this morning. I assume whoever you were chasing wasn't interested. Anyway... It wasn't something that made a big impression."

"So, I owe you one? Or you just sure I'm not the guy?"

Lisa smiled and pinched his cheek.

Somewhere, in the back of Lisa's mind, as she drove and got used to her new car, she heard Payden yelling at her. Belittling her, defiling her and torturing her flesh with a righteous fury that made her want to submit so badly she nearly forgot she was starving.

And somewhere, in the back of Payden's mind, one drug dealer after another looked at him in shock and realisation before a bullet tore into them, their head exploded, and he tasted their blood and flesh in his mouth.

XXVI

Bryan and Mindy made it to the pub later than expected, to find Payden and Lisa hadn't yet arrived. Bryan looked around the parking lot and opened the trunk of his car, pulling out a plastic shopping bag, offering it to Mindy and asking her to change. In response, she highlighted her conservative grey cotton dress that hugged her body so tight every line of her less-than-conservative underwear showed through it. Dressed, as always, for attention, which was the last thing Bryan wanted her to draw that evening.

Mindy refused to change, and they agreed they'd enter the pub, and drink, separately. He'd find a table out of the way, once she was safely inside, so she could enjoy her usual spot at the bar. He shook his head as he secured the shopping bag in the trunk of his car and watched her enter the pub, winking and saying hello to a gentleman on his way out. A gentleman who looked her up and down, found his second wind and followed her back inside.

Bryan waited outside until he saw the vehicle he and Payden used to share pull into the lot. He moved toward it rapidly as Lisa parked, and knocked lightly on the hood when he reached it.

Payden and Lisa opened their car doors and got out. Payden was dressed the same as he had been earlier, keeping his jacket closed, though Lisa was wearing drab, loose blue jeans and a long, wide T-shirt a size too large for her, with her hair mussed and her face dirtied. Presenting herself in a way that made her look like she was short and chubby, with an unremarkable face. Nothing worth a second look. Which was the point.

"Hey, Verrill," Payden said, pointing at Lisa. "We stopped by Reid's place so she could dress up extra special. Just the way Mindy likes it. Tell me, does she pass the test? You know your woman better than anyone. Is she trailer-park trash or what?"

Lisa shook her head, scowling. "Not funny, Beck." Her gaze shifted to Bryan. "And you'd better say yes, Verrill."

Bryan nodded. "You did as good as you could and, when it comes to this place"—he pointed over his back with his thumb—"it doesn't really matter after a certain hour. But, yes, Mindy will definitely think less of you when she sees you looking the way you do. She'll probably assume that's how you look when you're not made-up, though you never have been that I've seen. Not to say that—"

Lisa held up a hand. "Thank you, Verrill. I was going for the 'please don't offer to buy me a drink' look." She messed with her hair to make it appear more unkempt and unwashed. "But—I have to ask—what are you doing with a woman like Mindy?"

Payden replied. "It's a long story. They met when we were phase one field trainees. Pretty much right after the academy."

Lisa asked, "You two have known each other that long?"

Bryan nodded in reply, putting his hands on his hips and letting his gaze float between Payden and Lisa.

"So, what's the plan? If everything's as normal as Mindy prefers, she's sitting at her regular spot. As usual, she's dressed to get looks, which might actually help the situation. We're spending the night in there apart."

"Bully for you. The play is this." Payden looked to Lisa. "Correct me if I'm wrong, or help make the plan better, if anything I lay down sounds like a bad move, yeah?"

Lisa nodded.

Payden brought Bryan and Lisa in closer, gesturing with his hands, so he could speak more discreetly. "Here's the play."

Payden ran down how things would go, and in what order they'd happen.

Lisa and Bryan pitched in with their own ideas.

Fifteen minutes later, when they all agreed that if they spooked James it was as good as a confession, Payden walked around back and into the pub alone.

Bryan and Lisa stood next to each other, keeping in the shadows as they watched the front door, and the lot, to make sure James didn't slip by them if he showed and got cold feet before he made the door.

Things got awkward within the first minute.

"So," Lisa said. "You and Beck have known each other since you were kids? Not in the literal sense, but, really?"

"We were in the academy together. Good times."

"Maybe. He's an intriguing man."

Bryan chuckled. "That's one way to put it."

"How would you put it?" Lisa asked, unable to mask the contempt in her voice but not showing it on her face.

"Well, I mean, he's got his own way of doing things, that's all."

"So, he's not a hundred percent above board. Is that what you're saying?"

"Pretty much. You figured that out already, no?"

"Yes." Lisa brushed her hand against Bryan's elbow. "You two ever do anything he wasn't supposed to together?"

"I'm sorry?"

"Like the energy between him and Mindy," Lisa said, though she'd meant something entirely different. "Do they have a past too? All that pent-up hostility? She doesn't hate him for no reason. Though, from what I know of her, I suppose that's possible. Just doubtful."

"What do you know of—" Bryan kept his voice low, though he was nearly as upset as Lisa had hoped to get him. "She had a crush on him when we all first met. It went away fast."

"So, she finds him attractive?" Lisa asked, feeling irrationally, but terribly, insecure, knowing two women—whom she believed were much better-looking than her—had their eye on the man she'd begun to fantasise about before their first day working together ended. And, unless Valarie and Michael had been lying, three gorgeous women would desire him before the evening ended. "Interesting."

"Not—No. She maybe did, and maybe she gave it a shot. I don't know. It doesn't matter. Nothing happened and it's the past."

"Good to know. If it would help, I could tell her he's a lousy lay."

Bryan replied, quicker than he'd meant to. "You two? Already—I mean, really?"

Lisa smirked. "That was telling. How many partners has he slept with?"

"None, thank God. We've been together the whole ride, until this week."

Lisa shook her head. "Well, that's good news. But, no, our relationship is strictly professional. I would, though. Sleep with him, I mean. In theory. He's objectively good-looking."

"I'm assuming you don't want me to say anything to him about that."

"That wasn't a given?" Lisa asked softly and slowly, shaking her head. "I trust you slightly less now."

"You didn't trust me before?"

"I don't trust anyone completely." Lisa bumped Bryan's elbow to indicate enough time had passed he should go into the pub. "There are only degrees."

XXVII

Payden entered the pub through the back entrance. He glanced around and caught sight of Michael and Valarie. Valarie was already looking at him and shaking her head slowly. After their eyes met, she waved him over to her and Michael's usual corner booth while keeping her gaze fixed on the back door.

Payden walked casually toward them and slid into the booth's seat to Valarie's left, with Michael sitting to her right.

"Hey," Michael said, taking a chug off his beer. "It's our favourite cop."

Valarie smacked Michael's hand and he pulled it back, looking hurt emotionally, but not angry. "Be cool. We don't want to scare Jimmy off."

"Okay," Michael said more quietly. "But, then, why did you invite him to sit with us?"

Valarie looked down, feeling like she'd ruined everything. Only calmed by Payden's gaze—which insisted she hadn't—when she looked back up. "I don't know. I guess I wasn't thinking." She gave Michael a sharp glance and he smiled back at her, which made her grin. "Enjoy the moment."

A woman with cream-coloured skin, wearing jeans that made her ass look too-perfectly round and a top that showed the pub most of her freed breasts, backed up toward their table and turned to take a seat to

Michael's right, only looking at the bartender. Attempting to get his attention with a wave that made every other man in the room take notice.

Michael glanced at Payden and shook his head slightly. "Sorry, man," he said, his voice low and humble. "Didn't know...."

"This ain't good," Payden muttered, giving Michael a curious look.

"Wait." Valarie grabbed Payden's wrist. "This is my friend from where I used to work. The one I was telling you about earlier."

Payden's eyebrows cocked. "When she turns around, my story may change but, as yet, I can't say you ain't the best friend a guy could have."

Michael chuckled as he rolled his eyes.

Valarie gave Payden a gentle elbow to the ribs.

"Layla," Valarie said, snapping her fingers. "We'll get you a drink in a second. My friend Payden could get it for you." Valarie smiled as she winked at Payden.

Layla turned her head to face everyone at the table. Still good-looking, as Payden remembered, but plain when contrasted with Valarie. Even less attractive when contrasted with Lisa. A thought that had either never occurred to him or had finally figured a way to get past his inner defences.

Layla smiled, her lips trembling slightly. "You're Val's friend?" She smiled wider, still subtly shaking. Looking like she wanted to run but didn't want to end up naked from the waist up if her shirt got caught on pretty much anything.

Payden shook his head, looking Layla in the eyes, wishing she were dead or, at least, anywhere else. "Pleasure to meet you, too. Lola. That's an interesting name. Reminds me of that one song...."

Michael moved Layla from her seat, and encouraged her to sit next to Valarie, so he could go order them drinks.

Layla stared at Payden, shaking as she found herself separated from him by only one warm body. Sure he could reach out, strangle her and never lift his ass from his seat, if he so chose, at any moment. "My name? It's not—"

Payden snapped his fingers. "It'll come to me, Lula."

Layla's expression turned sterile as she glanced away over and over. "My name's Layla."

"You two," Valarie said, pulling Payden close with her left arm around his neck. "I'll tell you what. If I can convince Payden to switch places with me—"

"That'll give me no easy out if Jimmy shows," Payden whispered quickly.

At the same time, Layla said no without thinking, sounding distressed.

Valarie nodded to Payden, indicating she'd heard him and understood, then faced Layla and opened her mouth to finish her sentence.

"I mean," Layla said. "Don't push. That could ruin things."

"Yeah." Payden scratched his chin, his voice returning to normal volume. "Wouldn't want to sour the atmosphere."

Valarie looked at Payden. "She's beautiful. Was I lying?"

Payden nodded, then shook his head. "Depends what you mean."

"What is with you?" Valarie removed her arm from around Payden's neck and put her mouth to his ear. Whispering. "I know you're working but, I mean, come on, I'm hooking you up." She breathed out warm and heavy. "And—" She gulped, then said what she felt. "You know I don't want to—I mean I don't like to—I mean, it still hurts to. You know?"

Payden shook his head slightly.

"Just, please, be cool with this. Okay?"

Layla cleared her throat. "Mickey's coming back, Val. Try not to tongue fuck my blind date's ear too much longer. He may catch you."

"Nice to know you care," Michael said, scooting Layla closer to Valarie and placing a tray with three beers and a triple-shot of scotch on the table. "Don't worry about that. She's always doing that. They're friends. It don't mean nothing." Michael raised his beer to toast, not waiting for anyone else to join him. "To my beautiful wife and the man who gets whispers for life." He whispered to Layla, "What the fuck are you doing here?"

"What was that?" Valarie asked, grabbing her beer and blowing Michael a kiss. "I hope you aren't pressing. Let them get to know each other."

Michael snorted. "Don't worry, Val. She ain't interested."

Valarie looked past Michael, at the bar. The little girl locked behind her eyes screaming to be freed from the trap of her own creation.

Layla tried her best to look apologetic as she spoke to Valarie. "I'm sorry, Val."

Payden's body language went loose. The jig, as it were, being up.

"It's just, sometimes you know, you know?"

"Wait," Valarie asked Layla. "Do you and Payden—"

"Bumped into her here not too long ago," Payden said. "It didn't end well."

"That's—" Layla said, her lips quaking. "I was just—"

"Yeah, you were just." Payden scanned the pub. "I don't get a smack before you walk away this time?"

Layla looked at Michael, who was nodding at Payden, which made Valarie somewhat happy though she was utterly confused at what was happening to her match made in heaven.

"I got to go." Layla looked at Valarie, who had begun staring at Payden. "Thanks for trying. We're just not—"

"Let her go, Mickey." Payden shook his head, then addressed Layla. "Have fun finding someone who'll put up with your shit attitude."

Layla didn't hear most of what Payden had said. She simply pushed against Michael. "Seriously, I need to go. I got this thing. Totally forgot."

Payden chuckled, looking at Valarie. "Unbelievable."

"Hey," Layla snapped. "I don't got to justify—" The words caught in her throat when she looked into Payden's smiling eyes. Seeing herself being tortured in them. Her reflection writhing in unimaginable pain. "I just, I got to go. The thing. I can't miss it. I'm sorry, Val."

A low voice broke in. "Don't apologise. Weak."

"Sorry?" Layla looked up as Michael slid out of the booth and James sat to box her in, moving her, Valarie and Payden slightly to their left. "You are?"

"Destiny."

Michael sat back down. "If it ain't the runaway. What's up, Jimmy?"

"Drinks," James said, looking at Payden, handling Layla by the waist to move her over a bit more. "This hard-on giving you trouble...?"

"I'm Layla," Layla said.

James rubbed her left cheek with his right hand. "Fuck, Layla, you are just... Fuck."

"Sweet talk her, Jimmy," Payden said. "She likes that. You got a shot."

"Thank him for the advice," Layla said to James, winking at Payden through her persistent fear.

James looked at Payden while Layla flipped Payden the bird and Valarie's gaze swept the pub, flabbergasted. "Thanks, faggot."

Layla kept her eyes on Payden as she kissed James full on the mouth. Not satisfied with Payden's lack of upset.

"What the fuck just happened?" Valarie asked, still looking everywhere but at the other people in her booth.

"Destiny." Payden patted Valarie on the shoulder and gave it a rub. "Seriously, though, it's not a big deal, this blind date not working out. Are you okay? Look, I'm not mad at you or nothing. Grateful, actually. It was sweet of you. Valarie? Come back to us. Destiny can be manufactured more than once. And I'm sure it will be. Very soon."

Valarie snapped out of it when Michael banged the table. "Val? You alive? It's cool. Your favourite cop's okay with things not working out. Why are you taking this so hard? Hello?"

"I'm." Valarie grabbed her beer and downed it in one chug. Tapping the table after and catching the bartender's attention. Ordering four more drinks with her fingers. "I just." She looked at Payden and took his hands in hers, glancing over her shoulder at James and Layla, who seemed to be getting along better than nicely, growing more daring with regard to public groping. "This wasn't supposed to happen like this."

Payden shrugged, more concerned for Valarie than he was about James. "Like Mickey said, it's okay. You were trying to help me out. I love you for that. You're a good friend. Seriously, it's not a big deal."

"I had no idea you two met before," Valarie said, certain—and correct—neither James nor Layla was paying attention to a word anyone else said. She grabbed Payden's shoulders, her eyes floating. "If I'd known—"

Payden looked to Michael for a nod. Receiving it, he kissed Valarie on the forehead. "It's okay, Valarie. I know a lot of people. Believe it or not, some of them don't like me."

Michael burst out laughing. "You really are my favourite cop, you crazy fuck. Val, take it easy. He loves you. You love him. It's never been more obvious. He knows you wouldn't set him up to let him down. Give him a kiss on the cheek and pretend nothing happened." Michael winked at Payden. "Trust me, she knows lots of really good-looking women who aren't complete bitches like this one."

Valarie looked at Michael. "You don't like her?" She gave Payden a kiss on the cheek, whispering, "I promise I'll do better next time."

"Never have," Michael said. "Easy on the eyes, but I'd kill her if I had to live with her." He looked to his left. "If Jimmy came here to ask for free room and board again, that shit ain't happening if she's part of the deal."

Payden looked at Michael. "Shot you down during your pre-marital marathon?"

Michael nodded. "The worst way. Touched me all over. Frenched me just to see the look on my face when she smacked me and screamed for help after. I'm going to stop talking because recalling that is pissing me off, and recalling it out loud don't look like it's doing Val any good neither."

James gestured for Michael to stand.

Michael got up from his seat and backed away from the table.

James slipped out of the booth, pulling Layla with him. She excused herself to use the bathroom and he smacked her ass as she giggled, then scurried away.

"You serious?" James looked between Valarie and Michael. "I'm back in if she's gone?"

Valarie nodded.

Michael nodded as well. "No Layla. Not in my home."

"Deal," James said. "She smells ready. I'll fuck her out back, see you two at home. Leave the door open. She gets clingy after, I'll change her mind."

Payden slid out of the booth. "Just one thing before you throw her that half-inch, Jimmy."

"She remind you of a guy you like?" James asked. "I can make her share."

"No." Payden shook his head as Valarie watched him like a lost dog who'd just found its master. "I need you to come with me to—"

James grabbed an empty beer glass from the table, swinging for Payden's head before he could finish his request.

XXVIII

Bryan walked into the pub ten minutes after Payden, watching his fiancée as she accepted free drinks from regulars who knew she was taken. Finding a spot to sit with Mindy—and Michael and Valarie's corner booth—in view. Counting the seconds as he imagined himself suffering a long, boring night watching Payden drink, and his fiancée lead other men on, with nothing to show.

As he focussed his attention on Valarie, Michael and Payden, to keep himself from speaking up every time a townie copped an accidental feel on Mindy, he saw another woman sit at the table with them.

The night got a little easier to take.

She was strikingly beautiful, and dressed for more attention than Mindy. Cream-coloured skin and a hypnotic way of moving. Bryan watched her as she, Michael, Valarie and Payden interacted. He couldn't hear them, but he got a bad vibe, which made him feel good and made him forget. About Mindy, about James, about the job and about why he was there.

As he dreamt of the mystery woman, he didn't notice Mindy throwing him the occasional look, trying to get his attention as discreetly as possible. Nor did he notice the look of anger in her eyes when she couldn't draw his gaze away from the booth where she, too, noted a shapely—and scantily dressed—young woman garnering the lion's share of attention from everyone, including Valarie.

An amount of time Bryan couldn't quantify later, he noticed Lisa enter the pub, flashing him a sign. Index and middle finger of her left hand extended down with her shirt's arm covering most of them. An upside-down peace sign or symbol of victory, he couldn't tell which, or if he was even close to understanding what she'd meant.

She moved slowly to the left, into his area of the pub, and he caught her drift when James entered shortly after.

XXIX

Lisa hung back after Bryan let her know he was going into the pub. She wished him good luck and reminded him — in the most polite way possible — Mindy wasn't of importance that evening. Unless the plan changed and they decided not to wait and hope.

When Bryan was out of view, Lisa approached a young man hanging to the side of the pub, around the corner from the front door. He wore a dark, hooded sweatshirt and seemed intent on catching everyone's eye as they entered the pub. Not doing well but, if Lisa was reading him correctly, he'd picked a bad spot to set up shop. The drugs behind the door of the pub were legal and, unless folks were on their way out and not thinking clearly, they wouldn't be buying whatever he was selling. Their minds were already set on their poison of choice.

She walked past him, noting his gaze following her as he twitched. Then she leant against the wall farther away from the front door, chewing her fingertips lightly. "You holding?"

The young man looked at her eyes, his own clearly visible even in the shadow of the pub covering the shade of his sweatshirt's hood. "How much?"

"Gramme. Three?"

The young man shook his head. "Too much weight, fat little boy."

"Balloon?"

The young man nodded, then looked past her, letting a quick whistle go.

An older man popped his head from around the corner leading to the pub's service entrance.

Lisa looked at him, then back at the young man by her side, who held out his shaking hand.

"Twenty," the young man said.

She nodded and walked away, toward the back of the pub.

The young man tried to stop her with his voice, being careful not to raise it. "No. You pay me, tall boy."

Lisa glanced over her shoulder and kept walking. She was around the corner before the young man could fully insist she stop. When he made it to the back of the pub, Lisa was standing in front of the older man, her quivering hand extended.

"You pay?" the older man asked.

"Walk, dude," Lisa said in reply, scratching the back of her head hard, making herself look worse. "There's fuzz on my back."

The young man from the side of the pub moved closer to Lisa, pressing his pelvis against her spine. "What you call me, *perra*?"

Lisa froze, genuinely disturbed. Feeling out of her element. Frightened. She glanced, over her shoulder, at the young man. "I was never here, okay?" She gave the older man a lingering look, whispering, "Seriously, walk. This guy's a cop."

"*Coño*," the older man said. "That shivering fuck's my man. No cop, *putita*." He exchanged a look with the young man.

"I'm sorry." Lisa's stare went blank as she stood between the two men. Noting they were out of everyone else's sight, no one would be able to reach her fast enough if she called out for help and the men she was dealing with were more serious than she'd expected. "I'll go." She backed away from the older man.

The young man blocking her path shoved her forward.

The older man retreated slightly. Drawing her farther from the corner of the building, then stopping her with a smack to the left temple. "Maybe you're a cop."

"Yeah," the young man said. "You running a game? Do I know you? Playing dress-up, faggot?"

The older man chuckled. "Calm down. She definitely a bitch. Stinky, too. Maybe she like you."

Both men lifted their shirts to expose guns tucked into the waistbands of their jeans as Lisa turned sideways, her back to the wall, to keep them both in view.

"No," Lisa replied, her lips and cheeks trembling. "I never saw you. Okay? This was a mistake. I don't know what I was thinking. I'm sorry."

"Apologise for real," the young man said, growing visibly excited. "If you a man, I kill you after."

The older man grabbed Lisa by the neck hard, after noticing her scar. "Nice mark. Who your pimp?" The older man looked at the young man quickly. "Tell you what. Suck my boy's dick. Clean my pipes, too. Do that, we don't make you uglier, dirty pig." He glanced down. "Put that tiny mouth to work, all's forgiven. But swallow, or it's Emergency for you, again, *yonqui*."

"You first?" Lisa nodded as she turned to face the older man. Dropping to her knees shortly after, when he gut-punched her.

XXX

Bryan looked away after seeing James walk into the pub. Keeping track of him out of the corner of his eye — as was Lisa, who took a seat close enough to Bryan she could whisper and he could hear.

"We should take him now," Lisa said, her knees shaking as she rubbed her neck and stomach.

Bryan didn't look at her, but shook his head in reply. "We move when he does something illegal. So we can bring him in and hold him. Make him sweat." Bryan dropped his left hand, placing it flat on a tiny invisible desk to his left. "This guy lost it in broad daylight with you, sober. He'll likely make a mistake here tonight after a few drinks."

"Fine. We'll do it the boring way."

Bryan nodded, honing in on James and the girl he'd never seen before kissing and petting each other in Michael and Valarie's corner booth. Coming as close to undressing themselves in public as they could.

Eventually, James insisted on Michael standing so he could, presumably, leave with the young woman Bryan found himself wanting more desperately the longer he took her in. He became lost as he watched her ass bounce away into the ladies' bathroom.

Then Payden slid out of his seat and stood, which prompted Bryan to.

Lisa got to her feet slowly when she noticed Bryan moving.

Only Valarie remained seated at the booth.

Payden and James began to talk, though neither Lisa nor Bryan could hear their speech clearly.

Bryan saw James scan the pub, not noticing him or Lisa, and grab an empty beer glass from the table. Before Lisa or Bryan could react, James swung the glass at Payden's head, cutting short whatever Payden was in the middle of saying.

Payden dodged the swing and spun James away from him, grabbing James's hand and twisting it, causing him to lose hold of the glass, which shattered when it hit the floor. Then slamming James's forehead onto the table as James struggled and punched at air.

Before the bartender could grab the bat hidden beneath the counter, Bryan had his gun out and Lisa produced a pair of cuffs from her back jeans pocket.

James pushed Payden away from him, turning to fight, his forehead bruised and his back to Bryan and Lisa.

Bryan roared at James. "Stop. Do not move or I will drop you where you stand."

Lisa licked her lips. With everything leading to this moment—especially watching how easily Payden had turned James into a plaything to torture and beat—coming upon her at once, her eyes glazed over.

Mindy had no idea Lisa was thinking of Payden when she saw her appear to give Bryan a good look.

James raised his hands.

"Turn around," Lisa said, moving past Bryan and quickly scanning Payden from his crotch to his face and back down. "Remember me, Jimmy?"

James glanced over his shoulder, his hands still raised. "Who forgets you, stubby? You finally ready for a big kid's ride."

Lisa kicked James in the back of his right knee when he didn't lower his hands immediately—though she hadn't requested he do so—dropping him to the floor. His knees made a dull smacking sound when they hit.

"You're dead, scooter."

"Perfect." Lisa slammed James's chest into the side of the table with a right forearm to the back of the neck, and snapped a cuff on his left wrist, tight. Leaning into him and spreading his legs with her own—kicking the insides of his thighs—to keep him off balance before she released the pressure on his neck, cranking his right arm behind his back and up to slap on the other cuff. Making sure it hurt when she did. Putting James's arm in a position close to one it couldn't move into without breaking. "You're under arrest, Jimmy. Threatening an officer. Battery against an officer. Enjoy your big kid's ride to the station."

James grunted.

Bryan moved to ensure Payden was okay and Payden shook him off.

As Bryan and Lisa pulled James to his feet, Layla exited the bathroom. The look on her face turning from subtly sexual to utterly terrified. She looked away and walked out the back door.

Bryan kept her body and face tracked with his peripheral vision. Ensuring nobody, especially Mindy, caught him doing so.

Layla was gone before Bryan could finish assuring Michael and Valarie all was well.

Mindy stood as Bryan and Lisa lugged James past her, looking at Bryan with disgust. "Does this mean you're spending the night with"—she gave Lisa a condescending stare—"the dumpy midget?"

Bryan gave Mindy an ugly look and Lisa chuckled.

"Mindy," Lisa said, giving her a start. "Would you care to accompany us?"

Mindy didn't move, dazed and scared witless. "I'm—No, I'm—No."

Payden walked to stand beside Mindy, giving her a pat on the back that moved her forward a step. "You okay, Princess?" Then he whispered, "Stay out of this or our deal's off. Understand?"

Mindy nodded, terrified.

"Thank heavens," Payden replied to Mindy at normal volume.

Valarie stepped between them, draping herself on Payden's shoulder. "Jimmy didn't hurt you, did he?" Valarie asked him, combing the hair out of his face and touching him everywhere he might be wounded.

Michael pulled Valarie off Payden and assured her he was fine. "My favourite cop. Thanks for taking care of that crazy asshole." He looked at Mindy. "Mindy, right?"

Mindy nodded. Her eyes looking everywhere and nowhere. "I really should make sure—"

Payden snapped, "Leave it alone. This ain't about you."

Mindy stopped speaking immediately, her entire body quaking.

When Payden spotted Lisa and Bryan taking notice of Mindy's response to his ill-timed outburst, Payden continued to speak. "Sorry to bark at you, but, seriously, give your man, and everyone else, a break. We've got work to do. This isn't a game."

Mindy looked away, still shaking, and moved back to the bar to grab her drink.

Payden followed Bryan and Lisa out the door after saying good night to Michael and Valarie. Receiving a handshake from Michael and a loving kiss on the cheek from Valarie.

Payden, Lisa, Bryan and James all exited the pub and got into Payden and Lisa's car.

It was a short distance to the station, but it was a long drive back.

XXXI

Bryan, Payden and Lisa carried James in through the front door of the station, held open by the new guys on the night shift who enjoyed watching Lisa move as she struggled to keep up and her loose-fitting jeans hugged her ass tight. Though they lost interest quickly once Lisa caught them looking and returned their gazes with an angry squint, inadvertently exposing her neck's scar. The men on night shift headed to the back door to stand half-outside and smoke cigarettes.

Within a few minutes, the trio of detectives had James in the interrogation room, facedown on the floor. All of them too winded to make sure he was seated properly in a chair, and James not willing to cooperate, even to that degree.

Bryan stood at the opened door and wiped the sweat from his brow. "I'm going to go back to our—my office and give the captain a call, in case. If we can get something out of this guy, maybe it'll hit the early edition and the captain won't want us dead anymore."

"Sounds good," Lisa said, adjusting her clothing.

"I'll try not to beat this asshole any harder than I have to," Payden said, grinning, though Bryan didn't find the attempt at levity humorous.

Bryan pointed toward the door to his office and shook his head. "No. We can't have anything go sideways, Beck. And you're too easy."

"Too easy?" Payden asked. "You're going to give my partner ideas."

Lisa smacked Payden's back. "The day I start chasing after you is the day I've given up. Though I'm this close." She gave Payden a wink.

Bryan shook his head. "Better idea. You make the call, Beck. And close the door. Nobody knows why we brought Jimmy in. Let's keep it that way for now."

"Whatever." Payden walked down the hall and into Bryan's office.

Bryan didn't put his eyes back on James until he saw Payden enter his former office and close the door behind him.

"Get the door?" Bryan asked Lisa.

Lisa walked from her space, farther inside the room, and closed the door so no one could look in or hear. Locking herself in an enclosed space with no definite backup. Another test, she presumed, but one she didn't appreciate since Bryan wasn't her partner. "Too much for you?"

"I'm sorry? No. I just—"

James turned his neck to look up at Bryan. "Smelt your woman? At the pub?" He nodded. "She's ready. Ain't going to wait for you."

Bryan's hands balled into fists and Lisa backed up a step.

James continued to beg for an ass-kicking.

XXXII

Mindy stormed into the police station, waving off the two night-shift officers. Begging them to put her in cuffs and lock her up—or shut their mouths and let her speak with her fiancé—as she hurried by.

Mindy reached Bryan's office and swung open the door. She stopped cold. Watching. Listening to Payden explain whatever she'd just been a part of at the pub. Closing the door quietly behind her.

"Yes, Captain," Payden said, looking over his shoulder at Mindy and rolling his eyes in frustration as he turned his gaze away. "We have a guy in interrogation right now. Based on crime-scene evidence and eyewitness testimony, we think he may be the doer."

The captain's voice howled on the other end of the line. Anger and happiness.

"Yes. Of course. I, Verrill or Reid will keep you posted as this develops. Just brought him in. Keeping you in the loop. Thank you, sir."

Payden hung up the phone and turned to face Mindy.

"Look," she said, visibly shaking. "I had no idea you'd be—"

"What did I say to you at the pub?" Payden asked, his voice a menacing whisper.

"I heard you. I understood. I only wanted to apologise for—"

Payden moved to the door. "I thought you just said you didn't know I'd be in here."

"Where is Bryan?" Mindy asked. Realising, for the second time that evening, how thankful she was to be free of Payden and how completely terrified she was of their brutal, intimate relationship continuing as it had for the last few years.

Payden kept his voice low. "He's in the interrogation room. With Reid. Where we're going now, unless you don't want to live a happy life. Got me, birdy?"

"Yes," she said, her focus going fuzzy. "Why did you call me—I mean, I promise. And you'll keep your word? I have my freedom? Forever?"

"When have I ever lied to you about us?" Payden walked her to the door, opening it and marching her across the hall, holding her upper arm with his hand.

"How do you mean?" Mindy replied, pulling herself together.

Payden opened the interrogation room's door and guided Mindy in before him, leaving the door ajar. "Guess who couldn't resist seeing Jimmy again?"

Bryan looked up from his seat across the table from James, who was cuffed to his chair with his hands behind his back, and rolled his eyes.

Lisa—who stood at the side of the table farthest from the door—looked at Mindy like she was a pest while letting out a sigh of relief directed at—and noticed by—no one.

James gave Mindy a good ogling. "All done?" He bobbed his eyebrows at her, sniffing the air, and she shuddered. "Oh, yeah. Just finished." He tilted his head toward Lisa. "Don't like to get your knees dirty, though, huh? Shame."

Lisa spoke with authority, gulping quickly and glancing at her dirtied jeans first, noticing nobody else had paid strict attention to James's final remark. "Remain silent unless answering direct questions, Jimmy."

Bryan stood and walked to Mindy as Payden moved to stand behind James.

Payden gave Lisa a roll of the eyes, which she returned.

"What are you doing here, Mindy?" Bryan asked. "I'm working. You know that. A fellow officer is dead. This isn't a traffic violation—"

James interrupted, looking ruffled for once. "Dead cop?" he asked. "Not me."

Lisa looked at Mindy and Bryan. "Either close the door or take it outside, please."

Bryan looked at Lisa, incensed with Mindy but taking it out on the wrong person, as usual. "Detective Reid, please escort my fiancée to her car. Come back immediately. Detective Beck and I will continue the questioning until you return." He looked at Mindy. "Please, honey. I'll see you at home, sooner than you think."

"I'll wait up?" Mindy smiled. Selling it well.

"Yes, dear."

She gave Bryan a peck on the cheek. "I love you."

Bryan flushed while he smiled. "I love you, too."

Lisa put her hands on her hips. "Seriously?"

Payden gave Lisa a nod when she looked to him for direction. "Your call."

Lisa walked around the desk, took Mindy by the left arm with her right hand and walked her out of the room.

James clapped behind his back, watching Bryan. "Your bitch took a real pounding. Walking all fucked-up. Be asleep when you get home. Bet."

GO

Lisa slammed the door closed and the sound of whatever Bryan had to say in reply became muted immediately.

"You can take it easy," Mindy said as Lisa fast-walked her to the station's front door. "It's not like this is—"

"You heard Detective Verrill," Lisa snapped.

When the door closed behind them, Lisa continued to march Mindy into the parking lot. "Where's your car?"

"You can knock off the act now," Mindy said, the smile gone from her face as she struggled to free her arm. "No more boys to impress, you crazy munchkin."

"Your car."

Mindy pointed to it with her free hand and walked at the same pace Lisa did.

"This case could make me in this precinct. You don't want to fuck me up."

"I was just noting—" Mindy said as they approached her vehicle. "For God's sake, cover that hideous scar. It's not doing you any favours."

As soon as they escaped what Lisa had determined on her first day to be the outside security cameras' range, and Lisa saw the night-shift officers close the back door, she released her grip on Mindy. "I'm not fucking around. Drive away. Do it now. I don't got time."

"Listen," Mindy snapped. "I'm sorry you're deformed, but that doesn't give you the right to—"

Lisa punched Mindy in the stomach, causing her to double over and cover her mouth with her hands. Ensuring Mindy's insides begged to vomit but not putting enough force behind her punch to allow for it.

Mindy paused for a moment as she rubbed her stomach. Feeling the pain she knew wouldn't leave a bruise. Lisa's punch hurting her as much as possible without damaging her, just like Payden had done to her for years. Like she had just finally found relief from, probably.

Lisa put her mouth to Mindy's ear. "I have the right to kick your ass so bad you wish you were dead."

Mindy stood straight, still feeling her stomach ache, but wearing a sneer. "As if. You carved-up circus dwarf. I'd love to see you try—"

Lisa backhanded Mindy so fast, her head spun before she could move her hands to block the threat she never saw coming.

Mindy felt the pain spread from her cheek and down her arms. Stumbling and nearly falling.

"It don't matter how tall you are, pretentious cunt." Lisa punched her fists together. "I'll work your body all night if you cost me."

"I don't want anything to do—I mean," Mindy looked around, lost and confused. "I never meant—What has Payden done to you?—I mean, I'm sorry. I'll go." Mindy hopped into her car, closed the door, cranked the ignition, put the car in drive and rolled down her window. "Say goodnight to Payden, you pudgy, filthy runt. Good luck finding any man who'll—"

Lisa grabbed Mindy's hair and yanked her head out through the car's opened window.

Mindy pressed on the brakes and put the car back into park.

Lisa released her grip on Mindy's hair, shoving Mindy's face forward. "Make this the last time I hear you mention my wound." Lisa's voice dropped to a growl. "Mark my words or, so help me, I will beat the shit out of you wherever you think you're safe. I will put you on the ground and my fists will fuck your face ugly while everyone watches. Before they can stop me from breaking you into pieces. Because, from me, you ain't safe nowhere. Now, get the fuck out of my sight."

Mindy didn't look back, or dare say a word, as she put her car in drive and sped away from the station. Watching Lisa hustle back inside. Feeling more helpless than ever, knowing Bryan would never believe her if she finally, fully confided in him about Payden. That Payden's new partner wouldn't, were she to, either. No one, except she and Payden, knew the truth of them. Exactly as he'd planned it. And every attempt she made at righting the multitude of wrongs done to her only buried her deeper in her figurative grave.

Mindy cried as she drove home. Praying Bryan would get a confession—or clear James—soon and come make her feel like she might be free, though she would never know, for the rest of her life, if she truly was.

XXXIII

Lisa re-entered the interrogation room, hurrying in after escorting Mindy to her car, closing the door behind her. Feeling like she'd missed out on the action. Thinking, if anyone should have seen Mindy to the door, Bryan should have. Mindy was his fiancée, the mystery of who was whacking drug dealers left and right wasn't his to solve, and, though he'd only been Lester's partner for a day, he couldn't own the case since he was considered too close to it to be objective. Getting to the bottom of Lester's execution could make Lisa's career. With a partner like Payden, it could make her pension. And that made her resent Bryan — and despise Mindy — all the more.

James didn't look any worse for wear. Payden glanced at Lisa from his place across the desk farthest from the door, pacing. Bryan sat across the table from James. No one was saying a word.

"Finally wet," James said to Lisa's crotch. "Bring it here, punky slop. I'm starving."

Bryan snapped the fingers of his right hand. "Over here, Romeo. You have yet to explain why you were covered in dirt and looking beat-up when you came home to Mrs. Dooley's Monday night."

"Lawyer," James said.

"Soon."

James looked at Payden. "Question?"

Payden nodded.

"Lawyer?" James asked.

Payden kicked James's chair. "You begging me to beat you until you piss purple?"

James nodded, looking at the security cameras and grinning.

Payden punched the wall behind him.

"Lawyer." James eyeballed Lisa's breasts, licking his lips. "Going to take good care of you, nipples."

Lisa walked to James's left side. "With what?" She bent over to block the surveillance camera's view and smacked his limp crotch quickly.

James knocked his knuckles on the tabletop. "Ask the Chinaman's bitch when I'm done with her."

"I'm not Chinese," Bryan said.

James glanced up and around the room. "Lawyer."

Payden growled. "What?"

"Why am I still here?" James asked. "Not in lock-up?"

Lisa looked at Payden, who nodded, while Bryan shook his head as she ignored him. "We have a dead officer. You're our prime suspect."

"Don't know about no dead cop. Never seen one. That a crime?" James shook his head slowly.

Bryan continued. "We have it on good authority, you were—"

"You got nothing." James looked at Lisa as she moved to the side of the table closest the door. "Pussy don't make me stupid. No matter how tasty it stinks, or how used-up it looks. We're done."

Lisa's cheeks turned red. "We're done when—"

"Lawyer. Also, Miranda."

"I read you your rights," Payden said. "Ain't no one in this room remembers otherwise."

"Pub. Other people. Bet they noticed. Lawyer."

"Look," Bryan said, holding his hands together in prayer. "If you work with us, we're not going to see you go down for something you didn't do. But you're the best suspect we have. So if you don't start answering—"

James rolled his eyes. "Lawyer."

"If you don't start answering questions, we will see you put away for assaulting an officer. We'll fight bail. We'll get you a court date. As far in the future as possible. And you will be convicted. You say we didn't read you your rights? The judge won't take your word over ours. Or anyone's. Then you'll do a chunk of time. Do you really want to go to prison?"

"Lawyer."

Payden walked to the table and rested his body's weight on it, propping himself with his arms. "That all you got to say, Jimmy? Think hard."

"Lawyer."

Payden stood straight.

Bryan got out of his seat, waving Lisa and Payden to him, speaking softly. "Look. He isn't going to talk. And what we've got is circumstantial. But we'll hold him for as long as we can. No need to trump up charges. We've got him on battery. We can find out more on the streets while he's locked up here. What do you say we stop wasting our time with him?"

"But—" Lisa began.

Payden shook his head. "Verrill's right. This fuck is either too stupid or too smart to spill."

Lisa looked at Bryan. "I appreciate your summation, Verrill, but let me remind you of something you seem to have forgotten, ordering everyone around. You're riding shotgun on our case. Mine and Beck's. You're here because the captain doesn't know what to do with you. You're here because you used to roll with Beck. But that's over." Lisa snapped her fingers. "Like that. I can get you pulled from this case if you cross my line again. Beck will back me."

Bryan looked at Payden. "Really?"

"She's got a point, ex-partner," Payden said. "I don't want to, but if Reid goes down that road, I got to put her first. You know me. We used to run together, not a few days ago. When didn't I have your back?"

"When didn't you have my back? When didn't you have me on my back?" Bryan shook his head. "I'll have the boys on night shift put Jimmy in a cell."

Payden shook his head in return. "Maybe you should just go home and be with Mindy. She didn't show here because she don't need you. Forget this. It ain't your battle. Not tonight. Go home and take care of your fiancée. Let us do our work."

Bryan backed up a step. "You can't be asking me to—"

"I ain't. I'm asking you to do the right thing by your woman. You know she's waiting up at her home. Waiting for you. Some word, at least. She just took you back. She makes you happy. You make her happy. Your relationship is solid. Keep it that way. We on the same page?"

Bryan nodded, then shook his head. "I can't just—"

"What?" Payden snapped. "Walk? Look the other way? We both know that's bullshit."

Bryan glanced at Lisa, fear in his eyes.

"Don't look to Reid for confirmation. Don't look to my partner for nothing."

Bryan nodded.

"You know I ain't threatening you with information. What we got on each other? Everything over the years? Not a word from me to Reid about any of it. Not a word from me to nobody. Not now, not ever. Our secrets die with us. Yeah?"

Bryan moved back another step. "Okay... I'll just—Look, we have to give this man his—"

"And we will. He'll get his, but good. Maybe. You don't know nothing. You won't see nothing. Go home to your woman. Bang her until you forget. You'll feel better, she'll feel like the fuck of the century. Win, win."

"This isn't right." Bryan glanced at the door. "But I'll go. Just promise me you won't take things too far. If he did do it, we can't let him walk. Not on a technicality."

Payden grinned. "You and I know that shit don't happen no more. Ain't going to start again now."

James shook his head. "Audio? Video? Off?"

The door to the interrogation room cracked open behind Bryan and he turned to hold it steady out of instinct. Only allowing the officer from night shift to see what he wanted him to. Which, at that point, was nothing. "What is it?" he asked, an edge in his voice. "You don't announce? We're in the middle of questioning a suspect. What can't wait?"

"Sorry, sir," the voice from outside the room said, sounding servile. "I didn't mean to interrupt—Just thought you'd want to know the news we just dispatched."

"News? What news?"

"Another dead dealer. Alley, back of the pub."

"Another one?" Payden asked, moving to the door with a spring in his step. "Another one down?"

"Another one down," the night-shift officer confirmed. "But, different. Sternum crushed. Died bad. We got a lead on another dealer. Says he almost bought it. Can ID the killer. Not sure it ain't bullshit. He won't say where he is. Called from a pay phone. Units heading there now, but he's likely gone. Said he'd turn himself in if we guaranteed his safety. Not sure how we can if he ain't waiting for pick up. Could be anybody. Could be a crank call. Could be there's no victim. We'll be sure soon. For all we know, it was the killer himself calling it in. It's a possibility. You think?"

"He tries," Payden said, catching Lisa's slight grin out of the corner of his eye. "One day, maybe, he'll get the hang of it."

Bryan gave Payden the finger, not bothering to conceal it, as he opened the door another crack and continued to address the officer. "It's definitely a possibility. It's happened before. You said a car's headed that way already?"

"Several," the night-shift officer responded.

"Fuck it." Bryan looked at Payden, then at Lisa. "Have a car pick me up here. I'll ride along. To find out if it's a hoax. If it's not, we'll see if we can locate the caller. Call in CSI, too. Put it out on the wire no one is to touch the pay phone until they give it a look-over. Make sure they know to dust for prints."

The night-shift officer grunted. "That'll just piss them off, sir. No offence. They'll do that without us asking. And we've already called them in. This case is priority number one. May be the same guy who did your partner. It's a possibility, no?"

"Everything's a possibility." Bryan opened the door wide enough he could step outside. Looking back at Payden and Lisa. "You two want to come along? We're not getting anything from Jimmy. And this makes him look like the wrong guy."

"I disagree, Verrill," Lisa said, scratching her neck's scar unconsciously. "Until CSI determines the time of death, we don't know the murder didn't occur before Jimmy showed at the pub."

Bryan nodded to Lisa. "True. Good point, Reid. But I'm thinking it's best we all get on this. Put Jimmy, here, in the tank?" He looked at the night-shift officer—who nodded in reply to his question—then back at Lisa and Payden. "What do you say? Give Jimmy some time to think about assaulting an officer. Let him stew on that while we make it known we're on to whoever's dumping bodies in our town. Worst case, the captain finds out and gives us a pat on the back."

Lisa shrugged, keeping the look of disappointment and anger from her face. Disappointed she wouldn't be able to beat the answers she needed out of James. Enraged at how blatantly Bryan was ignoring her previous directives with regard to who owned the case. "Agreed, Verrill. That's the smart play. Beck?"

Payden nodded as well. "I'm with you. But we all drive together, yeah? Don't need a car to pick us up. We got one. Just need directions."

"Fair enough," Bryan said. "Then let's roll."

Bryan opened the door fully and the night-shift officer walked into the room, uncuffed James from his chair, stood him up and cuffed him again.

Lisa's eyes went dead. "Don't forget. This man could be the one. Don't treat him like he's special. He's already assaulted two officers. Get him in the cage. Do it fast and keep your guard up."

Bryan moved closer to the night shift officer, his voice low. "I'm going to need you to do me a favour and call my fiancée. Her name's Mindy Hayden. Her number's in my file. Call her and let her know I won't be home until we clear the crime scene. Can I count on you?"

The night-shift officer nodded and walked James out of the room.

Within five minutes, Lisa and Payden were headed to their car, Bryan having decided to have a squad car pick him up when he caught a glimpse of Lisa's threatening squint. Since the case wasn't technically his, he made sure to state loud enough everyone on shift could hear him, it would look better for all of them if they covered more ground, and no one would get busted down if the captain saw them pull up in the same vehicle and reckoned they might be muddying the waters and putting a viable suspect on freedom's path. Something, to Bryan's knowledge, he and Payden hadn't done since they'd caught their first big case as detectives in their precinct. Though neither of them intended for that to happen again, the stench of that situation would never leave them, and the captain would never forget.

Things were moving fast, and they were looking up.

Lisa couldn't have been happier, or more concerned.

XXIV

Lisa opened the driver's side door to her and Payden's car, motioning for him to throw her the keys. He didn't think twice, tossing her the keys, asking for a quick second and running back into the station.

Lisa thought twice as she accepted the keys and got into the driver's seat, closing her door and putting on her seatbelt. She thought twice about why Payden had been so quick to allow Bryan to break the agreement they all three stick together, and she thought twice about why Payden had decided he needed to make a call—what she presumed, since they'd already gotten the crime-scene location from dispatch—before they left. Wondering if he was going out of his way to keep Valarie apprised of her brother's situation when they both knew Valarie wanted nothing to do with him. Something was off and she didn't like it. Not that she didn't trust Payden, more that she knew he was like her. To a degree that made her feel vulnerable. He didn't always say what was on his mind, and he made his own plans. He had his vision and he followed it, filling everyone else in later. The same qualities she possessed which had made it easy for her to get transferred from her old precinct to her current one, on demand. At the same time, she trusted Payden's judgement. Mostly because he hadn't lied to her—that she knew of—from the start. He'd messed with her head, but he'd only taken it so far. Always tests, always jokes. But never a flat-out lie. And, for the first time in her career, she feared that circumstance was inevitable. That he would, at some point, reveal himself to be as dirty as the scum he dedicated his life to putting behind bars. Another thing that made them equal. Another thing that worried her more terribly the longer he made her wait.

When he returned, he rushed to the driver's-side door and patted on the top of the car.

Lisa rolled down her window. "What is it? We're primary. If we show on scene after Verrill, it isn't going to look good. And, no offence, I don't want to blow this case. Are you coming or not?"

Payden stared at her as she talked, some form of disappointment in his eyes.

"I'm serious, Payden."

"You're slipping."

"What?"

"I'm having Valarie come out and pick up Jimmy. I'm not letting him go, but she can take me to the scene. Jimmy in attendance and none the wiser. We're going to want him there if that eyewitness shows, right? And, if I'm wrong and show separately, you won't take the hit. I'm giving you a gift if he ain't the doer."

"A gift." She gasped, looking awestruck, faking it poorly as she cursed her overenthusiasm. Blinding her to the simplest, most reasonable plan. "When you put it that way... Thank you. But I should be able to trust you without having to pull on your choke chain."

"Yeah, true. But when shit goes sideways for you—which it will, when you accidentally beat some poor son of a bitch to death or put him in the hospital—you'll thank God I gave you this present. Because you'll know whatever lies I got to tell, whatever shit I got to pull, you'll be bullet-proof. Once that happens, we'll both be."

Lisa shook her head. "You have a subversive way of looking at things, you know that? And, though I appreciate the surprise grand gesture, you still owe me one."

"I know, but—"

"If that's the way it must be." Lisa put the car into drive. "I'll see you at the scene."

Lisa sped off and Payden waved goodbye, shaking his head and feeling like, maybe, he'd finally met someone he could trust without having something on them. Silencing that voice immediately.

XXXV

Valarie arrived at the station just after Payden finished filling out the forms required for James's release. Payden refused to file assault charges and ensured the subsequent assault charge on Lisa was rejected since it hadn't been filed and was hearsay he wasn't willing to substantiate. The night-shift officers called Bryan on his portable radio and, though he sounded surprised, he agreed to waive the charges, as well, stating he couldn't be sure Lisa was, technically, assaulted—given the commotion at the pub—and, if Payden wasn't pressing charges and claimed nothing happened to another officer, he had no desire to force the issue.

James and Payden walked out to Valarie's waiting car and Payden got in the back seat, giving James the front.

Valarie put it in drive, having never turned off the ignition, and headed out of the station's lot.

"So, where are we going?" Valarie asked Payden.

"That's up to Jimmy," Payden replied, looking at him. "Where are you hanging your hat, now Valarie and Mickey put you out on your ass?"

"Fuck you," James said. He looked at Valarie. "You ain't letting me back in?"

"That's up to Mickey," Valarie said. "And he says no until you let Layla go for keeps."

"Fucking," James muttered, then raised his voice. "We sucked face, she took off. No worries."

Payden chuckled. "Just because she didn't want to walk into the middle of a dust-up don't mean she ain't interested."

James grunted. "How can I break it off? Nothing solid. Don't know where she is. Don't even got her number."

Payden patted James on the shoulder and he flinched violently. "We'll call her. Valarie knows it." He looked at Valarie. "It okay if you drop him with me at the crime scene? You feel all right giving him your friend's number? We'll call her from a pay phone. That way, you don't let him back in the house without being sure. That way, you know they're done."

James snorted. "You going to help me, cop?"

Payden caught Valarie's glance in the rearview mirror. "I'll vouch for you, Jimmy, if you don't try to pull nothing."

"Thanks, faggot."

Payden fell back in his seat. "You want to keep cracking wise, maybe upset me, and guarantee you sleep in a cell tonight?"

"Ain't stupid." James looked back at Payden. "Tell me this ain't a line-up you're taking me to."

"What do you mean?"

"Yeah," Valarie asked. "What does he mean?"

Payden shook his head. "What he means, Valarie, is he's thinking I'm having you drop him off to call Layla by the scene, in the hopes someone there can ID him from any of the other murder sites."

"What crime scene have you been talking about?" Valarie asked. "Another killing?"

"One less drug dealer," Payden replied. "Near the pub."

James shifted in his seat. "Sure you ain't setting me up?"

Valarie glanced into the rearview mirror at Payden. "Are you?"

"The thought hadn't occurred to me until now, but having you on scene could clear things up more quickly. Thanks, Jimmy. You ain't as stupid as you look." He gave Valarie a quick pat on the shoulder. "Let's head over there. Cool?"

Valarie nodded, and Payden gave her directions.

"Cunt," James said. "Pretend it was my idea."

"I'm only looking out for Valarie."

"I'll bet you are. I see you two. Flame moves to protect you. Don't realise it, but she does. Specially when your pocket pussy shows."

"Jimmy," Valarie snapped. "Watch what you say if you're expecting to live in my home."

James looked at Payden. "Wouldn't it be nice if Mickey went away?"

"Don't you ever suggest—" Payden held back, feeling the urge to strike James. "You ain't never met a man and woman who were friends before?"

"Never two who used to fuck."

Valarie slammed the dashboard with her left hand. "Where do you get this from, Jimmy? Knock it off."

"I got eyes. Ears, too." James bobbed his eyebrows at Payden. "Want her back? I can make it happen."

Payden gulped. "Do as Valarie says. Watch your mouth."

They pulled up to the crime scene and parked two blocks down, near a pay phone. Payden got out of the car and James exited with him. Valarie stepped out a few moments later.

Payden pointed to the pay phone. "Call Layla. Get her to come out here. I want to see you dump her ass. Watching you drop change into the slot, talk shit, then tell me it's over ain't good enough."

"Crazy," James said. "All homos this paranoid?"

Valarie gave James Layla's phone number. "Do it, Jimmy. Have her come out here. I'm not putting you up in my home if she's going to be coming by. Mickey won't allow it either."

"Bullshit." James began walking to the pay phone. "I'm family."

When James was out of earshot, Payden gave Valarie a pat on the elbow. "Sorry to put you through this. Thought you deserved some closure, given what went down earlier."

"It's okay," she said, resting her head on his shoulder and wrapping her arms around his waist. "And thank you. I just hope she offers to take him in. Though I don't know why she would. Then again, she seemed so normal when I used to work with her. And she never said anything to me about Mickey and her. I mean, neither did Mickey, but I made it a point to let him know I didn't want to hear any of his details. What he did before we wed. Guess I'm not as good a judge of character as I think."

"True," Payden said and Valarie loosed one hand to whack him softly. "But we'll see."

James was back moments later. "On her way. Happy?"

Valarie nodded and Payden replied. "Sure, Jimmy. Hey, because it's bugging me, where'd you stay the night you left Valarie's?"

"Up," James said. "Didn't sleep. Having too much fun."

"How so?"

"Killing cops." James grinned.

Payden shook his head. "That shit ain't funny."

Lisa called out from down the street, and Payden waved to her and Bryan. She moved at a brisk pace toward Payden, James and Valarie, with Bryan following.

"Oh, for Christ's—" Valarie said. "Seriously? Is your new puppy still in love? I get it but, I mean, the bitch—she could try to be less obvious."

Payden whispered, "Don't confirm Jimmy's bullshit."

Valarie looked into his eyes, whispering in return. "You mean you don't think about us? Not anymore? Ever?"

Payden frowned slightly. "Course I do. But does talking about how I fucked up with you do anything good for either of us?"

Valarie looked away and shook her head. "I'm sorry. It's stupid and irrational, I know, but some of what he said is true. I didn't want you to hit it off with Layla. Not really. And I don't like seeing you with other women. It's two-faced, or a double standard, I know, but I can't help how I feel. A part of me still wants you to be mine. But I won't ever keep you from happiness if you can find it with someone else."

Payden kissed Valarie on the forehead, which Lisa noticed, making her walk even more aggressively. "You'll always be the best at making me feel good. Even when you're killing me inside."

Valarie smiled sadly as she stopped holding Payden around the waist.

"And thank you," Payden said to Valarie at regular volume.

James rolled his eyes.

"Hey," Lisa said when she got close enough. "Good you're here. I was afraid you wouldn't show."

Bryan stopped beside Lisa, looking at James hard. "What the hell is this? I get that you dropped the assault charges, but why is he here?" Bryan paused, glancing up. "Oh, I get it. And, yeah, good idea."

"The bullet train's arrival never fails to impress," Payden said, giving Lisa a look.

"We'll walk Jimmy around," Bryan said, squinting. "There are a lot of folks here from the last few scenes. Maybe a good citizen will point the finger if we put him on show."

James growled, looking at Payden. "Can't trust a cop."

"Shut the fuck up," Payden snapped. "And calm down. I didn't break no promise. We're waiting for your woman. If you do the right thing when she arrives, Valarie and Mickey take it from there. If I didn't say it perfect before, fuck yourself."

"Works." James stood behind Valarie and Payden, not looking Lisa or Bryan in the eyes.

Bryan shook his head. "You're going to let this guy walk?"

Payden waved his hands, cutting through the air horizontally in both directions, giving Lisa a wink she didn't react to on purpose. "We're reuniting Jimmy, here, with his current interest. So we'll know where he's at, no matter the outcome. We're not walking him through the crime scene. Best case, if he did do it, he's going to act like an asshole and contaminate the fucking thing with his prints. Shoe, finger, etcetera. Follow me? If it makes you feel better, Verrill, you have his consent to put men on him." Payden looked at James. "That right, Jimmy? Shouldn't be a problem since, like you said, you got nothing to do with all this drug dealing, murder and that, yeah?"

James nodded. "Watch me. Learn."

Payden smiled, closed-mouthed, then raised his hands in victory. "There you go. Does it get any better?"

Bryan shook his head and looked away. "Yeah, fine. I'll be right back. Like you said, Beck—and you consented, Jimmy—I'm going to have some of the patrolling officers keep a car on you. I'll bring some witnesses to see you, too."

"Fucking care," James said. "Do what you want."

Bryan trotted off, engaging the nearest officers who were, essentially, loitering and contributing nothing to the ongoing investigation.

A few minutes later, a car pulled up a block away from Valarie's and parked. Layla stepped out, dressed in jeans and a top that was basically lingerie. Catching sight of James, she quickened her pace. When she got close enough that she recognised Payden and Lisa, she slowed her walk, looking back.

James called to her. "It's okay, baby. Val just needs to see. Cops don't want nothing. Be cool."

Layla walked to James and took his left hand in her right. "Pigs. I could file a complaint."

"Why haven't you?" Lisa asked. "I can take it for you if you'd like."

"As if that's going to—"

James held up a hand. "Forget the toy cop."

Layla chuckled. "Come on, Jimmy, let's go. Back to my place. I got music and plenty of booze. Ready to have a good time. Finish what we started." She meowed, which made Valarie's eyes roll. "I can't wait to—"

James gave her a punishing smack with his right hand. He jerked her back to him with his left, causing her to stumble. "Here's the deal, chippy," he said to Layla. "One word: Not interested."

Layla looked at James, questioning, and he slapped her hard again, releasing his grip and chuckling as she fell to the ground.

"So," James asked Valarie, "I come home now?"

Valarie looked at Lisa, who seemed confused by Payden's non-reaction to events, then at James. "Of course not. What was that?"

"You talk to Mickey," James said, anger in his voice. "He said I come home. Long as no Layla."

Valarie looked down. "I know what he said, but, I mean—"

Bryan rushed back, having seen Layla being knocked around. When she attempted to stand, James kicked her in the stomach.

"Dogs lie," James said. "Stay."

Lisa finally snapped and rushed James, putting him in an arm-lock and spinning him around. Pulling up on his elbow to drop him to his knees, then slapping on the cuffs and reading him his rights

Bryan moved to ensure Layla was okay. Helping her stand and wiping the blood from her mouth. Walking her away from Payden, Lisa, Valarie and James.

Lisa looked at Payden. "What are you doing?"

"Didn't see that coming." Payden shrugged. "But it worked out okay."

"What do you mean?" Valarie and Lisa asked, almost at once.

"Well, you're taking this fuck back to gaol, putting him in a cell where he belongs, and Valarie don't have to worry about him stopping by and waking her kid."

Lisa shook her head. "I thought I understood why you were bringing him here, but wouldn't it have been easier to leave him in the tank?"

"Sure. But this is better. Witnesses. They see him now. Maybe they seen him before. And we established a pattern. Yeah?"

Valarie looked dumbstruck. "I'm glad he's not going to be living with us, but I don't get it either. The pattern. Not really."

Payden let out a frustrated breath. "You both know I love you, right?"

Lisa and Valarie nodded, each of them stopping when they saw that the other noticed.

"The fight at the pub was reaction. This was intentional and premeditated. He could have just told Layla things were off, but—"

"You said to make her show," James barked. "You said—"

"What I told you, Jimmy, was I needed to see you talk to Layla. To hear you brush her off. That's what I said." He patted Valarie on the shoulder. "Instead, even better, we now have verified proof you're violent and act with intent. So, Reid, you take him back to the station. He's a multiple-assault violator and a murder suspect. And he's ours."

"Yes, sir," Lisa said, her expression serious, giving Payden a weak salute.

"I mean," Payden said, fighting not to stutter. "If you're good with that. I wasn't ordering you to—"

Lisa chuckled, giving him a wink. "I'm good. You need to loosen up, though."

"What about—" Bryan asked, standing with Layla, a safe distance from James.

"Bring all the witnesses you want by the station's tank. I give a fuck."

Lisa grinned. "Nice work slipping in the extra behind my back. I guess I should just trust you now?"

"You don't?"

Lisa smiled, which made Valarie frown, which made Lisa smile wider. "I think I might. Anyway, I like the way you worked me." She threw Payden a wink which made Valarie hold herself and look down. "I'll be right back, as soon as I process our new guest."

Lisa wrestled James to his feet and walked him off through the crowd of police.

Valarie smiled, her eyes misty. "You did what you had to do. I can't say I'm upset about the outcome. But, if you still haven't noticed, your new partner likes you. Maybe she'll make you happy."

"No one ever will," Payden said, and Valarie's eyes went softer, sadder. "Not like you. But maybe I'll enjoy spending time with her. We'll see. She's a little—"

"Off? You two are perfect for each other."

"Not what I was going to say."

"Keep pretending. It doesn't work."

Payden looked around. "What the fuck happened to Verrill?"

Valarie scanned the area, unable to spot Bryan. "Maybe he took Layla back to her car? Too many people here. Too many police lights. I can't see."

"Could be. You good to drive back to your place alone? Mickey waiting for you?"

Valarie nodded. "Yes, he's there with Charity. We sent the sitter home after we got back from the pub."

Payden kissed her forehead again and she kissed him on the cheek as they hugged goodbye. Valarie was in her car, headed home, moments later. Lisa was out of sight and, however hard Payden squinted, he couldn't spot either Bryan or Layla.

Then Layla's car raced up beside him. Bryan was in the driver's seat. "Hey, Beck. Jimmy fucked this girl up pretty good, but she doesn't want to press charges. Still, she's in no shape to drive. I'm going to get her home. Can you follow me, pick me up there?"

Payden noted Layla was keeping her face out of sight. "I came here to work the crime scene, not the passers-by. Call a car once you dump the trash. And hurry back. People might be paying attention."

"Fuck you, Beck," Bryan said, driving off.

Payden returned Bryan's one-finger salute and gave the tip of his middle finger a kiss. "You'd better not fuck me. If I go down, so do you."

XXXVI

Bryan drove Layla home. Almost the projects, where his badge meant nothing. The neighbourhood was rough. The houses to either side of Layla's were boarded up and looked to be abandoned or occupied by squatters. No lights were on in either, which was a good sign, he supposed. He'd never spent a night in the bad areas of town except for a handful of times on the job. He'd never considered what it must be like to rest his head there. To close his eyes and try to sleep.

He pulled Layla's car to the kerb and she opened her door, putting one foot on the ground, then looking at Bryan. "I'm going to need my keys."

"Oh, yeah," Bryan said, snapping out of his thoughts. Still thinking about the years he'd spent on the force, the times he'd spent in neighbourhoods like Layla's, and how badly he wanted to speed away from it. He turned off the ignition and handed Layla her keys, exiting her car. Locking it from the inside before slamming the driver's side door shut.

Layla closed her door, watching Bryan check up and down the street. "You not consider how you were going to get back when you turned chivalrous?"

Bryan shook his head. "But, while I'm here, I should walk you to your door. Make sure you get inside."

"I'm fine here," Layla replied. "Known. You're the one you should be worried about."

Bryan stopped at the base of the two steps leading to the small front porch in front of Layla's door as she unlocked and opened it.

"Stay safe." Bryan began to walk away.

"It's a long road back," Layla said, not raising her voice, but clearly audible in the dead air. "Come in for a second."

Bryan slowly turned toward her.

"Give someone a call. You got a woman, right?"

Bryan walked back to Layla's, climbing the stairs and entering her small home, closing the door behind him. Noting the phone in the kitchen to the right, and the bathroom to the left. Standing in the combination living room, bedroom.

"Not much, I know. Go ahead. Give your woman a call."

"Thank you, Layla."

"A gentleman." Layla removed her clothes, sitting on the couch and turning on the television. Watching whatever crap came on first, in her panties and nothing else, while Bryan picked up the phone. She looked at him and chuckled. "Nothing to feel guilty about. It's not like you're cheating."

"If I call my fiancée, and she comes to the door, she might think so, no matter how convincing your argument."

"Not married yet?" Layla looked Bryan up and down. "Must be your personality. You're distant. Anyone ever tell you that? I bet you keep a secret good, though. I don't even know your name. Maybe I'm confused from that fuck, Jimmy, slapping me around."

"If it's any consolation, you look good. I mean, unharmed."

"Yeah. I think that mother fucker was just making a point. To get back in Mickey's good graces. Another prick. I'll bet he and your partner are buddies, yeah?

Even though I'm sure Mickey knows that asshole fucked his wife before they tied the knot. Then again, Mickey was screwing around too. Said it was their arrangement, but I called bullshit and walked. Turned out it was true, but I don't regret blowing him off. He called me a whore. You believe that? I'm a whore because I wouldn't sleep with him? Tell me how that makes sense."

"It doesn't."

Layla looked at Bryan as the buzzing on the phone's line, indicating the phone had been off the hook too long, caught him by surprise and he hung up. "You still ain't told me your name," she said.

Bryan loosened his shirt's collar. "Verrill, ma'am."

"No, your name."

"Bryan," he said, moving to pick the phone up again.

Layla stood and walked toward him. Draping herself on his right shoulder, running her index finger around his cheek, her naked body's natural odour exciting his senses. "You look confused. Why?"

"It's nothing. History. Actually, more like fantasy."

"Oh, you're dreaming?" Layla rubbed herself against him. "About me?"

"Ma'am?"

"Layla." She dipped her tongue in Bryan's ear and he shivered, not looking her way, but beginning to dream a different dream.

Bryan turned to face Layla, feeling her sweet breath in his mouth. "Apologies. Layla."

"No worries." Layla removed Bryan's jacket. "And thank you."

"I'm sorry?"

Layla stroked Bryan's clothed erection. "You're cute."

"Thank you, ma—Layla. I really should—" Bryan felt his belt open, his zipper come loose and his pants drop to the floor along with his boxers and belt-holstered gun.

"Why spend your life wondering?" Layla asked, undoing the buttons of Bryan's shirt. Kissing and licking her way down his chest. "I could feel what you wanted when you lied to your cop buddy about me not being in any shape to drive. When you forgot all about the police radio in your jacket, I knew what I felt was real. You want to be here. With me. No shame in it."

"What do you—" Bryan grabbed Layla by the shoulders and she dropped to her knees. "This isn't—"

"No? You don't want me to—"

Bryan didn't need to cut Layla off as she took him into her mouth. Finding himself forgetting Mindy completely as he ran his fingers through her hair. "We shouldn't—"

Layla stopped sucking Bryan, pulled down her panties and stood, stepping out of them and dragging Bryan to the couch, throwing him onto it and mounting him. "You got a good reason?"

Bryan looked at Layla, speechless.

She continued to ride him, moving her hips and swivelling them as he swivelled his own to thrust up into her, causing her to moan as she spoke. "Jesus, I ain't been fucked in so long. Don't shoot too quick. I ain't there yet. Almost, though."

"Okay," Bryan said, looking at Layla in disbelief. Everything he'd ever wanted in a woman, physically. And everything he couldn't resist sexually. He felt cursed, and he felt lucky. "I promise."

"Good," she said, her breathing becoming constricted. "God damn. Tell me how bad you need me."

Bryan opened his mouth to speak.

"Tell me I'm the hottest piece of trash you've ever seen. Make me your good little girl. Tell me to cum."

Bryan bit his lower lip, fighting to hold back his ejaculation.

Layla let out a deep moan. "Tell me to cum or you'll beat the shit out of me. Tell me if I don't—"

"Shut the fuck up," Bryan snapped, and Layla's facial features loosened completely, tightening again immediately as she squeezed her eyes shut and began to push him deeper inside her, more slowly. "Don't be a naughty girl. Cum for me now or I'll fuck you up so bad—"

"Do it." Layla's body seized and the muscles around her vagina spasmed as her entire body shook and she let her upper body fall on top of Bryan's. Holding on to him with animal strength as he continued to thrust into her and she continued to orgasm. "Fucking pig. You fuck."

Layla's voice began to rise and Bryan felt himself close to ejaculation while becoming acutely aware of his position. Both on the couch, being straddled by his dream woman, and his position were anyone he knew to catch him there.

"Oh, shit," she breathed out, her voice choppy, panting. "That was so fucking hot. Don't take it out yet. But don't cum inside me. I'm not on the pill." She let out a contented sigh. "Bryan. That's a sexy name. Spelt with an I?"

"With a Y. But, I have to tell you, you're so beautiful. Jesus, I can't hold out much longer."

"I'm beautiful?" Layla asked, her tone belying her meaning. Making Bryan fear he'd been set up to use until she put her face above his, and began kissing and licking him from forehead to chin, finally finding his mouth with her tongue. "You really think I'm beautiful?"

"No one's ever told you that?" Bryan asked, feeling himself about to lose control. "Look at you."

Layla pulled Bryan out of her and slid down his body, dropping to her knees on the side of the couch and finishing him with her mouth. Lovingly, tenderly. Swallowing until he was empty. When she finished draining him, she held up a finger and walked into the kitchen to collect his clothes. Bryan sat and she dressed him in his shirt. Then she motioned for him to stand and she put back on his boxers and pants. Ensuring his clothes looked good and didn't have any wrinkles or stains. On her knees. Attending to the task with a devotion he hadn't expected. Just like he hadn't expected any of what had just happened to him.

Layla looked at him when she finished getting his clothes in order and his gun had its safety set on. "Tell me I'm your good little girl."

Bryan flashed on Layla, at a much younger age, being violated by a family member—possibly her father—and snapped out of it when she tugged on his pants waist and looked into his eyes with more expectancy. "You're my good little girl, Layla," Bryan said, believing the words he spoke but not believing he was actually speaking them.

"Thank you, daddy." She smiled, standing to dress herself.

Bryan watched her and marvelled at the perfection of her body. How she wasn't soft like Mindy, but she also wasn't tough. How her breasts moved and her belly wasn't slim, but it also wasn't fat. How everything about her seemed normal. Nothing about her intended to fool him into believing she might once have been on the cover of a men's magazine. Nothing fake about her at all. Not her body. Certainly not her attitude or her words. Not even her need for affection she'd voiced to him. Something he hadn't expected at all when she'd first begun seducing him, which he'd initially taken as the beginning of a rebuff.

After she was dressed and she'd walked Bryan into the bathroom with her to freshen their faces and bodies, she walked with him to the door, holding his right hand in her left, kissing his shoulder. "Let me give you a ride back? To end this right, or whatever?"

"I—" Bryan began as she opened the front door.

She put a finger to his lips. "Don't apologise. I wanted you, you wanted me. That's what that was. Was I a dream? For you, I mean?"

"Yes. You were. You are."

Layla smiled genuinely. "I can't believe this is happening. I love that you say what you mean. Especially the way you don't look at me like I'm different from anyone else. I can't, for the life of me, read your face. You're a closed book. I like that. A good man who don't talk. I need that."

"You've got it," Bryan said, almost smirking. "Or, you had it. Thank you for that. For everything."

Layla looked at her body. "I never felt beautiful before. No one ever said that to me either. They called me almost everything. But never beautiful. You did, though. And I believed it." She paused. "It's hard for you to lie, ain't it?"

Bryan nodded.

Layla opened the front door and walked outside with Bryan, locking it behind them and walking slowly with him to her car. Opening the passenger door for him and pleasantly surprised when she reached the driver's side and saw Bryan moving back into position in his seat, having just unlocked her door from the inside.

She got into the driver's seat and cranked the ignition. Putting the car into drive and making a three-point turn, heading back to the crime scene by the pub.

As they drove, Bryan struggled with what to say. Opting to remain silent.

Layla parked her car three blocks from the scene. Far enough away the police lights were visible but her car wouldn't be noticed. She turned off the lights and looked at Bryan, pleased he wasn't wearing his seatbelt either. That he hadn't been thinking to, just as she hadn't. That he was still dreaming of her though he'd just experienced her fully.

"This is the best place to let you off," she said. "So you don't got explaining to do. Especially if your woman's there."

"Good thinking. But I'm feeling conflicted about—"

Layla leant over and French kissed him passionately. Making it last longer than she'd expected she needed to. "Nothing to feel bad about, Bryan. I love your name. I won't ever say nothing to no one. And you can always—"

"I'm not—" Bryan said curtly. "I'm sorry. I didn't mean to lose my temper."

Layla chuckled. "That was you losing your temper? Jesus, I think I'm falling for you." She tilted her head. "I should have let you cum inside me. The world needs more people like you."

Bryan chuckled, finally betraying emotion with his features. "That's kind of you to say."

Layla smiled. "He laughs. I did it." Then her smile turned to a frown. "But I'm serious." She gave Bryan's cheek a loving rub. "You ain't honour-bound to be miserable. You know?"

"You really are beautiful," Bryan said, looking into her eyes. "And you're right. But I can't just—"

Layla nodded. "I know. It ain't easy. I ain't telling you what to do. I ain't even asking."

"Asking what?"

"You to be with me. I'm not what everyone wants, and I don't say what everyone wants to hear, but I'm true."

Bryan let out a heavy sigh. "I know you are. And...." Bryan looked away. "I want to see you again. May I?"

Layla shook her head. "I don't answer questions from people who can't make eye contact with me when they ask."

Bryan turned and looked deep into Layla's eyes. "Will you see me again? I know it's the wrong thing to do. Or maybe I don't. I just know, right now, I want to see you again."

"In public?"

Bryan shook his head. "I couldn't do that to Mindy. I'd be proud to be seen with you, but not until—"

Layla shushed him. "Don't promise me you're going to leave her. Not now. But, yes, you may. And I don't mind being your woman on the side, so long as you don't treat me bad. But I won't be ignored. Not completely."

"You have my word."

"And I got your number," Layla said, smirking. "I mean, give me a phone number I can call you at. I don't want you to have mine. Your woman might find it. Someone else might. It could put you in a bad spot. Give me your office number." Layla pulled a piece of paper and a pencil from the glove box. "How do you answer?"

Bryan gave her his office number. "Verrill, detective division."

"You're the cutest. When I call, I ain't going to answer if I hear a click. But when you answer the first time, I'm going to say something like, 'sorry, wrong number, sugar,' and hang up. When I do, you'll know it was me."

"I'm certain I will."

"And, when I call again, to ask to see you, you'll give me yes or no answers, like you're giving someone the runaround. Don't ever say my name. I ain't going to call you for a good while, neither, so no one can tie tonight to when we hook up again, if they're paying attention. All these little rules keep you safe."

"True."

Layla smiled. "One last thing?"

"Yes?"

"Say my name, so I can fall asleep hearing you speak it?"

"Of course." Bryan opened his door and blew her a kiss, which she returned. "Have sweet dreams, Layla."

"The best."

Within the minute, Layla was driving back to her home and Bryan was walking at a good pace to the crime scene. A place that now spelt more kinds of trouble than it had when he'd left.

XXXVII

Bryan made it back to the crime scene, which was still flooded with officers and loud as hell, looking around for Payden. He found him, standing alone, on the perimeter of the scene, and patted him on the shoulder. "Beck. They find anything? What happened to your partner?"

Payden turned to look at Bryan. "Technically, our partner. Since we took you on. She'll show again soon."

"She left?"

"No. She got smaller. You were there when she took Jimmy back to lock-up. Better question. What happened to you?"

Bryan looked away quickly. "So, she should be back soon, then. Good."

"Seriously. What happened to you? You jog back here? You smell like shit, man." Payden stared at Bryan, who looked everywhere but back at him. "Anyway, those CSI pricks are almost done corrupting the scene. Then we can take a look. The eyewitness has yet to show."

"Reid shouldn't have left. This is where we need to be."

"By that logic, you shouldn't have left, either, Verrill. Where you been? Where you at? And what do you give a shit what Reid does? She's my partner. She's putting a bad guy away. She ain't missing nothing. And — who knows? — maybe Jimmy lets something slip while he's eyeballing her and dreaming."

"Never. That guy's a brick wall."

Payden chuckled. "And Reid's a brick shithouse." Payden glanced around. "All these people. The place is getting dangerous." He paused. "And again. Where the hell you been? You took that hot slice home over an hour ago. Tell me you fucked her, so I have some respect for you."

"I can't tell you that."

"Saving it for Mindy, still? Or you just won't tell me?"

Bryan gulped as Payden looked away. "Should we go see what we can see? CSI has got to be finished."

"Fuck it, let's go."

As they began to walk, they heard the announcement. The eyewitness was on the scene. Another drug dealing piece of shit Payden would put in the dirt himself if he could, but, now, maybe the one person who could ensure his job remained secure.

XXXVIII

Bryan rushed to meet the eyewitness while Payden approached with a slow stroll, watching Bryan push his way through a wall of police and the citizens they were supposed to be keeping away. Add to that the fact local news had shown, and the crime scene was guaranteed contaminated.

Payden stopped outside the ring of front-line officers and turned to face away from them, not bothering to look at the rambling lunatic of an eyewitness to murder. He pulled the portable radio from his jacket and called Lisa.

She picked up almost immediately.

"Reid," Payden said. "It's Beck. Open channel. Hear me okay?"

"Yes, Beck," she replied. "Loud and clear. I'm on my way back from the station."

Payden turned to look at the crowd of people finally being dispersed as the eyewitness was walked around by officers, identifying every other person he looked at, then changing his mind. "The guy who called this thing in showed. Looks like he uses his product and took a header into an empty swimming pool. You close?"

Payden heard a car roar to a stop somewhere in the distance.

"Was that a yes?"

"No," Lisa said, a smile in her voice. "Stay where you are. I'll find you."

"You stay, Reid. Stick by the car. I'll meet you there."
"Staying."

Payden clicked off his portable radio, secured it and jogged away from the scene casually. Not running, lest someone notice and decide he was the guy.

When Payden spotted their car, he waved to Lisa, who sat on the hood.

She slid off as he got close. Her clothing the same, but looking cleaned and pressed. Her jeans hiked up, no longer appearing loose, and her shirt pulled down tight to flatter her form. Her hair combed almost straight, no longer a mess, showcasing her beautiful face, which looked fresh and clean. Almost as if she'd been wearing a hideous mask at the pub.

"Any luck with Jimmy? No way he could resist you getting all gussied up for him."

"What? The two-minute makeover?" Lisa looked down at her body to hide the smile she fought to suppress. "Anyway, I'm pretty sure he isn't the one."

"How so?" Payden replied, watching Lisa look away and inspecting the soft skin of her neck, noticing a beauty in the contrast its scar brought, as she made sure her hair looked its very best. He snapped his fingers in front of Lisa's face, but her eyes were fixed on the crowd.

Lisa stood firm, still watching the crowd, clocking the eyewitness, and beginning to tremble. "I did what I had to. Please stop staring."

"Sorry, I didn't mean—" Payden said. His speech halting when he realised Lisa couldn't possibly have seen him looking at her neck. Considering she must have felt it.

The eyewitness was making it to the outer ring of the crowd. Still blathering. Hopped up on something. Getting nearer.

Lisa didn't blink. "I know what you were thinking. Like all the rest."

Payden's face tightened, then his lips loosened into a penitent frown. "That's not what I was thinking—I mean, I was just—You got me wrong, Lisa, I—"

She punched him in the arm, her eyes still facing forward as she began to smile, sensing an affection in Payden's stuttered apology she hadn't expected, which erased her initial feelings of humiliation and anger. "Got you."

Payden looked at her as she gawked at the crowd. "That's hilarious." Then he smiled. "I think maybe we were meant for each other."

"Maybe. Seeing as you keep calling me Lisa. Which you shouldn't when we're in public."

"You going to tell?"

"And ruin us?" She smiled wider, her eyes still looking forward, her body language contradicting her face's easy expression. "Maybe."

"That works. Hate to break up a good... partnership."

She gave him a sideways glance, then fixed her eyes forward again. "Nice try, Beck. I don't crack that easy."

"I wasn't trying to—"

"Of course not." She grabbed on to his hand, then abruptly pulled hers away, trying to mask the look of embarrassment and discontent on her face. "That was your fault."

Payden looked her up and down. "You okay? Why so interested in the eyewitness?"

"He reminds me of someone I'd like to feed to a dumpster."

Payden grinned. "Bright side, if he tries to cop a feel, you can always break his arm when we follow up with him later. No one will see nothing."

"You're sweet," Lisa said, stopping herself from smiling and clearing her throat, bringing both hands up to cover her mouth as she did.

"Looks like I got you, too."

"You have no idea—" She gave him a glance that was, at once, hopeful and helpless. Something like love, as Payden understood it. "And that's the last time."

"Shame."

She smacked his arm. "Don't be... Just, don't."

The eyewitness, a young man being marched about by two officers—one for each arm—stood before them within seconds. Looking Lisa in the eyes intently, then sniffing the air in front of her.

"Recognise her?" the first officer asked the eyewitness.

The eyewitness shook his head and moved between Lisa and Payden.

"Eyes off the lady." Payden poked the eyewitness in the sternum to direct his gaze away from Lisa. "This is a murder investigation. You realise that, right, you junkie piece of shit? This ain't your fifteen minutes." Payden stepped forward, face to face with the eyewitness, trying not to cough from the smell. "You got something to say, say it or fuck off. And when you leave, make it for good. This town don't need you, it don't want you and, apparently, it won't tolerate you."

"Fuck you, cop," the eyewitness said. "You're too tall."

"That all you got against me? After what I just said? How fucked-up are you right now?"

The eyewitness scanned Lisa from toes to forehead. "Your bitch, though... Shortcake. Ready to suck cock. Catch some dreams. I remember."

Lisa glared at the eyewitness. "I've never seen you before. You're mistaken." She held up her hands, trying to keep them from shaking. Something the officers didn't notice but Payden caught immediately. She was scared.

The eyewitness looked lost for a moment, then shook his head. "Thought I—No, it's nothing. Too good-looking. Clean. Smell too salty. But you." He looked at Payden. "It was you."

"Looking to suck your dick?" Payden asked. "If balls to the chin is your thing, you have my blessing. But I don't play for that team."

"Yeah, no," the eyewitness said, looking more confused.

"Are you identifying me, sailor? Say I'm the guy." Payden looked at the officers after noting the bulge in the eyewitness's front left pants pocket. "You frisk this mother fucker? He's carrying. Secure that shit."

"Yes," the eyewitness yelled as the officers stripped him of his weapon, which he didn't notice or mind. "The voice. It was softer, but he was messing with us. Drag queen faggot."

The first officer shook the eyewitness and waved another pair of officers over. "Are you identifying this man as the person you saw kill your friend?"

"He's the one," the eyewitness said. "I see it now."

The two other officers came to stand beside Payden as the eyewitness was marched away to ensure he saw everyone else, in case.

"Sorry to have to do this," the first officer said, extending his hands to encourage Payden to do the same. "But it's procedure."

"I know it looks bad," the second officer added, "but you'll be cleared. That brain-damaged mess already ID'ed ten other people, then changed his mind. No hard feelings?"

Payden held his hands together and in front of him. "I don't see ten other people in cuffs. How do you know he ain't going to change his mind again?"

"I'm sorry?" the first officer asked.

The second officer chimed in. "You're a detective. It would look bad if we didn't—It's strictly procedure and—"

Payden shook his head. "Strictly procedure." He turned to Lisa as he noticed Bryan moving toward them from the crowd. "Meet you back at the station?"

She nodded, looking down.

"Chin up, Reid. Don't worry about how this looks."

"Not that," she growled to keep from whispering. "I just... I can't say. Not now."

The eyewitness complained as the officers charged with escorting him decided enough was enough and handed him off to be stuffed in the back of a patrol car, which sped away, presumably to the station house.

Bryan arrived, pushing the arresting officers apart, too late to stop them from applying the cuffs to Payden's wrists. "What's going on here?"

"Eyewitness made him," the first officer said.

"I'm sorry, but I won't allow—" Bryan snapped.

Payden shook his head, his voice clipped but menacing. "I didn't do nothing. Everything's fine."

"You're sure? Do you want me to let Val know?"

Payden nodded and walked away with the officers.

Bryan quickly called in to the station on his portable radio, to request they notify Mrs. Valarie Dooley of Payden's situation

Lisa moved to follow Payden, then stopped beside Bryan. Looking away from him for a moment to collect herself as he secured his portable. Watching her brand-new hero risk going down in flames willingly. Wondering if he was doing it for her or doing it for himself.

XXXIX

Bryan shook his head as he watched Payden being shoved into the back of a squad car and taken away. His eyes went glassy as he pondered all the things they'd ever done together. Since the academy. After Payden's first true love had been taken from him, he had never been the same, and their relationship had suffered as a result. And, though Payden had—in Bryan's estimation—a fairly solid moral compass, he was never one to do things by the book. As much as he hated to admit it, the thought Payden had grown tired of the state of his decaying town and taken matters into his own hands had crossed Bryan's mind more than once. Even the thought he might have taken Lester's life to preserve his own didn't seem unreasonable. The Payden Beck he knew did what had to be done when backed into a corner. For Payden, that corner was the mere threat of loss of things he held dear. While a part of Bryan prayed Payden wasn't the man behind the recent spate of murders and the execution of a fellow officer, another part of him was sure the eyewitness had identified him correctly. Whatever disguise Payden had been wearing hadn't been good enough, and he'd shot his mouth off one too many times. Guaranteed his end. And, as Bryan pondered those things, he prayed Payden wouldn't take him down with him, or use their long-standing partnership as leverage, if what Bryan was coming to believe was true. Payden knew things about him that could cost him his career, his fiancée, his life.

Bryan turned to look at Lisa, who had unlocked the door to what was once his and Payden's car. Taken by surprise at how drastically she'd managed to change her look without changing her clothes, and watching the way she moved. Slow, like she'd been knocked over by an elephant and left to drop in a weightless universe. "Hey," he called out, moving toward her. "I'm riding with you." He stopped when she opened the driver's side door fully and turned to face him. "We're both going to the same place, right?"

She looked up at him, squinting. "Are we?"

"What's that supposed to mean?"

"Nothing. Just get your story straight."

Bryan brushed the arms of his jacket. "What? I don't need a story."

Lisa shook her head. "We all need a story, Verrill. And we need to be able to tell it well. So, practise. Your time to show, then tell, is coming sooner than you think."

"Look," Bryan snapped. "You have no call to accuse me—"

"Of what?" Lisa walked to Bryan, standing so close the toes of their shoes touched. "You don't have your story straight?"

"Again. I did nothing wrong."

"I never said you did, and what's that got to do with anything? You don't think half the people who live in this neighbourhood believe my partner's been murdering drug dealers—maybe killing police—now? It doesn't matter the word came from the mouth of a dope dealer so high on his own product he could barely stay awake. Beck's been damaged. Nearly as bad as the half-dead junkie who fingered him."

"So what? He's not the only other detective—"

Lisa whispered in Bryan's ear. "Fuck. You." She sniffed and backed up a step. "The hint of bad is as good as the real thing."

Bryan glanced to his left and right, his cheeks pinking slightly before he regained control of his stony visage. "What is wrong with you?"

"Nothing. Breathe in my face."

"That would be inappropriate."

"You've got bigger problems."

Bryan's voice cracked. "I didn't do anything."

Lisa looked at the scene, seeing the captain making his rounds. "But you're guilty."

Bryan waved her off. "Beck's got you all twisted. He does that, you know?"

"I know." Her eyes grew misty for a moment.

"Just remember, when he offers you a gift, you're already fucked—"

Lisa's expression didn't change. "Your guilt reeks."

Bryan sniffed himself automatically.

"Knock it off, Verrill. You're not a woman. Your olfactory sense isn't naturally fine. But I can smell the girl you escorted from harm's way on you. She was a looker. I can't say I blame you."

"All I did was take her home and walk back here."

"Give me your hand," Lisa said, holding out hers.

Bryan extended his hand. "You're letting Beck turn you into him."

"Beck isn't changing me," Lisa said, locking eyes with Bryan as she took his hand in hers. "I'm not surviving in a man's world because I'm weak like you."

"I'm sorry?" Bryan asked, flabbergasted. "You've got no right—"

"I've got every right." She sniffed his hand, pulling him closer to her. "You're a liar and a cheat. You smell like sex. You smell like her."

"You were never close enough to her to—" Bryan snapped, stopping himself too late.

"That's true." Lisa grinned. "I never was. But I have gotten a good whiff of your fiancée. Her skin smells like baby powder. You don't smell like her anymore. And, if I can tell the difference out here, you can bet she'll be able to when you get home."

"We don't live together—" Bryan began again, cursing himself.

"Just keep talking yourself into a confession. Now, breathe in my face."

Bryan looked down as Lisa tilted her head back and he breathed directly onto her mouth and nose. "Happy?"

Lisa stepped back, releasing her grip on Bryan. "Christ." She coughed. "When's the last time you changed your underwear?"

He shook his head. "Enough with the parlour tricks."

Lisa waved her hands in front of her face. "Go meet Mindy with your breath smelling like you just gave yourself a blowjob and swallowed. Tell your woman she's mistaken when she calls you out. She's not as honest or forgiving as me. You're going to lose her if you don't get that stink off you." She paused as she moved to enter her car.

Bryan continued to shake his head. "I never—"

"Do you know what your problem is, Verrill?"

He shook his head one more time and stopped.

"You're showing me everything. Your body, your words and your breath are all telling me you just fucked around."

"Whatever," Bryan said, looking distressed. "Can I catch a ride with you?"

"Ask me later, when I see you at the station." Lisa slipped into the driver's seat, closing her door, locking the car's passenger side door and rolling down the driver's side window.

Bryan looked over his shoulder quickly to see the captain growing nearer. "What is this about, really?"

Lisa scoffed. "I saw you suppress a smile when they dragged Beck away in cuffs. A dream come true?"

Bryan opened his mouth to speak.

"Don't deny it. I can read you better than you think you can put one past me. I don't like that you did that. It doesn't sit well with me. Not just because he's my partner. In general. I don't trust you. Catch a ride with patrol. I'll see you, Verrill. Freshen up."

Bryan moved away from the car and Lisa cranked the ignition.

"Hey," the captain called out and Lisa looked past Bryan, removing her hand from the gear shift and letting the car idle. "Hold on."

"I wonder what he wants?" Bryan asked.

"Really?" Lisa replied. "That's so interesting. Tell me more."

Bryan gave her the finger behind his back and Lisa grabbed it, pulling it the wrong way just enough to make him squeak.

"All right, kids," the captain said, looking jolly. "No grabby hands. Especially you, Verrill. You're practically married."

Lisa released Bryan's finger as the captain put his hand on top of the car. "Don't worry," she said. "I'm done. Nothing to grab."

"Anyway." The captain chuckled as Bryan rolled his eyes and looked away. "CSI found so much evidence here, everyone who drinks or lives in the general area's going to be a match for the killer. What are you going to do?"

"That's the good news?" Bryan asked. "I hardly think—"

"It's true," Lisa said. "He hardly ever does."

The captain gave Lisa's cheek a pinch. "I like you. They told me you were bad news, but maybe that's what this town needs."

"So, the good news is...?" Bryan asked.

"Oh, the suspense," Lisa said, smirking.

The captain gave Lisa's cheek a light smack in good spirit. "Don't ever stop being you, kid. Anyway, Verrill, the good news is this. It don't matter what happened here. The results came back from your ex-partner's crime scene. They got DNA from there. And they say it's one person's." The captain bobbed his eyebrows, noting Bryan's scowl. "This don't make you happy, you friendless mope?" He looked off and waved to someone in the distance. "I'll see you two back at the station. No one gets the night off."

The captain rushed away and Bryan looked at the passenger side of Lisa's car. "May I ride with you now?"

"Sure," Lisa said, putting it into drive and pulling away.

It took Bryan five minutes to realise Lisa wasn't coming back to pick him up, and he tried to catch the last cruiser heading to the station.

In those five minutes, Lisa drove directly to the station house, worrying terribly. About Payden and about what evidence CSI had turned up at a murder scene they'd both visited.

Mostly, she was scared to death for her future. Though it had only been two days of almost non-stop rush, she'd grown attached to her new partner and her new home away from home. In the pit of her stomach, she felt everything slip farther away the closer she got to the station.

The first thing she determined she would do, when she arrived, was get Payden out of lock-up if they'd had the audacity to put him behind bars. If not to save James from being beaten to death — something she felt Payden would do in an instant, given the affection he still held for Valarie and couldn't hide worth a damn — then to ensure his night didn't end in utter disgrace. If there was anyone she'd ever met who didn't deserve to lose because perception became skewed to even the slightest extent, it was Payden.

And, she had to admit to herself if she was going to be any use to him at all, she loved him to a degree. He was a kindred spirit. Someone she'd been searching for over many years. Someone she'd not known she needed in her life, or known she'd been seeking, until she met him. And, if she was anything, she was loyal to her friends and loved ones. In both categories, he was the only contestant.

XL

Mindy drove from her parking space down a side street two blocks opposite the crime scene and honked as she approached Bryan—who appeared to be stuck without a ride—and stopped. Dying to know what they'd found at this latest crime scene. Not because she hoped drug dealers would stop dropping dead. Not because she hoped he'd caught a break in the case which might earn him a promotion. Mostly, dying to find out if Bryan had any news about Payden and why he'd been taken away in cuffs after what looked like an argument with a young man the chatter on the street said was an eyewitness to the latest murder.

Bryan raced to the passenger side door of Mindy's car and she motioned that it was already unlocked.

"Thank Jesus you got my message," Bryan said, huffing as he hopped in. "We've got to get to the station. They got DNA from Mansfield's murder. Quick compare results are back."

"I love you, too," Mindy said, showcasing her tight, white jeans and sleeveless pink top. Looking tacky as hell. "And I'll assume you meant to thank me for showing here, without being asked, after you left me to spend the night alone."

"I'm sorry, sweetie." He wiped his mouth, trying to look excited about the job and not nervous about anything else. "Thank you. I'd be hoofing it back to the station if it weren't for you. You're a godsend. I'm just amped. We could nail the son of a bitch who's been doing these murders, and maybe killed my new partner, by tomorrow."

"Yay," Mindy said, no emotion in her voice, taking her foot off the brake pedal and heading toward the station. "I saw the way Payden's little partner couldn't keep her hands off you. She's just like him. Was she trying to kiss —"

Bryan thought of Layla, and started talking fast. "What you saw was Beck's new partner telling me to go fuck myself. If you must know, she thinks I was happy to see Beck get taken away. And Detective Reid's not really a woman either."

"Looks like one to me," Mindy snapped. "Short, maybe, and grotesquely marked-up, but she's put together well. I'll bet you've taken a long look or two. She's a trap you'd fall into. Don't deny it."

Bryan slammed his hands on the dashboard. "What the fuck?" He took in a calming breath. "If she wants me, why'd she leave without me?"

"I assume because you said no," Mindy replied, looking satisfied with herself. "Which is a good thing. She may be moderately attractive, but she's dangerous and, good Lord, I can smell her on you."

"What are you talking about?" Bryan asked, trying to look insulted as he recalled Lisa's words more clearly. Thanking God Mindy hadn't insisted on giving him a kiss to greet him. "She got close to me, but —"

Mindy pulled up in front of the station, just outside the lot, and slammed the car into park. "If that's the case, I'm not coming inside. If what I'm smelling is her breath or body odour on you from standing near, I'll probably vomit if I have to spend time in an enclosed space with her. Jesus, she must sweat like the pig she is when she puts the brakes on trying to impress the boys."

"Christ, Mindy. It's not like you haven't been near her—" Bryan stopped himself as he realised he was trying to talk Mindy into probing deeper into his evening. She'd been walked out of the station by Lisa before and, if she put it together, the smell wouldn't make sense. Not Layla's smell. A smell everyone but he noticed—ostensibly, because he was a man—and a smell he wished he could.

"Yeah, but, like you said, she's all bothered tonight. And, if you keep denying she's beddable I'm going to get suspicious."

Bryan opened his mouth to protest.

Mindy put her hand on his left thigh. "Kidding. I'm not worried about that tomboy bitch. I'm not worried about you either."

Bryan let out a breath of relief, directed away from Mindy. "Good to know you trust me."

"I don't need to." Mindy looked away. "You've never cheated and you never will. I know you."

"So, this was all just for fun?"

She threw up her hands. "It got us from where we were to here, and then some, yes? Not much awkward silence. Why does it matter? Should I be worried?"

"Maybe."

Mindy let out a condescending laugh. "When you find this other woman who'll put up with you, let alone make it regular, you let me know. Until then, sweetie, you're not going anywhere." She called attention to her face and body again. "Let's be real. You know you're never doing better than me."

Bryan cringed slightly when she gave him a peck on the cheek.

"Go. Before I become physically ill. And stay clear of the funky smelling troll. I don't want to have to throw away a perfectly good pair of clothes because she doesn't bathe. I'll wait for you here, doors locked, and see you soon. Now, please, go."

Bryan opened his door as Mindy shooed him away. Closing it behind him and giving her a wave she didn't return as he walked toward the station. Thanking God Mindy took him for granted while he wondered how soon he could see Layla again, and — if necessary — put off the wedding so he could get her out of his system, if that was possible. As he remembered her, he wasn't sure it ever would be. Even if he and Mindy did finally get married.

XLI

When all the officers from the precinct were crammed into the station—with Bryan arriving long after Lisa—the captain calmed the crowd. Herding them into the bullpen and having them move desks toward the outside walls so he could deliver what he felt was compelling news, though almost every officer in the room had already heard. When everyone was in order, he commanded the patrol officers keeping Payden in line to remove the cuffs because, where the fuck was he going to go?

"First things first," the captain said. "Meet the young man of the hour." He pointed to the night-shift officers who brought out the eyewitness.

The crowd roared with glee as the officers stood the eyewitness to the front and left of Payden, who was flanked by Valarie and Lisa, both of whom wanted to comfort him with touch, but neither of whom wanted the other to witness them doing so.

"How are you?" the captain asked the eyewitness, who scratched his bruised arms furiously, looking around the room and sweating as he twitched. "If you can take a few moments and stop whatever it is you're doing"—he looked at the night-shift officers—"He ain't detoxing, is he?"

They shrugged.

"All right, we'll make it quick," the captain said, grabbing the eyewitness by the shoulders and walking him in front of Payden. "See anyone here you recall from the night your brother in the illegal sale of drugs was executed?"

The eyewitness nodded his battered head furiously.

"Can you point him out to us?" The captain cleared his throat. "Soon."

The eyewitness — still shaking — pointed at Lisa.

"That her," he said, grabbing his crotch. "I see her little mouth. Soft. Choking on my *polla*."

"What?" the captain asked, looking around, confused. "This is a line-up, you dumb fuck, not a cat-house."

The eyewitness moved toward Lisa, who focussed all her adrenaline, squaring up to knock him on his ass, and he backed away.

The captain groaned, pointing at Payden. "I understand you confirmed it was this man. More than once."

"*No sé*," the eyewitness continued, muttering more and more softly. "She, on her knees. Then the man, he appeared."

Payden shook his head. "You sure that was me, you half-retarded drug-baby? And why are you mumbling? Speak up. Some people give a shit what comes out your mouth."

"No," the eyewitness said, fear in his eyes. "It was him. Said *niñita* his piece of — "

The captain rubbed his forehead. "Shut the fuck up, you worthless mother — " He pointed at Lisa. "Detective Reid, I have to ask."

Lisa nodded. "For the record, I've never performed fellatio on this man."

The captain looked at Payden, rolling his eyes.

Payden spoke. "For the record, Detective Reid is not — nor has she ever been — my piece of...."

The eyewitness looked around everywhere, panicking. "Why you talking about me? I try to help you, but you won't stop changing. Fucking spiders. I hear you. Not funny."

The entire room was silent as the eyewitness continued for another five minutes. Then he was escorted to holding, where he was placed in the same cell as James, who seemed eager to shut him up.

The captain rallied everyone afterward, bringing a sobering end to the night. "Looks like we still got a killer running around. Only thing I know for sure is... nothing. Don't give the eyewitness his weapon back. Let it stay lost in evidence. Until he stops having fits."

The crowd rearranged furniture in the bullpen and officers milled about, making their way toward the hallway leading to the front door.

"But," the captain hollered. "I need you all to hold for a little longer. Thankfully, we got more than one piece of news tonight. With regard to the recent killings, I mean." He grumbled. "CSI came through, for once. We have evidence from last night's scene which may be slightly more reliable than our eyewitness's testimony."

Everyone stopped and looked to him.

"So, pretty much everybody stays, for now. That includes our eyewitness and that other fuck in lock-up." He motioned with his hands and everyone drew closer. "We already got Beck's DNA. Too much. This department may have a child one day." The captain smiled, raising his hands, and everyone laughed as expected. "We also have one other officer positively identified as the single executioner with us tonight. Detective Reid. You may not know her, but she's an angel. Just transferred in. We have her DNA, too. Don't get the wrong idea."

Everyone laughed again, with less enthusiasm.

"The rest of you, I'm calling in CSI and have you all swabbed. If you're already catalogued, you can go home. But I've got the roster. So, if you want to keep working here and you're untested, don't leave until you've been swabbed. I find out you did, that's your job and your pension." The captain's voice grew louder as his aggravation became more apparent. "Mrs. Dooley is free to go. We may have to swab her later." The captain's voice petered out. "This is just so, fucking—God damn it."

Lisa walked out of the bullpen, in the mob of officers, well ahead of Payden. She didn't acknowledge Bryan as he gave her a wave.

Payden and Lisa met back up in the front area, after Payden quickly stopped by the evidence room, which was half-full, completely disorganised and ready to be looted.

Payden looked around for Valarie as he spoke to Lisa. "I guess we get to have fun for one more night, before the quick compares come back with inconclusive evidence, yeah, Reid? Big fucking show. Cuffing me in public."

Seeing no one was scrutinising them, Lisa took Payden's hands in hers to calm him and, though she rejected the thought of it, to bring herself down. She looked up into his eyes. "I can't believe I'm saying this, but it's going to be okay. I have faith in you."

Payden looked back in the direction of the bullpen and saw Valarie rushing toward them. "Thanks, Reid. You're good police."

Valarie moved to Payden's side, noting Lisa wasn't letting go of his hands or paying her any attention. "Payden?"

He looked at Valarie and nodded. "Thank you for showing. I appreciate it. You're my—"

Valarie put her hand to Payden's mouth and kissed him on the cheek. "And you're mine." She glanced at Lisa, no anger in her expression, but some form of sadness. "Let me know when you're cleared? Maybe stop by the house?"

Payden nodded. "You'll be the first to know," he said, looking at Lisa. "Unless Reid finds out before you." He gave Lisa a wink.

"For what it's worth," Valarie said to Lisa. "I'm sorry you had to go through this."

Lisa looked up at Valarie and smiled a muted smile. "Thank you."

Valarie nodded and gave Payden a quick hug, walking out the front door immediately after.

"I was wrong about her," Lisa said after the door closed. "She'll never let you go."

"Just marry other guys," Payden said.

"That too." Lisa released his hands, looking down. "But after tonight? This week? All that's happened? I really need to—"

Payden brushed her right hand with his left quickly. "Don't start drinking now. It won't help. But I appreciate the—"

"You haven't even heard the offer. I just really need to talk. Make sure tomorrow doesn't go worse. My place?"

Payden nodded. "I'll start walking now. You hang around a bit, then take our car home. That way you don't got to explain nothing to nobody."

Lisa nodded, walking back toward the bullpen. "Maybe I can get Jimmy to confess before CSI shows. Want to bet?"

"Against you? Fuck no."

"Then walk," Lisa said. She stopped in place, praying she wasn't mistaken about what she felt, and whispering, "I'll see you soon."

XLII

Payden trudged along in the dark of night, keeping his walk slow in case his sense of direction had him heading somewhere other than Lisa's home. Life wasn't short, but it was limited. And he had no intention of letting an attractive woman's offer of shelter and comfort go wasted.

Fifteen minutes later, he heard his and Lisa's car driving behind him slowly. When Lisa pulled up beside him to stop, she leant over quickly and the passenger-side door swung open, nearly hitting him before he hopped in. As soon as he closed his door, she continued driving.

"Thought maybe you decided to start drinking like a cop, after all," Payden said, in the middle of putting on his seatbelt when he noticed Lisa noticing out of the corner of her eye and smiling.

She smiled wider when she noticed him noticing her and decided not to go through with it. "No. They ended up letting our accuser go back to wherever he calls home, which he ran away to as fast as he could." She grinned. "Then a fellow officer straight-up propositioned me. I turned him down. Had to give it some thought, though. Hung like a horse, that guy." She bit her lower lip, then giggled. "Messing with you. About the officer, anyway."

Payden nodded. "You don't have to tell me that. I get you. At least, better than I did when you started."

"Ah, you understand me. And so soon." She gave him a glance, pulling the car to the kerb beside her home, putting it in park and cutting the ignition. "I suppose that's what most women want."

"You prefer to be misunderstood?" Payden asked, getting out and closing his door as Lisa exited the vehicle and slammed hers shut.

"Not in the way your wise ass is implying." She moved ahead of Payden and walked to her front door. "I just don't need understanding from a man."

Payden gave her a quizzical look as she unlocked her front door.

"Sorry. Just making my boundaries clear."

Payden indicated he understood as he walked in and took off his jacket. Placing it on the floor to the side of the door, beside the closed closet, at Lisa's unspoken instruction. Folding it so it laid with its inside pockets secure and covered "No hangers in there?"

"None still worth a damn in the conventional sense, anyway." Lisa pointed him to the living room, moving to his jacket when he wasn't looking, dipping her hand into its only accessible outside pocket, and patting it back into shape quietly. She made sure the front door was closed securely. "Your jacket's better off, believe me. No need for them."

Payden gave her a curious backward glance. "Don't suppose they're necessities."

Lisa moved into her kitchen to the right, tapping Payden on the shoulder as she passed and motioning for him to sit on the living room couch, or use the bathroom at the end of the hall if he needed to. She didn't gesture toward the stairs to the left which he presumed led to her bedroom, and he took a seat. "I don't have any liquor. Do you want a juice?"

Payden declined with a shake of his head.

"Water? Maybe something to eat?"

"I'm better than good," he said, noting the dust on her television's screen.

"Are you?"

"What's not to love?"

"We'll see." She walked to the couch, taking a seat next to him to his right, brushing her hair away from her neck.

Payden asked, "So, what did you want to talk about?"

"Us," she said, realising she was still dressed in oversized, sweat-stained clothes which only flattered her form because they'd become stuck to it. Wondering how bad she smelt. Feeling unattractive. Knowing why it mattered to her now and cursing herself for not stopping by her home earlier to upgrade her look properly. Before racing back to the crime scene to make sure all was under control but, mostly, to be near Payden so the panic she'd felt building inside her would go away again, if only for a while.

"You asking if I'm the guy?" Payden looked at her and nodded. "I could be."

She traced the scar on her neck and looked away. "You are the guy."

Payden gulped inaudibly.

"Whether you're a murdering psycho, I don't know. But you're the guy."

Payden tilted his head slightly. "By which you mean...?"

She looked back at him, smiling weakly, feeling even less desirable when he didn't have to redirect his eyes to look into hers. "I don't want... Would you do me a favour?"

Payden grinned. "Who else do I have to kill?"

Lisa's smile hung on, looking somewhat sad. A little distant. Like she'd lost something she'd once adored and had forgotten, then found again. "Don't be an asshole, Payden."

"I thought you liked that."

"I do. At work, yes, always. But, now? Could you...? I mean, just don't, okay?" Her eyes searched his for understanding. "That isn't what this is about."

"What do you need?" Payden asked, his voice low, sincere. "If I can make it happen, it's yours." He brushed his right hand against her cheek and she tried not to blush. "No questions. No repercussions."

She glanced to the side, taking his right hand in her left and standing.

Payden sniffed the air. "Jesus, even your sweat smells good."

"It tastes even better." She grinned momentarily. "But that's not what this is about. I just need you to... I just need you." Her eyes looked into his, the hope in them fading. "I don't know how else to say it. Is that explanation enough?"

Payden nodded, standing when she gave his hand a slight tug.

Lisa walked Payden upstairs, into her bedroom. Directing him to close his eyes when they were both safely inside. Stopping him and unbuttoning his shirt before stripping him of it. Unzipping his pants, getting on her knees and pulling them down with his boxers so he could step out of them as she removed his shoes. Undressing herself as she stood. Leaving her socks on, as well.

"Open your eyes, but don't look at me yet." She put her arms around his waist, feeling him hard against her soft flesh—which only made her feel guilty—and kissed his chest tenderly. "When I ask, go to the closet."

"What do you need from—" Payden asked, not looking at Lisa, as she'd requested, which only excited him more.

"No questions." She released her hold on Payden, stepped away from him, pulled back her bed's sheets, then moved to her room's closet, opening it and standing inside with her back to him. Getting on her knees again as she instructed him he could look at her.

Payden took in the scar tissue which made up most of Lisa's body her clothes covered. Nearly every inch of her tender flesh he could see, beautiful and devastated. Feeling aroused and terribly saddened at once.

She looked back at him with trepidation, then turned her face away again. "I'm trusting you. Grab a wire hanger from inside this closet and close the door behind me. Wait a few minutes before you open the door again, and—"

"I don't understand—"

"When you open it, you won't say anything, but you'll use the hook end to cut my right cheek from the bone below my eye to the side of my mouth, but not so close you cut my mouth or damage my eyesight. You'll do it no matter how hard I beg you not to. You'll make me feel less than human with your words. You'll tell me I'm getting what I deserve. You won't put me in the hospital, but you'll cut deep enough the mark will never go away." She paused. "Please, no more questions? As you offered?"

Payden stood, stunned silent.

"If it helps," Lisa said, her lips trembling. "You owe me one." She glanced over her shoulder at him with shame, then down and away. "Please?"

Payden grabbed a hanger from inside the closet and closed its door, trapping Lisa inside. Standing and waiting until he felt the time was right. If there was a right time for what he'd promised he'd do. Unable to figure how, or why, Lisa would go to such specific lengths to set him up. Unable to understand what she hoped to gain from their 'talk'. Finally deciding to trust her, his sense of obligation and his feelings, though what she'd asked him to do contradicted everything his logical mind considered worth the risk he'd be taking.

Five minutes later, he threw open the closet door and Lisa looked up at him, terrified. She screamed and begged as she cowered, while he grabbed her by the hair and did everything she'd asked. When he finished, she ran to her bed and lay down on it with her back to him, not covering herself with the bedsheets.

"I'm sorry," she said. "Please hold me?"

He wiped down the hanger with her clothes while she wasn't looking, then lay beside her on the bed, turning to spoon her.

She lifted her upper body to pull his right arm beneath her armpit, rested on it, wrapped his other arm around her on top and gripped his wrists as she cried. Not in physical pain. Her breathing steady and slowing. Peaceful.

"Thank you," she said, panting and bringing his hands to her mouth to kiss, lick and suckle his left index finger. Exciting a part of him he couldn't feel. The damage to his finger's tip that he owned, and a numbness they shared.

"Are you okay?" he asked, confused and genuinely concerned.

"That was a question," she said, a smile fighting to own her bloodied face. "But, yes. I own you now."

"And I trusted you," he said, trying to pull away as her grip grew stronger. "I can't believe—"

She kissed his hands, licking her blood from them. "I only meant, you'll always be a part of me now."

"What?" Payden asked, relaxing.

She bit her lower lip. "No questions, no repercussions."

"Okay." Payden let out a breath she interpreted as disappointment.

"I'm sorry. I fucked everything up, I know. But you're the only person I've ever met I thought might understand. You're marked too."

"You didn't fuck anything up. And I understand." He stopped speaking momentarily, feeling her body tense, rejecting the notion he could ever comprehend what she felt. "I wish it had never happened to you. If I could take your childhood back and return it to you without the punishment, I would."

"Jesus. You really do understand me. Like you live here." She pressed his hands between her breasts. "In my heart, somewhere. Hiding for so long. In my dreams."

Payden inhaled deeply.

Lisa clutched him tighter, lifting her head but not looking back. "Kiss my neck. You know where. Don't kiss my cheek yet. Not until it heals." She nodded. "Promise you will when it does?"

"I promise," Payden said, planting kisses from her right shoulder to her right ear and she rested her head again, contented. Not stopping him when he kissed the rest of her body's damage his mouth could reach without moving. Only closing her eyes as she enjoyed the lack of sensation.

"Don't feel sorry for me. I'm not a good person. But I am grateful to have finally found you."

"I'm grateful too."

"And God bless you," Lisa said, finally focussing and feeling Payden's lack of sexual excitement against her back. Thankful he wouldn't be leaving disappointed, after she didn't come through on the subtle suggestion of sexual intimacy she'd used to get him into her bedroom. Sensing that, though his body wasn't telling, he really did find her attractive, at a level deeper than the physical, as well. "For making this night good. Beautiful. Something I'll never forget."

"I'll never forget you, either," Payden said, wondering if she was saying goodnight or, possibly, goodbye.

Lisa smiled as she felt tears roll down her cheeks, not letting her voice betray her. "I know it sounds strange, but I feel like if you're here when I wake, it might ruin what we have now. And that's not an excuse. I really want to hold on to this feeling. Yes?"

"Yes."

Lisa looked down slightly. "Would you stay with me until I fall asleep? Then take our car—I'll drive my personal car to work tomorrow—so you can get home? I put the keys in your jacket by the front door already. In its outside pocket. Whichever side was facing up." She paused. "I hope that doesn't upset you. My actions weren't meant to. I just needed this night to end the way—"

"I'm not upset with you, Lisa. Just curious now, I suppose. How do you need this night to end? Ask. As I said before, if I can make it happen, it's yours."

Lisa kissed Payden's left index finger's tip. "Would you let me fall asleep feeling this happy, this peaceful?"

"Yes. Of course."

"Then, if it wouldn't be asking too much, would you also tuck me under the covers before you go? That's all I need for this night to end perfectly."

Payden grinned. "Now you're pushing it."

Lisa smiled, hearing the playfulness in Payden's voice. "Thank you, Payden."

"Sweet dreams, Lisa."

He held her until she drifted into sleep. Taking pains to not wake her as he manoeuvred her body, ensuring she was well tucked away under her blankets before he sat beside her bed and stroked her hair. Loving her with his hands until he was sure she was fast asleep. Fighting his wakening sense of arousal. His need to possess her body. Doing so with comfortable ease, which gave him pause.

Then he dressed, walked downstairs quietly and committed her phone number—typed on the piece of paper inside the plastic housing on her kitchen telephone's base—to memory. He made sure the door was locked from the inside before he grabbed his jacket and keys, closed it and drove home.

Lisa woke several times that night. In a cold sweat, terrified. Each time, she felt the pain on her cheek and fell back asleep with peace in her heart and a feeling of deep love and understanding to keep her warm.

XLIII

Payden arrived at work the next morning, hoping James was still locked up. Wanting to stop by Valarie's on the way to work, to let her know he cared about her. Why he'd felt the need to, he couldn't explain. Except that the previous night with Lisa had changed him. Awoken something he hadn't felt before. Not the same love he'd felt for his first, but just as bracing. In his heart he knew it wouldn't change who or what he was, but he also knew it would define him more clearly. Help him understand why he was who—and what—he was and how he'd become that way. In a manner he'd never before considered and with a perspective he'd lived his life, to that day, without.

Bryan was in his office when Payden walked by, stopping him on his way to lock-up. "Hey, Beck. If you're looking for Jimmy, he's gone. The captain let him go. They already had his DNA, and the private lab CSI uses can do a quick compare. They've got to do more work, but they could rule him out. No matches, or repeats or whatever they look for. I argued against it. For all we know, their rush job caused inconsistencies. Stuff that won't show until they finish thorough testing. They say it's good enough to rule out a suspect, though. Or earmark someone for further investigation." Bryan looked away as his desk's telephone began to ring. "Oh, and the captain wants to talk to you. Let's hope it's not a CSI maybe."

"Either way," Payden said. "I could use a vacation."

Bryan looked at him funnily and Payden continued walking.

Payden knocked on the captain's door and two officers exited shortly thereafter.

"Get the fuck in here, Beck," the captain said. "Close the door behind you. Got some news."

"Yes, sir." Payden did as he was told. Moving to stand in front of the captain's desk as the captain took his seat. "Good?"

"Can't be worse than last night's. Where's your better half? Did you not invite her along? What kind of man are you?"

"I didn't realise you wanted to see her."

"Seriously, where is that beautiful piece of ass? I thought you'd have her on a leash by now. She's an eager little beaver. She'd probably go for that shit. You should run it by her."

Payden shook his head. "Sir?"

The captain slammed his right hand on his desk's top. "Fine. You want to get right to the point and your new partner will be along shortly. By which I mean, in a moment or two. She arrives everywhere shortly." The captain's chuckle died when Payden didn't return it. "Jesus fuck, are you falling in love with that short-stack psycho? You know she'll castrate you if you make a move. She's damned good-looking, though. I'll bet she's a fuck and a half if—"

"Sir. Don't mean to interrupt, but shouldn't we be out working leads? We still got a murderer killing criminals—and fellow officers—at will, walking our streets."

The captain waved Payden off. "Yeah, okay. Good news. Your quick compare cleared you. Apologies for last night. That was unacceptable."

Payden nodded. "Thank you."

"Yeah, fuck you, too. Anyway, when the elf gets in, send her to me."

"Her quick compare come through?"

"Yeah," the captain said. "Just wanted to keep her apprised."

"I can't do that?"

"No." The captain rubbed his chin. "Well... maybe. She's a possible. Nothing damning. The quick compare is bullshit if someone ain't way off, like you. And that huge fuck locked up here last night. Heard the pipsqueak brought him in. That true?"

Payden nodded. "I can break the news for you."

"Would you?" the captain asked, looking suitably grateful. "I mean, I'll have to deliver it officially. Take her gun and badge, all that. But, hey, I'll owe you one. Calm her down before you bring her to me. Call it paid time off, or whatever you think she needs to hear. You'll do that for me, yeah?"

"Of course. She should be in shortly. By which I mean soon."

The captain shot Payden a hard glance. "Hilarious. Get the fuck out of my office."

"Yes, sir," Payden said, exiting the room and closing the door behind him. Walking through the bullpen and hearing the whispers. Still a suspect even though he'd been cleared.

"Beck," Bryan asked, stepping into the hallway after Payden passed his office on his way to the front door. "Good news?"

Payden flashed his badge. "Depends how you look at it."

"Where are you headed?"

Payden continued walking, looking back. "My office. It's still a car. Enjoy the free space."

"Come on. Hang in my office. Our office."

"Why?" Payden turned and walked to Bryan. "They making this three-partner train wreck of a shitshow a regular thing?"

"Beats me. But we are both attached to the same case, and—"

"Let me stop you right there," Payden said. "I only work with my partner. I share information, but I don't work directly with anyone else. You do your thing, I'll do mine. We'll exchange notes from time to time."

"Don't be hard about this."

"What about the way I'm acting is hard?" He looked away. "If you'll excuse me, I have to meet my partner when she arrives."

"She isn't here yet?"

"You'd miss her?"

"You know what? Fuck you, Beck."

"Smile, Verrill," Payden said, which made Bryan's face go even more emotionless. "We'll talk later. And say hi to your permanent freezer burn for me."

Bryan gave Payden the finger and slammed his office door closed.

Payden walked out the station's front door, through the lot, to his car a block away, and sat on its hood, waiting for Lisa.

An hour and a half after she would normally show, he called Lisa on her portable radio. When she didn't answer, he called Valarie and asked if he could come by to visit her baby girl, Charity. The answer, of course, was yes.

As he drove to Valarie's, he shook his head. Cursing the fact Lisa would be getting paid leave because of sloppy preliminary DNA work. Cursing the fact he'd be delivering the news to her. Most of all, cursing the fact he'd connected with her so totally the previous evening, it hurt him physically to think of hurting her emotionally.

XLIV

Payden knocked on Valarie's door as quietly as possible. Unsure if Charity was napping and not wanting to upset his only real ally if things went south and he had to cover his new partner's ass. Lisa, now the closest thing to his long-dead first love, Ana. A girl who complemented her and was, perhaps, better for him. What Ana would have desired for him, he liked to believe. Whether out of knowing or guilt, he couldn't tell.

Valarie opened the door before he could knock twice, dressed in another pair of generic blue jeans and a white T-shirt with no bra to counterbalance Payden's jacket, buttoned shirt and slacks. Holding a finger to her lips and ushering Payden into the living room, encouraging him to sit before she took a seat beside him.

"Charity asleep?" Payden asked.

Valarie nodded. "What's up, Payden? Did you fall in love with my little angel or are you here on business?" She smiled, batting her lashes. "You can always tell me that — ever since you saw me after avoiding me and Mickey for so long — you can't imagine a day without me in it. I won't beat you too badly for suggesting you still want me."

"That may be true, but—"

"Which part?"

"You know which part."

Valarie sat, silently waiting for Payden to continue the sentence he thought he'd completed.

"Your life's good," he said, looking down. "I should be happy for you, right?"

Valarie nodded, looking somewhat sad. "I understand if you're not, entirely. I get it. It's okay." She placed her hand on his left knee. "Let's hear the but."

Payden glanced at Valarie's lips, then into her eyes, as she did the same to him and they each noticed the other noticing. Turning the atmosphere exciting and awkward all at once. "The but is this. My new partner's DNA came up as a possible on Detective Mansfield and a dead drug dealer. Nothing conclusive, but she's going on vacation."

"Say her name in my presence? It's okay. If you like that—her, it's okay."

Payden looked to Valarie, who nodded in return. "Lisa ain't around. Hasn't shown at work yet. Can't get hold of her. I didn't want to call her from the station. In case."

"In case she's moving on?" Valarie asked, looking concerned.

"If she's making trails out of here... I don't know. I feel mixed up about it. If she's the doer, I'd let the drug dealer killings slide. I'd fix it so someone more deserving walked that plank. In a heartbeat."

Valarie rubbed his knee. "I love that you trust me now." She looked down. "A part of me so wishes you'd been this open years ago."

"I know. And thank you. By the way, you hear anything from Jimmy?"

Valarie shook her head. "He left his stuff here. My guess? He's already skipped town."

"Fuck. That counts him out, maybe. But, Lisa? If she's guilty of killing a fellow officer...? I'm not sure I could turn her in. I feel like—if she did that and I knew for sure—I'd help her escape if I could. Is that wrong?"

"You know the difference between wrong and right," Valarie said, looking up.

Payden shook his head. "I only know what my gut tells me. Wrong and right. There's degrees. If she did it, it was a crime of necessity, depending on how you look at it. I could forgive her that."

Valarie moved her hand to Payden's chin. "You don't know what you'll do if you see her face to face, especially if you've slept with her. Have you?"

"It's not—"

"It's okay, Payden. I know I'm over-protective. And God knows I still want you all for myself, but I get it. I'm not yours and you're not mine. She's a beautiful woman. Even if you haven't slept with her, she's got you to some degree. I can tell when I see the way you look at each other, the way you act when you think no one's looking." Valarie took in a breath. "But she's not here now. What does your gut tell you when you look into my eyes and not hers? What does it tell you when her energy isn't here to influence you? If you're unsure, I can listen to your heart and tell you if you're lying to yourself."

"Any excuse to snuggle," Payden said, and Valarie tilted her head to the left, unconsciously nodding.

"And, so you know, if you decided Jimmy was the guy, and you removed him from my—and my child's—life, it wouldn't hurt me. And I would never tell."

Payden nodded, feeling the truth in Valarie's words.

"What does your gut tell you right now? About your new partner?"

"Given chance, she'd open the driver's side door for me now."

Valarie let a soft laugh go. "What?"

"Like you always do, when I open your passenger-side door to let you into my car. Before I can get to my side to unlock it."

Valarie's smile quivered slightly. "You know what I meant."

Payden nodded. "My first instinct is to make her disappear."

Valarie looked at him quizzically. "How do you mean?"

"I wouldn't let them punish her."

"Only you?"

"I didn't say that."

"Okay." Valarie pointed to the kitchen phone. "Call her at her home. That's why you came over, right? Call her and see if you can get her to meet you. If anyone asks, you were never here. But, if you need, I am here. For you. Always will be. You know that, right? I'll never tell, like I promised. Whatever you decide you need to do."

Payden nodded. "Thank you, Valarie."

Valarie smiled weakly. "Of course, Payden. I love you. What else could make me do something so stupid?"

Payden grinned, his eyes misting. "Can I ask you another favour?"

Valarie nodded without hesitation.

"Would you talk for me? Can't have my voice on her answering machine. That would end us both. But deepen your voice."

"What should I say?"

"I'll whisper in your ear."

Valarie nodded and took Payden's hand, standing him up with her and walking him to the kitchen. She picked up the phone and dialled the number he gave her.

Valarie waited as the phone rang on Lisa's end until an answering machine picked up. She tilted the phone slightly, so Payden could hear the pre-recorded message.

After the beep, Payden put his mouth to Valarie's ear and began dictating, turning her white cheeks pink from the second his warm breath began bathing her ear.

"Yellow, this is Blue. We met the other night. Projects. Had an argument. Two blocks from 'softie' street. You know that place? There's a pay phone nearby. I don't have my own phone, but I want to talk." Payden gave Valarie the number of a pay phone he used near the station and she repeated it into the receiver. "Call me back, and delete this message. My ex-wife will end me if she hears."

Valarie stopped looking up, and realised she'd been absently rubbing her crotch, when Payden clicked his tongue.

"Wait ten, fifteen minutes before you call."

Payden touched Valarie's hand and she hung up the phone.

Valarie turned to face Payden, their noses touching, feeling the warmth of his breath on her lips and tilting her head like she was ready to receive a kiss. "If she did what you think she did...?"

"Say her name, Valarie. It's okay."

"If" — Valarie gulped — "Lisa did what you suspect, won't they check her incoming and outgoing calls, even if she does delete your message. Because if they trace it back here, I'm going to have to — "

Payden kissed Valarie's nose and her tongue licked the bottom of his chin quickly, involuntarily, making her skin flush. "They got no cause. But I won't make you lie. If you get involved, I'll cop to trying to draw her into the open. Easy to justify. If she's fleeing, I did what I had to do to flush her out. I had to lie to her to get her to show, so I could bring her in."

Valarie nodded. "That makes sense. But what if — "

"I decide to let her go?"

Valarie nodded, her lips twitching as she fought not to fall back into a pattern that felt perfectly natural and kiss Payden full on the mouth.

"They still got no cause, for the same reasons, and they'll never know I helped her flee. If they do catch me, I'll tell them I threatened your life if you didn't do what I asked. And they'll believe me. Besides, for all I know, she may still be at home sleeping. I, obviously, shouldn't go back there."

"You did sleep with her?" Valarie shook her head. "I mean, that's good."

"I know where she lives. And I would have. But it wasn't the time."

"Thank God," Valarie said, kissing his chin. "I mean, I'm sorry."

"Just remember, even if she meets me and puts out my lights to make good her escape, you're golden. And—"

"Don't say that. Not to me, okay? I don't like to think about you being hurt, much less dead."

"We all have an expiration date. It's just the stamp from when we were born is too faded to read anymore."

Valarie smiled involuntarily. "I love you."

"Me too, Valarie."

She grabbed his chin, hearing levity in his voice. "I mean it, Payden. If this is the last time I'll ever see you, I want you to know it. I really do love you." She placed his hand between her breasts. "In here. Like I said. I always will. No matter what. I love you, Payden. Always and forever."

Payden touched his forehead to hers. "I love you, too, Valarie. Sincerely." He looked in her eyes. "Hopefully this ain't the last time I can tell you. And, when I see you next—if I see you next—I'll tell you again. No matter who's there."

"Even Lisa?"

"No matter who."

"Okay." Valarie sniffled. "But be careful. Promise."

"I won't let you down."

Valarie's cheeks pinked deeper. "I never—I didn't mean—"

"I know what you meant. Don't count me out. Not yet."

"I don't understand," she said, her breathing choppy.

"I got ten minutes to get to the phone, wait and pray Lisa does the right thing." Payden walked to the front door. "The clock started ticking the second you hung up the phone."

"Not about that," Valarie said, desperation in her voice. "I meant about not counting you out."

Payden opened the door and gave her a wink. Soft, which didn't match his character and made her feel even more uncertain, yet filled with hope she didn't feel she should be experiencing with anyone other than Michael. "I meant that. Exactly."

Valarie nodded as Payden closed the door behind him and she moved to it to watch him through her door's peephole. Eyeing him intently as he rushed to his car, her body shaking involuntarily. Feeling, deep inside, she was watching him leave her world.

LXV

The captain knocked on Bryan's office door once before barging in. It was nearing eleven in the morning, and he still hadn't heard from Lisa. Worse yet, Payden wasn't returning his calls over his portable radio. Mindy sat, facing the door, on Bryan's desk, wearing a dangerously short sheer white skirt and matching crop top, no underwear. Looking better than a pin-up on the wall, but not regulation.

"Verrill, what the fuck is going on with—" He stopped screaming the second he noticed Mindy. Especially the way she involuntarily exposed herself, her legs spreading open slightly with surprise and shock. He looked her in the eyes immediately after. "Pardon me, Miss, but when did visiting hours begin?"

"Captain," Bryan said, caught off guard, as well. "You've met my fiancée, Mindy."

The captain tipped his imaginary cap. "A pleasure, but if you wouldn't mind, your boyfriend is at work and I'd rather not speak—"

"You may speak freely in my presence." Mindy looked into the captain's eyes, then at Bryan.

"That's not—" the captain replied, his face turning red, stopping himself short of explaining procedure to a civilian, especially with regard to sensitive information. So far beyond pissed off he decided he didn't care what Mindy heard. And that, if she insisted on being there, he wasn't going to speak politely to suit her.

"Apologies," Bryan said. "If you'd like—"

"What I'd like?" the captain asked. "What I'd like is for you to let go of your sex life during working hours."

Mindy looked at the captain, upset.

"I'd also like an update. I haven't heard shit from Beck since he left to go find Reid and bring her in to surrender her fucking weapon, her badge and sign papers. You understand me, you half-breed fuck?"

Mindy put her hand to her chest, outraged. "Excuse me, but I will not—"

The captain pointed at the door with his thumb, not looking back. "What you will not do is interrupt me again, you insufferable, meddling cock tease."

Mindy looked at Bryan and he shrugged, unable to think of what to say in her defence as he inspected her nipples through her crop top.

"We have murders we're working and a possible suspect who may be a runner." He gave Bryan a sharp stare. "So, what's the news? Where the fuck is Beck? And has he made contact with Reid yet? This ain't Take Your Woman's Vagina to Work Day."

Mindy pressed her legs together, ensuring their knees touched.

"This is Get Shit Done Day. If we don't find and stop whoever's out there killing whoever they think needs killing, on schedule, we're looking at more bodies by tonight, latest. This ain't over yet. I want results."

"Sir," Bryan said, apologising to Mindy with his eyes. "As yet, I have not been able to get a response from Beck and I've heard no news regarding Reid, nor have I seen her."

"You should be out on the streets looking for your ex-partner. Or his new partner. Whatever we're calling this triple-bill of one fucking lunatic, one fumbling moron, and one possibly lethal pygmy. Now."

"Yes, sir." Bryan stood, grabbing his jacket from his chair's back, putting it on. "Understood."

"Good. Don't take all fucking day." He pointed to Mindy. "And lose the tail."

The captain left, slamming the door closed behind him.

Bryan looked at Mindy. "I'll take you home and go find out where Beck's at. Then tonight, we can meet at the pub."

Mindy fussed with her outfit as she slid off the desk. "Forget that. I'm riding with you. Since you'll most likely be working with Payden again, we should stop by Val's so I may talk with her. Lord knows it will be difficult, but that fence needs to at least appear as though it's been mended. May as well get it over with now, so you don't get in trouble because of me again later."

"You just heard the captain—"

"In his parlance, fuck him. What he doesn't know doesn't matter. If he asks, you can say we went to her home to look for her brother. He's a suspect, is he not?"

Bryan looked at her with incredulity. "Cleared on initial—"

Mindy cut her hand through the air. "But not cleared entirely. You'll be stopping by to advise him not to leave town. Agreed?"

"I suppose. But—"

"After which, I'd prefer to be dropped off at home and picked up after you get off work. Deal?"

"The captain wasn't negotiating."

Mindy scoffed. "Neither am I." She motioned to Bryan. "Come on, let's go to Val's. Hopefully, Payden's grotesque little girlfriend is hiding out there and you'll get to shoot her." She bounced on the balls of her feet. "This is exciting."

Bryan rolled his eyes the moment she looked away. "Yeah, this is going to be fun."

"No more sarcasm," Mindy said, opening the office door, then raising her voice as she walked toward the station's front exit. "And I want to be taken directly home. Then, as the captain said, do your job, do it well, and collect me afterward. I'm a lady, not a police dog."

Mindy winked at the officers at the front desk and gave them a smile as she made sure to sway her hips and stretch her arms above her head to show them the undersides of her breasts. Loving, as always, the look of lust in their eyes that turned to mock-respect and genuine worry when she assumed Bryan caught them looking. Though their fear didn't keep them from ogling her essentially nude backside as she struggled to push open the front door.

XLVI

Payden parked two blocks away from the public wall-mounted pay phone one block catty-corner from the police station, so he could keep an eye on the front door and parking lot from his relatively safe hiding spot in the recessed corner of the building, which was dark every hour of the day, whether by night or shadow. He'd watched Bryan and Mindy leave the office together. Bryan looking beat-down. Mindy looking like the oblivious shit she was.

After they got into Bryan's car and sped off in the wrong direction, the pay phone rang once and Payden moved out of the shadows to pick up the receiver and pull it back as far as he could. Concealing himself to a lesser degree, but hopefully for only a short time.

"Yellow?" he asked.

"Blue," Lisa replied, sounding deep, but still feminine. "Three words in order. Go."

"Had an argument." Payden tapped his feet.

"Who is this? Middle name."

"It's me. You erased?"

"Remotely," Lisa said, her voice rising in pitch. "Yes. But that can't possibly be your middle—"

"Trust. You calling from the spot?"

"Yes."

"On the way. Will talk."

"Understood," Lisa said and the other end of the line hung up.

Payden slammed the phone back on its receiver and headed to his and Lisa's car. Taking the long way—stopping by his apartment on a quick errand—to the fixed point at which he and Lisa could safely meet. He only prayed nothing he'd said had spooked her, since he now knew she wasn't at home and she hadn't come into work intentionally.

XLVII

Lisa waited down an alleyway, her personal car—which Payden had seen before but never noticed—parked in a lot in the projects four blocks away. She stood in a recess along the alley wall, dressed in black jeans, a black T-shirt and a black hooded sweatshirt. A bit much for the daytime, but good for remaining relatively invisible in the dark. Ready to beat hell out of any daylight criminal scum who might mistake her for easy pickings. A little girl out of her element, ready to be taught that her life used to be easy.

Payden drove blindly past her in their car and turned the corner at the intersecting alley, stopping shortly after. Within a minute, she spied him walking around the corner, back into the alleyway heading out to the street, and she waited. When he got close, she grabbed his right arm and pulled him to stand with his back against the wall, as she was, to her right. Not giving him a start, which concerned her.

"Payden," she said, checking up and down the alley, looking into his eyes when he turned his face to meet her gaze. "Good."

"You okay?" he asked, glancing at her lips, at the stained napkin taped to her right cheek, finally back into her eyes.

She nodded. "Still needs to scar."

"You should change your bandage. It's getting a little heavy."

Lisa shook her head. "When I really need to. I have extra tissue and tape. What are you saying, really?"

"Let's make a deal. Whatever this is about, we tell each other the truth. If we been lying in any way before, it stops."

"How does that benefit either of us?" She glanced at his lips.

"It keeps us honest. It puts us both in a bad place if one of us is."

She smirked. "And if you're already in a bad place and I'm not?"

He returned her smirk, as lost in her eyes as she was in his. "Baby, I was born in a bad spot. I'll go first. Whatever makes this easy for you."

"Start by leaving the 'baby' talk for Mindy and Val."

"Of course. I didn't say that to make you feel—" He touched his right cheek, shivering slightly, feeling a phantom pain.

"I know. Just remember, I'm not them. Nothing like them."

"I will—I do." Payden fought to keep from touching Lisa, noticing her nostrils flare and feeling her reaction wasn't one of anger. "First, though, last night, why did you insist I—"

She shook her head. "Too fucked-up. Long, complicated. Maybe later."

Payden nodded. "You have great instincts, Reid."

"Lisa," she said, smiling weakly. "And that may not be the case. You first. Go."

"Mindy Hayden. You know that name?"

"Verrill's fiancée?" Lisa glanced up, confused. "What do you have on her? Did you two—"

"Not on her." Payden pulled a micro-cassette out from his jacket's inside pocket. "What I've got's on me. That's the deal."

"And this is...?"

"Her home security. Audio only. She broke off her two-year engagement to Verrill and it upset me. I made her take him back. Threatened her life. Nearly took it. It's all on there. My career. My life outside of prison. Some of it, you may not find excusable."

Lisa took the micro-cassette and shoved it into her jeans pocket after giving it a good look. "You didn't bring a player?"

Payden shook his head. "Don't own one."

"I'd have to buy one to listen to what I supposedly have on you. Which I'm not in the position to do now or we wouldn't be purposefully lost in the middle of a work day."

Payden let out a heavy breath, looking truly helpless, which Lisa felt. "That's all I've got."

She nodded. "This is good. I really do own you now. In the sense you mistakenly inferred last night."

Payden nodded. "You do." He looked up and down the alley quickly. "More than you know. If ever I turn my back on you when you need me, which I can't see happening, remind me you have that tape—someplace you'll never reveal to anyone, especially me—and you know I'll do anything to make sure you walk away clean."

"The tests are finally over?" Lisa looked down, not taking a defensive posture. "Is this the part where you kill me?"

"What? And why would you ask that? What the department has on you is good enough for me. All I want from you—to hang over your head—is an explanation."

Lisa looked up into Payden's eyes. "I don't understand."

"You had your transfer on hold at your old precinct, no?"

Lisa glanced away.

Payden nodded. "You picked a great time to push it through. Starting the day after bodies began dropping here. Couldn't have timed it more perfectly."

"I couldn't have known about—"

"I know that. According to the captain, you pushed your way in the morning after. The day we met. Anyway, I'm positive you weren't the guy. Or girl."

Lisa nearly smiled. "How so?"

"You didn't do it."

"What are you asking?" Lisa's eyes fixed Payden's and went wide.

"What made you go copycat?"

"Copycat? They haven't even—"

"But they will," Payden said. "Innocent people don't run. And your DNA is going to match the second scene. You're like me. You saw your shot and you took it. The opportunity was perfect. And I know you didn't do the first murders. The triple."

"How?"

"You know the answer to that."

"Then why did you give me the tape?"

Payden shrugged. "So you'd have more than my word to bury me."

Lisa nodded. "I still only have your word but... fair enough." She moved closer to Payden and touched his hand, holding it when he accepted her gesture. "The only question that remains at this juncture is what do we do now?"

"We get through this. We do it smart. We forget the past and focus on the outcome. Getting through this with you free. So you never have to worry about it again."

"How do we do that?"

"There's one question. If you knew half the things I've done since I became an officer, you'd think I was a real piece of shit. You might want to take me out, clean up the force. I'm not a good person. I know who I am. More importantly, I know what I am. And, maybe, I don't belong in this world. Or on the police force. Maybe some of what I've done is beyond forgivable. But, I swear to you, if you trust in me and I trust in you? If we work together, we will get out from under this. The only real question that remains is what are we willing to do? And I'm swearing to you now, if you have to ruin me to keep yourself clean, I won't stand in your way. I'll let you."

Lisa shook her head. "That's not fair, and I could never—"

"End a cop?"

Lisa's face froze.

"Don't worry. If you're concerned you've crossed my line, you haven't. If you have it in you to kill a fellow officer, the only difference between you and me is you didn't fuck it up when it came your time. The only thing I won't ever suffer are people who hurt children. You wouldn't kill a kid to get out of a jam, would you?"

"Of course not," Lisa said without thinking. "But this still isn't fair to you. And, to finish my sentence, I could never do that to you."

"You don't know what you can do. If you crash into a dead end, the only way out being me taking the hit, I want you to promise me you'll throw me to the dogs."

Lisa got on her tiptoes and wrapped her arms around Payden's neck. "I'd rather die. Then my final memories of you would still be good. We may not see eye to eye on a lot of things, but I'd like to think you wouldn't sell me down the river to save your ass." She stared at Payden, piercing, probing his soul. "You wouldn't do that, would you?"

"I would never—I won't have to."

"How can you be sure?"

"Because no one would believe me." He put his arms around Lisa's waist, the tip of his left index finger tracing the dimples above her buttocks. "Anything I say about you would sound insane. If they put me under a microscope and nailed me for the triple, even if your DNA did match at Mansfield's murder scene, I'd be discredited already. And the more I tried to deflect everything that happened after that? It would only make me look more guilty. No one would go out of their way to make sure I didn't do all the other murders, because it would make too much sense that I did, even if I didn't. They'd close the case and wrap it up with a bow. Trying to pull you down with me would look weak, at best, and it wouldn't work."

"What now, then? I'm sorry to ask. I'm just confused. Why would you do that for me?"

"Why wouldn't you do anything bad to me?"

"Because," she said, a tear falling from her left eye she was committed to acting too tough to wipe away, much less acknowledge. "I couldn't. I don't know you, it's true. But, from what I know of life, and my experience of it...." She shook her head. "You must feel that way about me. Maybe you'll never speak it, but you can't deny you feel something."

Payden nodded.

Lisa looked around, trying not to smile. "Then let's do what's got to be done. And what was that again?"

"We use what we have and we put it in overdrive. We press the right buttons and we mash those fuckers until they break."

Lisa chewed her lower lip momentarily. "Step one, you use this. I know, for a fact, your ex-partner cheated on his fiancée with that girl he rescued from Jimmy last night. Mindy may already be suspicious. She's a cunt, to be sure, but she isn't stupid. We can use that."

Payden nodded, grinning. "That's good. But that's step two. Step one is you disappear and I work alone — or with Verrill so I can keep him in line with the information you just gave me, combine the steps — to find you. You'll meet me later tonight."

Payden continued talking, not asking questions, not requiring answers. Something for which Lisa was grateful. He understood her. Knew her. Again, giving her exactly what she'd told him she didn't need from a man before they'd become closer to one another than she'd ever been with anyone. The pain in her cheek reminding her. Making her feel safe, even if she wasn't sure she truly was.

"As soon as possible. After working hours. I'm going to give you a relative address, because where I want to meet is off the map, and it's in a dangerous part of town. But that's going to keep you safe and you can handle what that part of town throws at you if you get in a bind. Just lose your car somewhere that doesn't link you directly to it and get there as fast as you can. I picked something up for you before I stopped here. Something you'll need, eventually. You got your gun?"

"No. I left it at the station, where I can't go back. If it comes to that, I wouldn't be discharging, anyway. I assume they're looking for me in numbers and I'm not suicidal."

"With that in mind, where I'm sending you, don't mess with anything you don't have to. Definitely don't drink the bottled water. Much too acidic. It will, literally, kill you."

Lisa nodded, looking concerned.

Payden handed her a tied-off black plastic bag with what felt like a somewhat-heavy square plastic container with rubbery edges inside..

Lisa gave the bag a shake, her eyes losing focus. "It feels light. Was I wrong?"

"How do you mean? And about what?"

Lisa shook slightly. "I don't know. I just... I need to tell you something about—"

"Only one thing I need to know for certain, Lisa."

"What's that, Payden?" Lisa kissed his chest, snuggling her head against it.

"Are you the doer? The other alley dealer? Mansfield? Behind the pub?"

Lisa looked up into Payden's eyes, tears streaming from her own.

Payden looked back at her, a softness in his gaze he felt his stiff countenance wasn't able to hide.

XLVIII

Payden walked back into the station calmly, looking beat-down, a strangely hostile energy surrounding him. Enough that people noticed him when he passed, then shook their heads and looked away. Exactly what he was going for. He made his way to the captain's office, knocking on the door and opening it before he received an answer.

"Come right in," the captain said, looking up from his seat, putting down his newspaper and motioning for Payden to shut the door. "Did you find her?"

"No, sir," Payden said, closing the door. "But—"

The captain proceeded to chew him out for a good fifteen minutes. Payden didn't speak, looking at the floor in mock-shame, until the captain ran out of breath.

At that point, Bryan rushed in through the door, opening it without knocking.

The captain threw up his hands, exhausted. "What the fuck happened to common courtesy? First, I have to deal with this prick and now your mongrel ass is knocking down my door? Shut the fucking thing and give me five minutes to catch my second wind, because you've got some words coming. Especially if you brought your fucking woman with you again."

"Apologies," Bryan said, closing the door. "I saw Beck's car outside and was hoping for some good news."

"Holy shit." The captain slammed his hands on his desk and stood, his vigour renewed. "You mean you came busting in here hoping someone else had done your job for you?"

Bryan didn't reply.

"Well, I'll tell you what the news is, Verrill, you rice-paddy mother fucker."

"Sir," Bryan said. "I'm not from—"

"Beck... What the fuck did you come here to tell me, anyway?"

Payden looked up slowly. Padding the time he needed to buy and the captain had purchased extra of already. "Are you speaking to me?"

"Is there another Beck in this office? Is there another Beck in this world? Please, Jesus, tell me the answer's no."

"The answer's no."

The captain moved to Payden, waving a finger in Payden's face. "Don't you get smart with me, you... fucking... I've run out of original shit to call you. Just don't be a wise-ass. I need a situation report."

"Sir," Payden replied. "While I agree the situation is urgent, the value is being overestimated. Real DNA results won't be available for at least a week."

"So you don't got Reid, then?"

"No, sir, but—"

"Didn't we just have this discussion?"

Payden cleared his throat. "If by discussion you mean, didn't you just run me into the ground for what felt like forever, yes, we had this discussion. But, if you'll pardon me, the discussion is not closed."

"Well, Beck. You've convinced me I should find a reason to fire your ass. But, enlighten me. What have we got to discuss further?"

"Sir. We may have a runner."

"Really? Thank you for the insight—"

"And you'll never catch her if you don't stop running your mouth."

The captain gave Payden a long, hard stare which scared the hell out of Bryan. "Continue, Beck. What's your status on our runaway caboose?"

"Our status is this. Detective Reid—who has not been convicted of any crime, nor has she been found guilty of anything other than being tardy—ain't at her home. Her car ain't nearby, either. I attempted to phone her direct line and police portable radio. No answer. After tracing her possible paths since last night, I determined she may have fled town. On the chance she'd had an accident or fallen victim to attack, I entered her home and searched it. Front door was unlocked. No warrant necessary. Given Detective Mansfield's murder, I had reason to believe her life was in danger. I'm assuming a description of her car has been put out? All units?"

"I know how to do my fucking job. The reason you work for me, and not the other way around. Continue."

"I cleared her home. She wasn't present, nor hiding. None of her belongings appeared to be missing. No mess in the bedroom. No closets or dressers open. No clothes on the floor. No indications she's running. I locked her front door after the search, in case she's still in the area and returns home. It's possible. In any event, as is generally accepted by everyone in this room, Detective Reid is, or was, aware she was to report to work this morning and she failed to. I believe her not showing for work today was a conscious decision. I believe she's made herself highly suspect by not making herself available. Given the timeline, she's out of town already."

"Well," the captain said, staring at the floor. "That's depressing. Everything you did was justified. I'll back you on the search of her home. Concern for a fellow officer's safety. Nothing about this has gone outside yet. We protect our own. Reid may very well have taken advantage of that. Still, it remains one of our guiding principles. I won't punish good men because some easy-bake muffin saw her shot and took it. If she's guilty and not dead." He looked at Bryan. "What did you get from your morning, Verrill? Please tell me you don't have more sad sack bullshit coming up."

"Sir," Bryan said, looking forward. "I ran routes similar to Detective Beck's, though I did not visit Detective Reid's home. In addition, I paid a visit to the Dooley household, since I wanted to ensure Mrs. Dooley's relation, Jimmy, was aware he was a suspect and advise him not to leave town. It's my understanding, as Detective Beck can confirm, he is — or was — living at her home."

"That's all you got extra? You made Jimmy aware of his status in this investigation? Told him not to leave town?"

"Sir, he was not at the Dooley residence."

"You realise Jimmy's as clean as Beck, right? Not who we're looking for?"

"Yes, sir."

The captain scratched his chin. "So, what was your working theory? When you stopped by there looking for Jimmy? Or Reid, who's the only person we need located. Give me a good reason you bothered law-abiding citizens to find someone we don't need to see immediately, and whom I can't imagine would go anywhere we'd think to look."

"Sir," Bryan said. "Reid had been there to arrest Jimmy previously. Val and Mickey are also close friends with Detective Beck. It was my belief she may have sought comfort there."

"I'm following your logic. But it makes no sense. Are you suggesting Detective Beck's close friends would give aid to a fleeing suspect merely because of their relation to someone whom she previously arrested?"

"No, sir, I—"

"Hold that thought."

Bryan and Payden glanced at each other with suspicion as the captain dialled Valarie on his phone after grabbing a telephone directory from his desk drawer. He got more information he didn't want to hear from his brief talk with Valarie. Then he hung up and stared straight through Bryan. His eyes lost. "You showed to question a civilian about our missing detective with your woman?"

Bryan cleared his throat. "Sir, I took her home immediately after—"

"Immediately after I told you to get her out of the office? Don't get smart with me."

"No, sir. Immediately after visiting Mrs. Dooley. I was going to take her home, but it was on the way—"

"Don't lie to me either."

"She wanted to be there, for personal reasons, and I—"

"You caved. I get it. She's a looker, but, once more, so you understand, she ain't a police officer." The captain pointed at Bryan, his entire body shaking with rage. "You keep that crazy little exhibitionist out of this. You keep her anywhere but where you are during work hours or you're walking a beat. Indefinitely." The captain put his hands together in prayer. "Here's how the rest of the day is going to play out."

Bryan looked down. Payden didn't move.

"Verrill, you're to continue sweeping. Men are already out with Reid's personal car's description, but I want you to manage them. Beck, Reid is your objective, too. Go where your gut leads you."

Bryan shook his head.

"And don't act upset, Verrill. Reid could be dead, or hundreds of miles away by now if she's running. Maybe because of your woman. Now, both of you idiots, get the fuck out of my face. Pray this ends soon."

Bryan and Payden nodded.

Bryan exited the room and the captain halted Payden, motioning for Bryan to close the door.

"Sir?" Payden asked, as they listened to Bryan hustle his way to the front of the station and call for situation updates on his portable radio.

"I need you to help me out."

The captain picked up his phone and called Mindy. Informing her that her life may be in danger and Payden would be by to watch her until other officers could make it, though she could refuse the offer of protection if she wished. She agreed to having Payden guard her without hesitation.

Payden looked toward the captain's office door after he hung up. "What was that about? She doesn't need protection."

"No she doesn't. But I need her contained and Verrill proved he ain't up to the task. It's only fifteen, thirty minutes of your life. If Reid's dead or running, we're too late, anyway."

Payden saluted, sulking. "I'll head to her home immediately."

"Yeah, you do that."

Payden left the office and walked out of the station, cursing Mindy's name under his breath. Upset he wouldn't be able to meet with Lisa as soon as possible, though it wasn't necessary, to ensure she made it to her proper hiding place securely. Certain she could take care of herself and follow his directions, but still worried terribly. A feeling he wasn't sure served him well. A feeling that, possibly, might serve her worse.

XLIX

Payden pulled up outside Mindy's home and quickly walked to her front door. Knocking loudly, impatiently. Thinking of Lisa, alone in the projects. Worried she'd catch the jitters and run before he could get her someplace no one would ever find her. Get her the cash she needed to move around and ensure they remained in touch, so he could keep her up to date on the search without compromising her. Lisa trusted him, which he thanked God for. He only hoped she trusted him enough to wait at least until dark.

Mindy opened the door a minute later, wearing a see-through white nightshirt and beige G-string panties.

"May I come in?" Payden asked, looking her up and down, his face puckering.

"Of course, Payden. Please don't worry, though they say my life may be in danger."

"Not that that ain't always the case for everyone." Payden walked inside, closing the door behind him as Mindy turned away and moved to her kitchen. "Apparently, you're special."

"True." Mindy shook as she looked over her shoulder and turned to open her kitchen's refrigerator. "Your promise still stands, yes?"

"What promise?" Payden asked, looking around for the recording devices or security cameras the new sticker beside the front door had assured him were protecting the property. "Can't hear an echo anymore. Security system all set? Video and audio? They did a good job."

"Yes." She paused. "I'm still free?"

"You can leave your home, and the force's protection, whenever you wish," Payden said, leaving his jacket on. "Please, mind your tongue and keep your distance. Maybe put on some clothes. Regular police are coming by soon and I'm pretty sure Verrill wouldn't approve, even if it was just me guarding you."

"So, we're okay, then?" Mindy asked, smiling more genuinely. "You promise?"

"As long as you do as the captain says and stay out of this whole mess with Reid, you won't have any more problems. But, this ain't about me, you, Verrill or any of us. It's about a department manhunt."

"Thank you, Payden." Mindy looked down, moving toward him. "I can't tell you—"

Payden held out a hand, stopping her in place. "Distance, remember? And, seriously, cover yourself. If the guys who come to relieve me see you looking like that, Verrill will never hear the end of it. You want him to be happy, right?"

Mindy looked into Payden's eyes, finally noting he wasn't ogling her. "Yes, and I'll change into something more proper. I promise. But do you think I can still make him happy? With the trouble I've caused him lately? I mean, I'm done with that, I swear, but I'm not sure I haven't already taken things too far."

"You want him, right? For life?"

Mindy nodded a little too eagerly.

"Then remember this name and don't say I never did you no favours." Payden rubbed his chin. "Layla. You may have heard it before. At the pub, when we nabbed Jimmy."

"I have. I heard you and your friends talking. Are you suggesting Bryan cheated on me with her?"

"Just her?" Payden chuckled. "No. He went through more than his fair share after you cut him off. Women love cops who can keep their traps shut."

Mindy opened her mouth to speak and Payden motioned for her to remain silent.

When Payden finished rattling off a list of names, he took in a breath. "Mention any of those broads to him, and see how he reacts. Though I'd start with Layla. She's still fresh."

"He would never—"

"What an upside-down world this will be, yeah? You and Verrill well rid of me, and him stuck to you for life. What you've always wanted."

Mindy began to object again.

"Just make sure, once my backup arrives, you switch out the tape in your security system. Or buy a cheap tape recorder at the store and record the audio. That'll be Verrill's ass, as long as you want it. Play it for him if you need to. I don't care if he hears. He can't like me much less. Now, go put on some God damned clothes."

Mindy held her head in her hands, looking at Payden. "This is the kindest thing anyone's ever done for me."

Payden looked away, rolling his eyes. "Happy to oblige." He turned away. "Change into something that won't get back to Verrill. Do it now. We don't know how soon my backup's going to show."

After Mindy excused herself to go upstairs and quickly change into thick black jeans and a beige sweater top, she and Payden said nothing to each other except to exchange pleasantries and remark about the condition of the neighbourhood. Mindy, all the while, curious as to whether Payden was truly giving her back her freedom or just playing for the cameras. Still confused at his total lack of interest in her body or face.

Fifteen minutes later, a sharp knock came upon Mindy's front door.

Payden opened the door to greet the two officers sent to relieve him. He pointed over his shoulder. "You see that lady there?"

They nodded, giving Mindy a glance and a wave.

Payden walked them outside and closed the door behind him, patting the two officers on the shoulders as he instructed them with regard to their protection detail.

Payden hopped into his car after, and left. Ready to do what needed to be done in preparation for his evening.

First, he hunted down Bryan. Checking in with him, comparing notes, though he had nothing much to offer. Staying busy after, cruising, and not reporting his whereabouts. Wanting desperately to go to Lisa, but now certain Bryan was having the men on his detail keep an eye out for him while he could spare the wasted hours.

After a good end-of-shift ass-chewing from the captain, Bryan and Payden went their separate ways. Payden promising not to interfere with Bryan's investigation and search. Doing so gladly, though acting as if he felt the opposite. Certain Bryan knew he had no intention of staying at home that evening, though the captain had finally issued an edict stating Payden was too close to the case and couldn't work it directly. The fact Bryan was also too close to work the case wasn't addressed or questioned.

They both knew the captain wanted results. And they both left the station determined to get some. The only difference between them being their interpretation of that word.

L

Lisa waited in the basement of the building Payden had assured her she'd be safe in, and that he'd come to meet her at as soon as he possibly could. She'd promised him she'd keep the door closed and stay on the ground level by the stairs and, for a good while, she did. Aware of her space and the unopened plastic bag she kept near, still not having opened it.

Though Payden had said she could probably catch some rest, she was too jacked to take a nap. And, after hanging on the ground floor for an hour or so, she decided she'd be much safer in the basement. If she couldn't see a damned thing, she reasoned, no one else would be able to either. In the basement, where no light entered or escaped and no shadows formed, she could remain perfectly hidden and, if need be, take down whoever happened to find her hiding place before they saw her coming. Then, if need be, use their weapon to defend herself against them. The basement was at least twenty feet down from the ground floor, and smelt of dust, wet meat and mildew, though the floor was dry. But fighting her way to freedom became her last option the moment she decided to descend into the depths of the abandoned slaughterhouse and make her own chances.

As the day turned into evening, she began to lose hope. Wondering if Payden had forgotten her, though she knew that couldn't be true, and hoping he wasn't too caught up in the search for her or her vehicle he'd end up showing later than she could stand to wait. But, if she knew him like she believed she did, he was taking his time. Ensuring her safety. Making everyone think he was going one way, then seeming to go the other while heading where he'd been going originally. However many layers of misdirection he had to lay down, he'd lay them. However much bullshit he had to spew to keep people confused, he'd spew. If anything kept her from considering escaping town in the dark of night, it was thoughts of him.

She sat on the floor in the corner, placing her plastic bag next to the plastic bottles of what Payden had warned her not to drink while she waited in that basement. That basement which reminded her of a gigantic closet. The way her bedroom closet had seemed when she was very young and hiding from her father. Her eyes on the only point of entry, through which very little light shone, fighting to keep from breathing too loudly, in case that gave her away. Her father had always found her, usually quickly, because she chose the best hiding places when the abuse started and, once her father learnt them all, she could only hide herself away in near-plain sight. Though she was secure in the basement of wherever in the projects she'd ended up, she still felt scared. Like a little girl. Waiting to receive her punishment for being alive, and being female. Born to a mother who didn't want her and a father who did, much more than any father should. In ways that had twisted her young mind beyond repair as her flesh grew host to more scars.

As she looked up, waiting for Payden to enter the exact way he'd said—parking near the abandoned slaughterhouse and honking once, softly, then opening and closing the door slightly three times before calling out 'Jerry', which she didn't understand but figured that name was as good as any that wasn't hers—she began to feel fear. Fear she'd been keeping at bay for hours. Fear that he might never come to rescue her. Fear, mostly, that she'd put herself at the mercy of another deceptively kind and viciously cruel man. Though he wasn't her father and, she imagined, he would never decorate her flesh with a wire hanger without her consent, he was still the enemy to a degree. A threat, for certain. Not only to her body but to her identity. He'd made her feel the future might not be so dark and, though he'd given her something solid to hang over his head, she'd destroyed the tape almost as soon as they'd parted ways. Partially because she couldn't verify it. Mostly because it didn't matter. She'd bought the possible lie because she'd run out of options and Payden, in his way, had made her believe he knew what atrocities she'd committed in the name of the law. And he'd done so craftily enough she may as well have confessed. To anything and everything she'd ever done wrong in her life. And Payden, the only man in her life now, held power over her, like her father had. The only question was whether he'd abuse it. She rested her head in her hands as she stared into the black, watching the figures her mind drew in the absence of visual stimuli and reassuring herself, though they might not have known each other long, she and Payden had been destined to meet. And he'd been destined to deliver her from evil. To wherever she belonged. And, when it came to that, she felt she'd end up exactly there. Not where Payden believed she ought to end up, but where her mind would put her. Where she felt she deserved to be. At the end of everything, she didn't love herself enough to spare herself punishment. Not for being bad. Not for being good. But she believed, somewhere inside her she was too numb to feel, Payden did. And, if it were at all possible, he would spare her. From punishment. From a lifetime spent confined in the haunting closet that was her soul. Her safe space. Worst case, from having to exist with her misery any longer.

She pushed away from the wall, lying on her side and tucking her knees to her chest, wrapping her arms around them and thanking God for her hooded sweatshirt as she felt cold night air blowing in from somewhere she couldn't see. Empty ducts. Old sewage pipes. It didn't matter. So long as it remained dark.

Then she heard what sounded like a car horn's low beep. She sat once more and pulled the hood of her sweatshirt up, covering her face in the black that disguised even it. And she waited.

Several minutes later she saw a sliver of light crack through the darkness above her, somewhere near where she was sure the door should be. Her sense of direction, relative location and certainty lost after moving around for too long and fidgeting. Then she saw the faint light again. And once more. Each time without an accompanying sound. No creak, as she'd heard when she entered the building, and she kept her gaze fixed. Wondering if perhaps her hallucinations had grown more intense. Then she heard a voice.

"Jerry?" it asked. Very calmly, very quietly. Yet so loud she felt it might deafen her. A stark contrast to the silence in which she'd spent twelve hours at most. A period of time during which she'd begun to hear the things that lived behind the walls, distant backfires which sounded like gunshots, and the voices of people who may or may not have walked by outside. All of their speech distorted, none of it making sense. Her solitary confinement taking its toll.

The fact the voice had asked a question set off alarms inside her body, kicking in her flight reflex, though her conscious mind knew the distinction was too fine to make a difference. The odds anyone would call out that random name after performing a very specific action thrice were beyond her comprehension. So she did as she'd been told. She moved backward to the nearest wall and knocked once, waited three seconds, then knocked five times. One, three, five, and she remembered. From her days at the academy poring over books, learning codes. Escape. And, recollecting that, a smile grew on her lips, its brightness erased by the abundance of dark. She stopped herself as she began to rise, wanting to call out her location so Payden could find her, but well aware, even if it were Payden at the door, her escape wasn't yet guaranteed in any way. Not by word, not by conclusive deed.

She heard the sound of feet entering the building on the ground floor, causing the door to creak as it had when she'd entered, giving her peace. Then the sound of the door slamming shut. Thudding. Heavy. Over and over. Then the sound of feet making their way down the stairs slowly. Jolting her as they did. When they grew near enough, a soft, yet firm, voice cut through the din.

"Jerry?" it asked in a whisper, once more. "I'm going to turn on my flashlight. Don't be alarmed. Please don't break my neck, either."

Lisa's smile grew wider and she stood, almost bouncing in place. Looking up at where the door now stood closed, no light shining in. Then at where her ears told her Payden was. Still not responding. Playing it as carefully as possible, as Payden had instructed her, though she knew well enough not to give up her position until all the facts were in. When he'd told her that, she'd wanted to give him a smack, if not just a playful one. But she was sure he was only being thorough, and she couldn't well punish him for that. If any situation called for the utmost discretion and attention to detail, this one did. Her life did.

She felt Payden's feet hit the floor when he made it to the basement, still unable to see him. Still with the hint of doubt in her mind he might be someone else. Still ready to beat that someone to death to keep from drawing attention. Considering how effective a good chokehold would be in her situation. Keeping her assailant quiet while slowly, surely draining the life from him, or her, without making a sound anyone at street level could hear even with the abandoned slaughterhouse's door open.

A flashlight clicked on, its beam pointed at the floor, exposing shoes she knew and moving slowly left and right until it lit the spot before her feet and she moved back slightly.

"No one else here?" the voice asked.

She shook her head.

"Jerry?" the voice asked, sounding disturbed, confused.

Realising her face wasn't in the light, she responded softly. "Tom?"

Then the flashlight's beam made a wild turn and she heard its owner bump into the wall opposite hers. The beam shone straight up. To the level of flooring which made up part of the ceiling of the basement and held a junction of the stairway in place. Illuminating the area well enough she could see Payden's face and the outline of his body while keeping her hidden in the absence of light her temporary safehouse seemed designed to ensure and maintain.

"Payden. What was all that noise when you came in? Is everything okay?"

"Don't worry, Lisa, he said, switching off and holstering his flashlight. "I was just making sure the door didn't come loose. It opens out, remember?"

The look of doubt erased itself from her face immediately and she rushed Payden, pushing him back against the wall and wrapping her arms around his waist. "Thank God you showed. I honestly wasn't sure—" She stopped herself speaking, chewing on his jacket, feeling the withdrawal from hours of pumping adrenaline.

As she did, she remembered the crack of light from the closet door opening and her father's hands crippling her before he anally penetrated her as she cried, ejaculating inside her soon after. Then scraping her flesh with thin steel for making him the monster he was. And, when those thoughts, visions and feelings visited themselves upon her, against any outsider's reason, she began to kiss Payden's jacket. Softly, slowly.

And she continued to kiss it, though there were much more important things to do first. Vulnerable, yet strong, in the caress of a man. The last thing she ever imagined she'd feel. The way he treated her as an equal, and not like an object. Though he'd faltered in that respect many times, it had only assured her that he desired her completely—mind and body—despite what she considered her physical shortcomings. The reason she'd fallen so hard, so fast and risked everything by asking him to mark her. To replace the hateful torture of her youth with a torture born of understanding and affection. And he'd acquiesced to her request, brutal and tender at once. Holding her after. Making her, in one night, realise her life wasn't necessarily going as it was supposed to. That the way she'd been living it wasn't the only way it could be lived. That she could feel pleasure fully and wholesomely if only she allowed herself to. That she deserved to. And that she deserved to be loved, not just feared or respected. Truly loved and cared for, even if she didn't need it. Everything she'd ever believed about herself and her self-worth, turned on its head so soon after she'd engaged in a course of action intended to ensure that state of mind would never die.

She pulled her head back slowly as she continued to plant soft kisses on Payden's jacket. "Can we stay here forever?" she asked, trying not to frown. "I know it's not possible, but would you please say yes?"

"Yes." Payden smiled, which Lisa felt. "But I'm pretty sure you'll get tired of the digs, soon. I know you're not a girl with many needs, but you deserve better than this." Payden looked around the room, blind.

"No worries," she said, snuggling. "But, if I may ask, what's so bad about the bottled water down here that I couldn't drink it? What about it would have killed me?"

"It's sulphuric acid. Ninety-eight percent concentrated."

"The good stuff." She looked around the room at the darkness. "Where's the drain?"

"It's over... I can't tell right now. But you were sitting pretty close to it if you were against the opposite wall."

"Is that how you rid your world of crime?" she asked, not laughing but with a smile in her voice. "Or how you used to? Why'd you stop?"

"Too much noise. The neighbours kept complaining."

"Still, no one calls in a gun shot." Lisa ran her right knee up the side of Payden's left leg. Her hands touching his body everywhere they could reach. "No one's looking for you, are they?"

Payden glanced down at his jacket. "No, but we can't afford to...."

"What?" she asked. "I can feel it's still not time." She breathed out heavily. "Is it?"

"I can't be sure," he said, comforting her and gently restricting her arm's movements, which made her feel fear again, if only slightly.

Lisa brushed Payden's jacket open with her face, now acutely aware of the portable radio in its inside pocket. "Advanced warning if they want to find you?"

"Or a bell hanging around our necks."

"True. But who'd come to look for you here?"

"Verrill's on the case. He's running the patrols. If he comes up with nothing, he'll end up here sooner or later. He's been here before. Only once for the show, but he knows what this place is."

Lisa shivered, feeling pathetic, then feeling all right with being scared given her situation and the lack of judgement she felt in Payden's presence. The same thing she'd felt that had driven her to take him to her bedroom the night she'd learnt she'd have to go. "You think he'll stop by? Can't you just turn your radio off?"

"I already have," he said, stroking her hair. "But that's not good enough."

"Why? If they can't reach you then, if you're off-duty, what are they going to do? What's Verrill going to do but stop by your place? If he's been here before—for the show, as you put it—he's not stupid enough to come anywhere near here. At least, not tonight."

"You met Mindy."

"What about her?"

"She's way off. You know that, yeah?"

Lisa nodded, which Payden felt.

"She went on patrol with Verrill earlier today, hunting for you. The captain found out."

Lisa tilted her head. "What's the problem, there?"

"The problem is, now Verrill's getting it both ways. Shit at work from the captain, shit at home from Mindy. The captain made me watch her repulsive, infantile ass before I could start looking for you. Believe that?"

Lisa reflexively kissed Payden's chest. Feeling even more confident all would be well. Knowing Mindy was no longer a threat, though she couldn't imagine why she'd ever considered her one. "Ridiculous."

"Had to babysit her until uniforms arrived so she'd stay away and not ruin her man's career. Anyway, now Verrill's got to please someone, you see? And he ain't walking away from the woman he's spent most of his adult life trying to tie down, though you can believe I've begged him to dump her more than once."

"How is this a problem for us?"

"He's going to be looking extra hard. He don't want to go home, and he don't want to go back to the station empty-handed. In short, his woman's bullshit has made him our biggest problem. He's going to come here eventually."

"But not for a good while, right? Not tonight." Lisa nodded. "I mean, have they even found my car yet?"

"I'm not sure," Payden replied.

"I hid it well, I think. No place they would look."

"Nowhere near here?"

"No. I walked through the projects on foot. Right after I made my way through my town."

"Where'd you park it?"

"In the impound lot. At my old station house."

Payden chuckled and Lisa let out a laugh. "I guess they wouldn't look there, would they? Great thinking."

"Then...?" Lisa hugged him tighter. Feeling his involuntary excitement, which made her heart race.

Payden pulled back slightly. "We should go elsewhere. Verrill's still going to come here. There's no way out."

"None whatsoever?" Lisa shook her head slowly while staring up at where she swore she saw Payden's eyes looking back at her.

"Only up. If he traps us here, we're done."

"You mean, I'm done."

"No. We're done. If you go down, so do I."

Lisa let out a sad breath. "We both know what you gave me on you wasn't real. Though I do appreciate it. You can still walk."

"No, you got me, dead. The only thing that ain't real is what I got on you. But that don't matter. What matters is what things look like. And us together here, with me knowing you're to be brought in to surrender your gun and badge, makes us both look guilty. Which we are."

Lisa rubbed her nose on Payden's chest and smiled, feeling a tear fall from her left eye. Flinching before she realised it wasn't from pain. More like joy. Deep love and surrender. "Tell me what to do. Be straight with me, like I know you always have been. Tell me and I'll believe you."

Payden kissed her on the top of her head. "You still have the present I gave you?"

She pulled away from him, stumbling around in the dark, and was back moments later. Laying her head on his chest while she handed him the bag.

Payden opened it and she felt him place a plastic container in her hand. "Keep the bag. I put something extra in there for you. For much later. You trust me? Really?"

Lisa nodded, taking back the bag, which felt empty, and touching the wet bandage covering her cheek's fresh scar.

"I need you to do exactly as I tell you, after I leave. It's not much, but it will mean the difference between us — you making it out of this good."

"Tell me."

Payden pawed at Lisa's cheek and pulled the bandage from it quickly.

"Was that necessary?"

"Everything I do and everything I instruct you to do before I leave is absolutely so. Though I'm truly sorry to have caused you physical hurt, I had to do that."

"Why?"

Payden folded the bandage and slipped it into his jacket's inside pocket. "Because birds fly into windows. Closed or open."

"I don't understand, but... okay." She took in a heavy breath. "Still, if you get too much more mysterious, I may be better off disappearing. Going it alone. Unless there's something you want to say? Something you need me to hear, if this isn't over already?"

"How do you mean?" Payden asked, his body shaking, deep yet subtle.

"Keep pretending."

"I don't—"

"I do. Take your time. I get it's difficult for you to say, because we're the same."

"I've already got you covered on the blame. Double if Verrill doesn't back off." He looked down, shaking his head. "It's your choice, if you want to vanish. If you don't feel comfortable."

"I feel safe. And I can wait for you to tell me."

Payden looked down, feeling Lisa's subdued, intense energy becoming more powerful. His heartbeat slowing as his throat grew dry.

"Until then?"

Payden moved Lisa back to where she'd been waiting before he arrived and sat, moving her to sit beside him, holding her close and comforting her. "Until then, you tend to your wound." He touched at the plastic container. "And we pretend."

"Pretend what?"

"None of this means anything."

Lisa looked in the direction of Payden's eyes, another tear falling from her left. "That's as good as I can ask for right now, I suppose. I understand." She kissed him softly on the neck and rested her head on his shoulder. "I do."

Several hours later, the night sky pitch black, Payden exited the abandoned slaughterhouse, opening the door carefully and checking the surrounding area as he left. Looking behind him, down the stairs into the blackness, and nodding. Hoping Lisa trusted in his plan more than he did. Hoping, mostly, the exact plan didn't matter to her and that she truly trusted in him as she'd said she did. That she knew he'd do anything to keep her alive. That he'd part with his life to keep her from feeling any more pain.

LI

Payden made his way through the cold night air, checking to ensure no one was around to see him breathe as he kicked at random pieces of litter on the ground. When he was satisfied he was alone in one of the worst parts of the projects, he turned his portable radio back on to catch the chatter. Voices back and forth. None of them with anything to say except what he expected to hear. Or, what he'd hoped to: Nothing. *Haven't found her yet. No sign of her. Can we go home now? Technically, all she's guilty of is not showing at work. Can't the captain just write her up and let us get some sleep?*

When he reached his car, he heard the sound of another vehicle in the distance. Running over gravel. Heading his way. The second he heard the sound, he stopped in his tracks. A few seconds after that, he got down in the heavier garbage to the side of his car. Not a perfect disguise, but better than good at that hour.

A car roared up beside his. Coming to a quick stop. Like the driver knew where to look for it, but not exactly.

Payden silenced his radio before the driver opened his, or her, door. Then he heard more radio hiss as the door of the car opened. A car he wasn't certain he recognised, but a figure he did. Bryan in his new work vehicle.

Bryan looked around the area as Payden remained still. Then Bryan's portable radio erupted with chatter. *Car's been reported found. Plates match. You'll never believe where it is.*

Bryan didn't bother to silence his radio. "Come back," he said in a loud, firm voice. "Repeat. Suspect's car has been located? Definitely Detective Reid's?"

Three different voices agreed. They had the car.

"What do you mean it's been reported found? By whom? Where? Have you got eyes on it?"

"No need," an officer replied. "It's in the impound lot of Reid's old station. The place she transferred from. We don't need eyes on it immediately because her town's police force is watching it for us. We can waste our time on better things."

Bryan shook his head. "I want units out there. Two. You decide who. Don't fuck around. This is serious. If her car's been there since before she transferred, it'll be obvious. Make sure you ask whoever took the BOLO seriously if they know if it was there yesterday. Copy?"

"Copy," a second officer responded. "And, so you know, she's not in it or anywhere near it. The search continues?"

"What do you think? Would you prefer we all call it a night? Grab a drink while that little psycho kills again when we might have been able to stop her?"

"Copy," the second officer said again, and the channel went dead.

"Fucking assholes," Bryan growled. Then he roared. "Beck, where are you? I know you're here. I know our old car, and I'm sitting on your mobile office until you show."

"Don't do that," Payden said, standing, pulling his right hand from his jacket's inside pocket and holding it in his left. "You might dent it."

Bryan turned quickly in the direction of Payden's voice, his hand on his holstered gun.

"Calm down, Verrill. It's too late now, anyway."

"What's that supposed to mean?" Bryan looked at the abandoned slaughterhouse, motioning for Payden to follow him as he walked to it. "Too late for whom?"

"You tell me."

Bryan stopped at the abandoned slaughterhouse's door. A door he hadn't opened — and a building he hadn't entered — since he'd first become an accomplice to what Payden considered a justifiable homicide. He glanced at the door. "Is Reid in there?"

"You don't smell her? Trust me, Verrill, the window's closed. Not like with you and Mindy. It's locked and nailed shut. You fly into this one, you're only going to hurt yourself."

"Your head games are getting weak," Bryan said, backing up. "How'd you spook her? How'd you convince her she was as good as done, for the bad shit you put her behind?" Bryan tilted his head. "Though maybe it wasn't so hard for you. After you reminded her of all the little details. Like how you didn't stop her from trampling on Mansfield's crime scene. How you didn't stop her from reacting to being snapped at, letting her sort her hair next to a dead body. Just like a woman, right? And she was good for all the murders. Unaccounted for. The night before she arrived, her first night after work and the night we moved on Jimmy, the last one into the pub. Just another ditzy broad, huh? Well, tonight, I'm bringing her in. And she'll walk when she gives you up. Which you'd better believe she will."

"You seriously can't smell her? She's dissolving. Not sure what she ate last, but, Jesus. You really don't smell her?"

Bryan shook his head and opened his mouth to speak.

"How about now?" Payden freed his right hand, rushing Bryan. Smearing blood and pus into his hair, yanking him by it and letting go, then wiping his fingers off on Bryan's cheek with a smack. Letting Lisa's bandage go as he did. Watching it blow away in the night breeze out of the corner of his eye as he kept his focus on Bryan.

Bryan loosed his gun from its holster, then let it sit. "You touch me again—"

"Smells like honey, don't she?" Payden grinned, fixing Bryan's gaze more intently. "Don't let Layla catch a whiff of your new little girl's stink on you. She might get mad. Start talking."

"Who?" Bryan asked, feeling at his damp, sticky hair with both hands. "The girl from the—All I did was drive her home."

"You drove her home? That's it? Tell me you didn't open her up like a can of sardines. I'll bet Mindy didn't give you a kiss on the mouth that night, did she?"

Bryan glanced away.

"Yeah. Women's sense of smell is a lot better than men's, you know that, right? I wonder how she'll take it this time? Not that it's the most important thing to consider right now."

Bryan shook his head, squeezing his eyes shut and opening them again. Touching at his cheek. Pulling back his hands, seeing them stained with blood and heavy, yellowish liquid. "Oh, Jesus."

Payden laughed as he backed up and watched Bryan inspect himself.

"What the fuck did you—Is this—What is this?"

"You don't know? To me, it looks like you didn't clean your hands after you finished, you filthy bastard."

"Finished what?"

"You know what. Can't believe I never saw it in you." Payden sniffed his right hand. "She's fresh, yeah? You'll never forget her now. And the discharge you rubbed into your skin and hair? That should keep you a blood match for a good, long time. Bryan Verrill, upstanding detective. Hobbies include making boring observations, taking long naps on the beach and protracted masturbation while manually violating the corpses of his victims."

"What are you talking about?" Bryan asked, panicking.

"I'm talking about us both going down," Payden roared. "I don't give a shit. Got nothing left. But if you jam me up, I'll insist they get samples from your Nancy ass. If I'm going away, I may as well do so watching you try to explain your DNA mixed with Reid's—on your face, on your hands and in your hair—while you insist I gave her an acid bath and you had nothing to do with it."

Bryan breathed heavy. "You fucking killed her. You didn't even use the acid first, did you? You butchered her, then you...."

Payden shook his head. "No, my friend. We did. Unless you get the hell away from here and let me end what I started."

Bryan stood, his head shaking. "I'll kill you."

"Go ahead. Fire away. Then wish I was still breathing to get you out of the double murder you committed. Stop me before I go back in the basement and mix your DNA with hers. Just remember the risk you're taking. Not everyone thinks you're golden, boy."

"This isn't...." Bryan moved to his car. "What am I going to—"

"Wash your hands, face and hair. Hot water and dish soap, rubbing alcohol, I don't know. This is your problem. Then drive back to your troops, tell them nothing's doing and fill in the captain. Close the case. You ain't flown into the closed window yet. Birdy."

"But, why?" Bryan shook, reeling with dread, and angry hearing Payden call him a very specific nickname he'd warned him to never use again. Feeling lost. Helpless. This close to breaking down.

"Why what?" Payden asked.

"Kill her?"

"Because I found her. And when I took her here to keep her safe? When I convinced her she had an ally? She confessed. I would have let the dealers go, but she killed a cop. Surely even you see the wrong in that. I couldn't let her live."

"But—"

"And I've known you long enough I knew you'd turn this into a problem. Making the right thing to do seem wrong so you could finally get what you wanted. Me, put away." Payden clicked his tongue. "And that time may come, but it ain't coming today, my friend. So go lie about what you have to lie about. Reid's gone. Whereabouts unknown. Unless you decide to tell the truth, which may get you what you want. I doubt it, but I guarantee you'll go away for the whole day, if they don't execute you nice and legal. So, do yourself a favour and remember, this never happened unless you say it did. Should you decide to, the clock on the veracity of your claim begins ticking the minute I put what's left of that tiny bitch's best parts in the tub. And I ain't going to waste any more time making her disappear. I was having fun until you came along. Now I got no choice but to finish her like homework."

Bryan stood, stunned.

"Oh, yeah," Payden said. "If I notice any police presence tonight, your problems multiply. One car or a hundred, I'll be here investigating you. And you don't want that. You know what I've got." He waved Bryan away. "Now, run. Get the fuck out of my face and make everything okay. Pretend until it is. I'll see you later." He paused. "And don't worry. Unlike you, I'll come through. As soon as all of her bits are melting, I'll call in my end-of-shift. You'll be untouchable. Just remember, there is no way you can fuck me on this without guaranteeing your own end."

Bryan ran away from the abandoned slaughterhouse at speed, hopping into his car and zipping away.

"Good call, birdy," Payden muttered. "You may make it through this flight in one piece after all." He licked his right hand clean, unholstered and turned on his flashlight, then headed back into the slaughterhouse, closing the door behind him.

LII

Bryan returned to the station with Mindy in tow. She'd been waiting for him when he stopped at his house and excused himself to go inside and clean what looked like cheap lip-gloss from his cheek, then washed his oily looking hair and strangely stained hands. She wore a sheer grey dress—with nothing underneath—that stopped at mid-thigh, but mostly wore a frown. A look that made Bryan think maybe Payden really did know about Layla. Bryan had spun a good story, though it hadn't placated Mindy. It had only made her feel more entitled to an answer about where he'd been that evening, and how he'd gotten messy. Only casually suggesting he might have been stepping out on her. When he'd finished calling the captain from his portable radio, getting the okay, sending everyone home for the night and promising he'd be in directly, she'd insisted on coming. Not to meet the captain, but to get an explanation. Something Bryan couldn't come up with before they arrived at the station.

Night-shift buzzed him in and he rushed to meet the captain, who made a point of looking at the clock on the wall and rolling his eyes the second Bryan closed the office's door behind him.

"I'm assuming you ain't bringing me good news," the captain said. "Tell me you found her."

Bryan cleared his throat. "Well, we did what we—"

"And you were out there hitting the bricks? Working the streets all night?"

"Of course."

The captain waved to highlight Bryan's face. "Then why are you looking so fresh? Or is this your woman? Tell me she ain't here with you."

"Well—"

"Fuck sake." The captain slammed his hands on his desk weakly, ready to take a snooze. "Just this once, could you tell me what I want to hear? Which ain't always the truth."

"I'm here, end of shift. Making my final report."

"Tell me I'm lying," the captain said, looking at Bryan. "Dogs are cats."

"You're lying."

"How can you be sure I ain't just misinformed?"

"Sir?"

"Nothing," the captain said, heaving a weary sigh. "Trying to make a point. Fucked that up, I guess."

"I'm sorry?"

"Reid's life is her own. Assuming she's still breathing. What do we know about her, exactly?"

"Well," Bryan began. "She's a possible match to—"

"This is what we know about her. What we can prove. She didn't show this morning, she ain't here now and, wherever she is, she ain't calling in and no one can find her. Sound about right?"

Bryan nodded.

"Here's what I think. She disappeared at a coincidentally conspicuous time. It's not a crime to be unreliable. She sure as fuck don't work here no more unless she has a damn good explanation when, and if, she ever shows her face in this station again. Best we can do is work our own missing persons. She could be in danger. She could be dead."

"So," Bryan said, pausing. "What do you suggest we do?"

"Go home, get some sleep, and come up with better bullshit."

"Sir?"

"You're saying what Beck wants you to. You know how I can tell?"

Bryan shook his head.

"Because he phoned in his report while you made the trip back. Indicated he bumped into you. Beck ain't supposed to be actively working this search. And you haven't mentioned him once." The captain walked to Bryan. "So, tell me, where did you run into that fuck while he was busy not doing the job? You two did just happen to meet, right?"

Bryan nodded.

"Go back there."

"Sir?"

"Just keep on making me repeat myself. You know how much I love that." The captain looked at Bryan sideways, giving him a wink. "I'm ordering you to check the area, or areas, the one member of our precinct who wasn't allowed to be on tonight's search cleared."

"Yes, sir. I'll head there immediately."

The captain, seeing Bryan was serious, stopped him with a wave. "Jesus, Verrill, are you allergic to catching a break or something? You know you don't have to go, right? It's dangerous and I just so much as told you it don't matter. Don't wake anyone else."

"Sir?"

"I will slap the life out of you if you ask me a question without asking me a question one more God damned time. Do as I told you." The captain winked again.

"Yes, sir," Bryan said, his voice cracking as his throat dried.

"Go."

LIII

Bryan hopped into his car, feeling panicked and confused. Putting it in drive and pulling away from the station as Mindy tugged on his arm.

"All done for the evening?" Mindy asked.

Bryan looked forward. "Just one last thing I need to do before I get the night off. I can drop you at your home."

Mindy shook her head. "No. You've still got questions to answer."

"Everyone and their questions," Bryan snapped, banging the steering wheel with his hands. "What is it that can't wait until tomorrow? Between you and the captain, I'm not going to get a minute's peace tonight, am I?"

Mindy pulled back, toward her door. "Excuse me?"

"Nothing." Bryan shook his head. "I'm sorry. It's been a long—"

"You don't have to tell me." Mindy looked out her window. "Ever since the police started babysitting me, it's been hell. You never think about that, though, do you? What I go through when you're out and about. Hunting for murderers, or...."

Bryan glanced at her as she crossed her arms in front of her chest and fumed. "Or what?"

"Nothing. Just something Payden said while he watched over me."

Bryan gulped, which Mindy noticed.

"You know I worry about you?"

He nodded.

"You're a good-looking man." Mindy showcased her body and face. "I mean, you did score this."

Bryan looked at her grim countenance, wondering if the lottery wasn't over yet. Wondering if he really wanted to win it. "I got lucky."

"That explains your loyalty," Mindy said, holding her hands and wringing them. "Or maybe not. Payden said you met a woman the other night. At the pub."

"Mindy. Beck was just saying whatever he could to—"

"You'll allow me to finish speaking, please," Mindy asked in the form of a statement. "Apparently, she had more of your attention than I'd wanted to believe."

"Look, Mindy, that—"

"I have a recording of him telling me, from my security system, if you'd prefer to hear the words straight from his mouth. Must I go there?"

"No. Not even if there is any such recording. You could just say what you mean."

"You son of a bitch," Mindy snapped, looking suitably angry as she thanked God Bryan had given her unspoken permission to 'lose' the micro-cassette. Her insurance. "Did you sleep with her?" Mindy paused, clocking Bryan. "I saw her. You must know that. Diseased, I'm certain, but I'll bet she felt as good as she looked."

"I never—"

"Think about what you say next. Because if you lie to me, I'll know it." Mindy glanced out the window as Bryan pulled to a stop, noticing they were in a very bad neighbourhood in the projects Bryan knew far too well. Empty buildings, garbage everywhere, plenty of places to disappear.

Bryan put the car in park and used his hatred for Payden to sell the lie. "That woman? She was there when we took down Jimmy. Before he arrived. A complete stranger. I saw her, that's true, but I didn't plan for her to be at the pub, and I couldn't walk away from the bust. End of story. Just because you hate Beck doesn't make me anything like him."

Mindy's eyes went wide and her mouth went soft. "I never... I mean, I'm sorry. I was just worried, that's all. Please, don't be—"

"Forget it."

"Are you going to call anyone to help you search for the handsy shrimp? This area is dangerous. Not the best place to be caught alone."

"No," Bryan said. "I'm just here so I can say I was, without lying, tomorrow."

"Work day's over?"

"Yes."

"Thank goodness," Mindy said, undoing Bryan's slacks' zipper. "You can finally unwind."

"Um." Bryan looked around the area. "As you noted, this might not be the best place—"

"This is the perfect place," Mindy said, an evil glint in her smiling eyes. "If you'll pardon the smaller, though infinitely more appealing, bust."

Bryan rolled his eyes.

"If you so much as think about Layla while I'm reminding you what a decent blowjob feels like, this one won't have a happy ending."

Bryan unholstered his pistol and threw it in the back seat the second he heard Mindy speak Layla's name. Hoping his impromptu actions disguised the guilt on his face and in his eyes, as he turned off the car's headlights.

Mindy shook her head, got on her knees in her seat, leant over and freed Bryan from his boxers with her teeth. Arching her back like a cat so her sheer grey dress's hem slid closer to her waist, exposing her soft, white, naked backside. "Hadn't thought of making you useless that way. But good to know you take me seriously."

As Mindy's head bobbed in Bryan's lap, he could think of no woman other than Layla.

LIV

Mindy swallowed, wiped her lips dry and French kissed Bryan after she finished relaxing him with her mouth. Zipping his slacks as he stopped dreaming.

"Yummy," she said, yanking her head back quickly, pulling her dress into place and seating herself properly.

"What's gotten into you?" Bryan asked, smiling.

"Surely you felt it too." She glanced away. "Look, I'm sorry if I've been crazy lately. I just want us to be a family. When we get home—you're staying at my place—we'll start trying. Deal?"

"Deal," a voice said as the car's back passenger-side door opened. "Please don't make me have to watch that, too."

"Payden," Mindy said, shocked. Wiping her lips again. "What are you—"

Payden—wearing loose black jeans, a black T-shirt, and a hooded black sweatshirt with a slightly bulging horizontal front pocket—got in the back seat quickly, closing and locking both rear doors. "Why is a better question."

Bryan turned quickly and he reached for his gun, feeling nothing but the material of his rear seats.

Payden slid Bryan's gun into his sweatshirt's pocket, waving his own gun at Bryan. "Way too slow, old man. You should jog with me some night. Get yourself in better shape."

"What do you want, Beck?" Bryan asked. "Except to see a show?"

"To see a good one," Payden replied, chuckling. "You can do better, Mindy. I believe in you." Payden winked at her. "You're getting sloppy. I mean, I assume."

Mindy gulped, nearly letting the feeling of terror at being exposed, in a much worse sense, creep into her facial features before she pulled herself together and glared at Payden. Neither reaction of which Bryan noticed. "Payden. Why are you pointing a gun at my fiancé?"

"Why don't you just call him your husband? The minor charm of that other word wore off years ago, when you started with the 'hands off' routine."

"Then, Payden," Mindy seethed. "I'll rephrase. What in hell drove you to point a gun at my husband?"

"I jogged here. Just said. Pay attention."

"Asshole. I was asking—"

"Why. I heard you. We'll find that out together soon enough. It'll be more fun that way. Tell your husband to drive. Tell him if he so much as brakes too quickly, an accident will happen. A really bad one. To both of you."

Bryan looked into his rear-view mirror. "Seriously. What the fuck?"

"My mobile office is parked outside my place," Payden said. "Where I'm busy sleeping."

"That's not what I—"

Payden waved his gun in Mindy's direction and she flinched. "Don't worry, Mindy. The safety's off. But do tell your long-suffering manservant I'll give him directions."

Mindy nodded.

"And, to answer your question, Verrill, I'm just here to see things through. Off the station's clock. Same as you, yeah?"

Bryan didn't reply, turning on the headlights, putting the car in drive and making his way, at the speed limit, into the town he and Payden policed.

"What I figured. Still, you've got to leave the gobbler at home every once in a while, or the captain's going to have your badge. He ain't fucking around." Payden gestured with his gun. "Turn here."

Bryan pulled into an alley in a seedier part of the neighbourhood. Far away from the station and far away from any of their homes. One block away from another alley. Parking there, killing the ignition, turning off the lights and exiting the car with Payden and Mindy slowly, at Payden's instruction.

Payden pulled his hood over his head and stood behind them, ordering them—softly, calmly—to not raise their hands as Bryan handed him his keys, which he then tossed down the alley away from the corner toward which they were headed.

"Look to your right, both of you," Payden said, and Mindy and Bryan looked down the intersecting alley at the light shining in from the street at the next alleyway. "Walk. Slowly. Quietly. Voices low."

"What are we doing?" Bryan whispered. "What is this?"

"Yes," Mindy said, whispering as well. "I don't understand—"

Payden banged Bryan on the back of the head with the butt of his gun. Enough to hurt but not do any visible damage. "Tell your disgusting, half-naked bitch to shut up," he whispered. "Then I'll walk you through what's about to happen."

Bryan asked Mindy to, please, be quiet, and she promised she would.

"Here's the plan," Payden said. Far enough behind both Bryan and Mindy there was no point in trying to rush him. "Mindy, you're going to walk ahead of Verrill, to his right. He'll lag enough you'll reach the corner of the alleyway first."

"Why?" she asked.

"Save your questions for later. Do as you're told."

Mindy and Bryan did as they were told. When they neared the corner, Payden whispered for them to halt.

"You got money on you, lips?" Payden asked Mindy, his voice barely audible as he moved into the brick-walled backyard to his right, keeping his gun trained on Mindy and Bryan.

"Why?" Mindy asked quietly.

"I'm going to need you to score."

"What?" Mindy asked, her voice slightly too loud.

Hearing a sound around the corner ahead, Payden waved Bryan into the brick-walled backyard across the alley from him. Pulling Bryan's gun from his sweatshirt's pocket and keeping Mindy in place with it.

"Hello?" a male voice asked.

Payden whispered to Mindy and she repeated Payden's words, looking worn out, as he commanded. Not touching herself or her clothing. "Are you holding?" she asked.

A man in dark jeans, a dark T-shirt and a dark hooded sweatshirt appeared from around the corner, glancing at the street. "You looking to score, *putita*?"

Mindy nodded. "I'm looking to... score. Yes."

"Cop?" the man asked, backing up slightly.

Mindy looked over her shoulder quickly, seeing Bryan's gun, in Payden's hand, sticking out slightly from behind the shelter of the brick-walled backyard, pointed straight across the alley. Its barrel tilted and focussed on Bryan. The message was clear.

"No," she said, scared out of her mind, looking like she was hurting for a fix. Moving closer to the man, who stopped in place. "I just need drugs."

"Drugs? Don't care what kind? You just curious? Show me cash."

"Well," Mindy said, sweat beading on her brow. "I don't have any on me, but—"

The man moved forward, frisking Mindy roughly, yanking her dress's hem up around her waist. "God damn. Nice, tight. Hate to ruin that."

"Thank you," Mindy said, flinching. "I mean, for not—"

The man released his grip on Mindy's dress and unzipped his pants, dropping them to his ankles. Pulling a gun from out of his underwear's waist and holding it to her head.

Mindy's gaze drifted down, as the man's gun insisted.

"Take it out. You know what to do. Smell it on your breath. Do it or I'll bust your—"

Bryan growled with rage and the man froze, no longer concerned Mindy wasn't going down on him yet.

"Fuck was that? Come out." The man looked at Mindy. "Smart bitch? Get drop on me? Not tonight. I call friends. Run a train on your bleached hole. Boyfriend watches. Boyfriend learns."

Bryan walked out from the brick-walled backyard with his hands up.

The man's gun fixed on Bryan. "I know you a cop, mother—"

Mindy pushed the man back and Bryan ran at him.

At the same moment, Payden stepped into the alley, fixing his gun on the man, who was in mid-reel, and stopping Bryan short. "Careful, scumbag," Payden snapped, pointing his gun at Mindy and Bryan's gun at the man, with Bryan in easy range. All three players well ahead of him and close. Sure kills. "Put your gun on the ground while the lady stands well to your side."

The man laid his gun on the ground as Mindy moved out of the line of fire.

"Mindy," Payden commanded as he pocketed Bryan's gun. "Walk to the weapon and kick it to me. Don't get clever or I won't end you, just make you wish you hadn't survived the gunshot."

"Don't do it," Bryan said. "He's bluffing. He can't shoot you with his gun without giving himself up."

Payden growled. "But I can always use your husband's." He gave Mindy a nod. "Want to bet your life he can stop that from happening? Kick the gun to me. Do it now."

Mindy kicked the gun toward Payden like she was afraid it might bite her, which ensured it reached him.

The man shook his head. "Mindy. I going to remember you."

"Verrill," Payden barked, collecting the man's gun from the ground quickly, jamming it into his sweatshirt's sagging front pocket as he kept one gun floating between his three targets. "Moved to the wall opposite Mindy. Now, or you die with this fuck."

Payden moved forward, both his and Bryan's guns under control again and lethal, and the man began to back up.

"Don't move or it's over."

The man shook his head. "Don't think so—"

Payden had Mindy by the waist within a second, holding her from behind with Bryan slightly ahead of him against the opposite wall. Holding Bryan's gun inches from the man's opened mouth. "What you think now?"

Bryan moved away from the wall slightly and Payden shook his head, putting Bryan's gun in Mindy's hand, jamming her finger into the trigger guard and closing his fist around hers as he released his hold on her waist and trained his gun on Bryan. "Point that thing anywhere but the dealer, Mindy, I paint the walls with you. And your future husband."

Tears jetted from her eyes. "Why?"

"You wouldn't want him to have to mourn your loss, would you?" Payden waved to Bryan with his gun. "Move to the dealer's side."

Bryan did as he was told.

Mindy shook as Payden forced her to push the tip of Bryan's gun's barrel into the man's mouth.

Bryan moved closer, though Payden had him in easy range. "This isn't funny, Beck."

The man nodded in agreement carefully.

"Nor fun. Not with an attitude like that." Payden pushed Mindy's hand farther forward, Bryan's gun's barrel fully in the man's mouth as Payden began to crouch. "Lighten up, Mindy, or this could turn—" Payden let go of Mindy's hand and gave her ass a quick, brutal smack.

Mindy flinched—her muscles tensing automatically—and Bryan's gun went off, blowing the man's head into pieces. Showering Mindy with brain, bone and blood. Staining Bryan thick with powerful spatter. Payden mostly clean as he ducked, using Mindy as a shield, then pulled the gun from her hand, spun her around and pushed her limp body toward Bryan, who instinctively grabbed on to her.

"What do you want to bet," Payden asked, "no one calls in that shot?"

"Why?" Mindy asked, her expression tortured.

"Yeah," Bryan asked. "Why?"

Payden shook his head. "You don't know? I warned you about the window."

Bryan shook his head in return, genuinely perplexed, then overcome with shocked realisation.

"What is he talking about?" Mindy asked Bryan, her voice strained and weak.

"He's just doing what he does," Bryan said, not putting any effort into selling the lie this time. Knowing Mindy was beyond comprehending any explanation, no matter how much sense it made.

Payden shrugged, wiped Bryan's gun clean and tossed it at Bryan's feet. "Maybe you'll find the bullet and its casing before daybreak." Payden's eyes scanned from left to right. "Came out at a funny angle. Still, it's possible. Though you really should consider carrying a more sensible weapon. Like a revolver. It ain't sexy, but it don't leave a mess. I mean, other than the one it was meant to." Payden directed his gun's aim at Bryan's forehead. "Don't get any ideas."

Bryan shook with anger. "I'll have your ass—"

Payden held up his free hand. "Save the speech, and clean your darling up. Do it fast, in case someone's looking out their window. And consider covering yourselves. Jesus, you two in this neighbourhood? Soaked in this scumbag's—"

"No one will believe—"

"Belief don't matter," Payden said, pulling his hood tighter. "Only what can be proved. And it looks like the killing ain't stopped. Who'd have thought it would all come down to a frustrated bride-to-be?"

Bryan and Mindy stared at him, trying not to look up in case someone was watching.

"Since I'm a nice guy, some advice. Take a long, soapy shower soon. But change your clothes, first chance. Burn the ones you're wearing. I'll be doing the same to mine and they're probably only spotted." He paused to glance at Mindy, grinning. "And don't forget about DNA, princess. It's a mother fucker. This sorry son of a bitch's is all over you. And Verrill. Not to mention the gunpowder residue your hands are stained with, from his police-issue piece. You may never be able to wash that off completely. Which leaves us with a question only you and your man can answer. Did the killings stop once Reid vanished, or did they continue? The second option is easier to cover up, and it practically sells itself."

"You can't...." Bryan looked away, his voice trailing off as the reality of the situation sunk in and he turned Mindy to hold her tight.

Before he could look back, Payden was gone.

LV

Payden got into work the next morning as the captain was rounding up the troops. Everyone on staff was aware, before the captain made the announcement, that there had been another murder shortly after they called off their search the previous evening. Since Detective Lisa Reid was determined to definitely not have been anywhere within range of the location of the fatal shooting, she was ruled out as a suspect. Everyone was, for the time being, since the scene and the body had been washed far-too-clean by a broken sill cock. In the meantime, Lisa's missing persons report was filed, though the captain wasn't keen to find her. He was more anxious to finish filling out the paperwork with regard to her permanent dismissal from duty in absentia.

CSI had been informed they were to treat their fresh crime scene with kid gloves worn over kid gloves. No officers were allowed on site, so no DNA evidence could accidentally be left behind which might accidentally point to the wrong person.

The only positive news was, this time—though no one called in a complaint until early morning, when someone noticed water running onto the street—they'd retrieved a bullet casing, along with a bullet, from the scene. The killer had finally made a mistake, it seemed, which gave the officers hope. If it weren't for lucky breaks, most serial crimes never got solved.

After the captain ordered minimum-triple patrols on the streets day and night, he excused everyone, being sure to let Payden know he and Bryan were working together again.

Bryan stormed past Payden to their office and Payden caught the door before he slammed it closed behind him, walking in calmly and taking a seat at his desk.

"That's something, huh?" Payden leant back and looked down, shaking his head. "Streets blanketed with bacon all night and the minute you walk away. Bam. The guy, or girl, behind this shit is back in business. Almost makes you wonder if one of ours is the doer. What you think?"

"What do I think?" Bryan deflated. "Mindy's still at home alone, in shock. Too horrified to get out of bed. And the killings are definitely an inside job."

"Interesting," Payden said, glancing up. "Go on."

"I think I know who's behind them."

"Do tell." Payden leant back farther.

"You don't know?"

"I know less than you. And you don't know shit. But, if you have any leads, I'm with you."

"I'm not—"

"What do you say? Take a drive while they run ballistics?"

Bryan stood and Payden followed him outside.

Payden drove, insisting they take their old car. Going nowhere in particular

Payden spoke first. "Look. If you want to hit someone, I'm right here and I'd understand. Better me than Mindy. It'd probably get her off, and she's confused enough as it is."

"You forced her to kill a man in cold blood, you sick bastard," Bryan said, unable to keep his cool. "You made her pull the trigger of my service pistol while you held me at gunpoint."

"Sounds like she pulled the trigger all on her lonesome. Shifting the blame, as usual." Payden pulled into the next alley and got out of the car, motioning for Bryan to follow suit. "Nice try, though. What are you implying?"

As soon as Bryan got close, Payden spun him around and slammed him against the alley wall. Frisking him, checking the places most people never did. Bryan wasn't wired, though Payden still wanted to wash his hands after.

Bryan seethed. "Touch me again and see what happens."

Payden chuckled as he got back into their car. "It's always the next time with you, ain't it?"

"Meaning?" Bryan asked as he got in the vehicle and closed his door.

"Meaning, why don't you show me what happens now? You're like every other tough guy. Say that again. Do that one more time. Always on the brink. Fuck you. And fuck Mindy's feelings."

"The only reason you aren't dead right now is because I know you."

Payden shook his head and backed the car out of the alley onto the street. "Seriously? You're giving me the 'I get a break 'cause we known each other so long' line?"

"No," Bryan said, looking ready to explode. "I mean, I know you. If you're this cool, you've got a clean way out. If I touch you, it'll end up coming back on me. Or Mindy. Of that, I'm positive."

"You give me too much credit," Payden said, shifting gears and driving forward down the road. "Or you're buying your mind's lie. I don't have an out planned. I don't even know what I'm going to have for lunch. But I'm thinking I'll hit the grocery. Get a roast beef sandwich. Plus, we'll get to see Mickey and, possibly, Valarie. Maybe her brother's back." Payden smacked himself on the forehead as Bryan stared out the windshield. "We should stop by Valarie's house, no? What if Jimmy's the guy? You're out all night looking for Reid, and he's biding his time. In plain sight. Waiting for you to clock out so he can get back to business and make us all look like incompetent assholes. You think?"

Bryan rubbed his chin. "You're something, Beck. You talk like you're being recorded even when you're certain you aren't."

"What are you talking about? Make sense, Verrill. You're all over the place."

"We both know Jimmy isn't the doer."

"How can we know that? The MOs were varied, sure. Could be he's smarter than he acts. It's worth a shot and you can see Valarie's baby. I forget if you've met Charity yet. Adorable."

"We're not going to Val's," Bryan said as they drove slowly past her home. "Jimmy isn't there. He bailed same as Reid. Or at the same time, approximately. Not the same way. You didn't have time for that."

"Time for what?"

"I don't know how the captain expects us to work together. We were at odds before this shit started. I don't know if I can do it."

Payden patted him with his free hand and Bryan brushed him off. "Sure you can, champ. You're the stone-man. Anyway, we're good."

"We'll never be good." Bryan looked out his window. "I can't touch you. For last night or anything before. You suckered me every time."

Payden heaved a sigh. "It'll all be over soon."

"How do you mean?"

"Jesus," Payden said, noticing Bryan going for his weapon. "Not that. Let's leave the brutal murdering to the one member of your almost-family who can lie convincingly. I just mean I'm putting in for transfer. To where Reid used to work. I talked to them a bit before I came in this morning. They haven't filled her spot and I'm thinking it's time to move on."

"Why?"

"You didn't just say? Anyway, I already live there and, quite frankly, it's not good for me to spend too much time with Valarie. Makes it hard to get on with my life. I can't really avoid her, since I work this town, even though I moved. And I really don't need this shit. The town's going to hell and we're looking for the one person with balls enough to do something about it. To put him, or her, behind bars. Because God forbid our boys don't make their side cash or our kids don't get hooked on dope. When I make enough money, I'm moving Valarie out. Help her and Mickey put a down payment on someplace in a nice neighbourhood. I can't have her kid growing up in this cesspool."

Bryan nodded. "That's what this was about?"

"What this?"

"You've been executing drug dealers." Bryan held up a hand when Payden opened his mouth to beg to differ. "You can talk all the shit you want, but I know the truth. You start remembering, about Val and what she's got. Your psycho ass loves her. Your first thought isn't to move her somewhere nicer. That's your fallback. Your natural solution to the problem is to kill it. If the drug dealers are dead, who's going to pollute our town with poison, right? But, what I still can't get past is why you killed Mansfield. He was clean. Of all the shit I know you've done—things you've made me an accomplice to—I never saw you taking out an officer. I should have, though. When your back's against it, you forget you swore to uphold the law."

"Some questions aren't meant to be answered."

Bryan looked out his window. "I get you have something on Mindy. On me. I know you didn't leave us with an easy out. You only do that for yourself. And Val, I suppose. Aside from her and her kid, you don't give a shit what happens to anyone. Except, on the outside, her husband. I mean, you didn't leave me an out. I couldn't retrieve the bullet Mindy fired from my gun. Couldn't even find the casing."

"The suspense is a killer, right?"

Bryan shook his head, frustrated. "Look. You wanted your get-back, you got it. You know I'm going down, so what's in this for you? What do you get out of taunting me?"

"Just working my way to doing you a favour."

"Are you going to magically make a bullet from my gun disappear?"

Payden shrugged. "It never happened before? But, no, that's not it. This favour is going to keep your mouth shut, and make sure you keep your woman in line when I drop you at her home shortly."

"What is it? Tell me or I'll—"

"The favour is this. That bullet they got? It ain't yours."

"Fuck you, Beck."

Payden looked at Bryan curiously. "That news upsets you?"

"I was there. What kind of an asshole do you think I am?"

"Shall I count the ways?" Payden glanced away. "Seriously. The bullet they got ain't yours. It's from that junkie who fingered me. He was carrying. I took his gun from evidence the night he couldn't decide if the doer was me or Reid. Fucking asshole didn't notice no one gave it back, same as he barely noticed we took it at the crime scene."

"Bullshit."

"No shit," Payden said. "I took it the night we brought him in. While everyone was at the station, even you. Nobody noticed. Nobody cared. Everyone's attention was on the fact they were going to get swabbed. Made them deaf, dumb and blind. What does that say about the quality of our department's personnel?" Payden sighed. "Anyway, his bullet's what they're examining now. The rifling won't match your pistol and the bullet ain't police issue. Probably."

"You put his bullet in my gun?"

Payden squinted with incredulity. "No. I put his bullet, and its casing, at the scene after you did your half-hearted search and gave in to Mindy's crying. Then I found your bullet, along with its casing, and I took them. Left that punk junkie's material where yours was. I'd already given it a test fire into some semi-solid garbage out in the projects before I took care of Reid." Payden gazed out the front window. "Check in the glove box."

Bryan looked at Payden carefully. "Are you—"

"You'll find out soon enough. When they're not dragging your ass off to gaol. When you're keeping mum. Then you'll know. Like I said, it'll all be over soon."

Bryan opened the glove box and the eyewitness's gun fell to his feet.

"It's empty. The serial number's not even filed off. Don't make me have to pull. That would ruin the gesture."

Bryan pocketed it immediately. "And you've got my bullet? Its casing?"

"On me?" Payden asked, forcing himself not to pat his front left pants pocket. "Fuck no. In my favourite garbage can in the projects? Not there either, but it's safe. Trust me. It'll be there for me should I need it. Unless you kill me, which would leave poor Mindy without a doormat. For life, or however long she's willing to wait. Not so easy to walk away from clean." Payden shook his head. "But focus. You're asking the wrong questions. The one's you should be asking are where's that eyewitness and, when they finish running tests on the bullet, how are you going to anonymously return the piece to him so he don't know he's being set up? Think. Your time is limited. And the favour I'm doing you is a real easy out. All you got to do is return stolen property and lie. With your stone-face, and that bullshit-machine of a fiancée by your side, you should be able to sell that fiction like water to a dead dealer in an alley. It's easy, trust me. Just don't forget to wipe down the evidence before you put it back where it belongs. And, you know, pray someone finds it and takes it. Best case, your now-favourite junkie lunatic. Worst case, some regular civilian takes the hit. But you can live with that. Ain't none of us innocent. Just eat the guilt like you eat Mindy's constant attitude. And, however it turns out, if anyone ever notices the gun's missing from evidence, you don't know shit. You didn't put it there, so that lie should be easy for you, if you have to tell it."

Bryan looked away as Payden stopped his car in front of Mindy's home.

"Remember, the window's closed. It'll never open again. So, go figure your plan, birdy. Run it by the conniving bitch inside. Your soon-to-be old lady may be a royal pain in the ass, but she'll get you out of this with a promotion. If anyone can do it, it's her." He gave Bryan a pat. "And try not to worry. As long as you don't actively fuck with my life, and the lives of people you know I give a shit about, what I got on you will never see daylight. I promise. And you know I keep my word." He paused. "Oh, and maybe steer clear of Layla for a bit, yeah? Mindy's killed once, already. No problems pulling that trigger. She's got a taste for it now. If she catches you stepping out on her, God knows what her pasty, fucked-up ass will do. She's already got your balls in a box so, you never know, she might just blow your brains out, too."

Bryan exited the car, broken.

LVI

Valarie waited in her kitchen. Wearing black jeans and a black T-shirt, and slipping out of a hooded black sweatshirt as she listened to the sounds of buzzing coming from the bathroom. Trying to calm herself as she wondered where Payden was and if he would return before whatever happened next happened. Like he'd promised. Like she'd believed when he'd shown with Lisa at her back door at an ungodly hour of the night.

Michael sat in the bedroom, on his day off, watching their daughter, Charity, as Valarie paced. Both of them waiting.

A knock came on her front door a few minutes later.

Valarie looked out the peephole, then opened her front door immediately. A muted smile on her face and fear in her eyes as she ushered Payden in and closed the door behind him.

"You good?" Payden asked.

Valarie shrugged. "Did you leave the baggage behind?"

"You mean, Verrill?"

She nodded.

"Yeah. He's at home comforting his woman. She had a rough night. Inconsolable."

"I'm sure you had nothing to do with that," Valarie said. "Heard another one bit dirt. Shortly before you stopped by last night, if I got my timing right." She looked at the bedroom door. "And don't worry about Mickey. He's cool."

"He knows?"

Valarie shook her head. "Doesn't want to. Leave it at that."

"Understood. And how's our passenger? You got the tickets?"

"She's fine. Better than I expected. And, yes. For a bus to anywhere far away. Cash transaction. You're welcome. I tried to move and act as much like her as I could. No one paid me any mind. I guess that says something, yeah?"

Payden smirked. "And you know what that is? You're so damned beautiful, nobody can do much more than glance at you. They feel guilty because they know they shouldn't be thinking what they are."

Valarie whacked Payden's shoulder playfully. "You'll never stop."

Payden shook his head and Valarie gave him a kiss on the left temple.

"God bless you for that."

The door to the bedroom opened and a short figure in black jeans, a black T-shirt and a black sweatshirt, with its hood pulled tight to disguise its face, walked out.

Payden looked in its direction. "You flush, girl?"

Valarie shook her head. "You're not talking to a dog, Payden."

"I meant." He motioned to his head. "Lisa? You did as we agreed?"

"Yes. I'm bald and ugly now." Lisa turned to face Valarie. "If your pipes clog, Payden promised he'd pay for the plumber to come out."

Valarie nodded. "He always pays."

Payden nodded, as well. "One way or the other." He looked at Lisa and she walked toward him. "Lose the frills."

Valarie looked at Payden and Lisa quizzically.

Lisa reached under her T-shirt and dropped a padded bra onto the floor. Then she flattened her chest. Smoothing her sweatshirt with her hands and making sure not to slouch while keeping her head facing forward and down.

Payden nodded and put his arm around Lisa's shoulders, checking out her profile, then checking out her behind, looking disappointed.

Valarie rolled her eyes. "The waist's padded. The only way I could make her ass look flat."

"Good thinking," Payden said. "Though you robbed me of the memory." He stopped and looked into and under Lisa's hood, seeing her smiling, reaching his hand in and feeling the coarse stubble on her head. "You get some good sleep? You ready?"

She nodded, speaking in a low voice. Guttural. Just subtle enough it was hard to tell it wasn't a man's. "And thanks for the extra, Payden. Though those rubber bands aren't much use anymore."

"They're for much later," Payden said. "Remember?"

Lisa kept Payden's gaze as she motioned to Valarie with her head. "Thank you, Val. For your aid and shelter, and for helping me figure how to finally get answers to my big questions."

"Of course," Valarie said. "I only wish I could have helped you more. But I've never known... Anyway, you're welcome back when they catch whoever's been doing all the killing. Though, I've got to say, I hope they don't find him—"

"Or her," Payden said.

Lisa chuckled, betraying her high pitch which Payden reminded her to watch out for.

"What questions?" Payden asked Valarie.

"We just talked makeup, hair care, the manufactured natural look. Tips and tricks. Nothing you're interested in." Valarie looked away quickly, changing back to the primary subject. "Anyway, I hope they don't find whomever. At least until this town is clean again."

Payden nodded, pulling Valarie close with his free hand and giving her a kiss on the cheek as Lisa crossed her arms in front of her chest. "I have a feeling they won't. Someday soon, this will be a good place for your child to grow up and, if that day doesn't come soon enough, I'm forcing Mickey to take a loan I'll shoot him if he ever tries to repay, and helping you two get out of here." He looked into Valarie's eyes. "And before I forget." He pulled her closer for a quick hug, whispering, "I love you, Valarie," though something behind his words had changed. His love for her was genuine, but different. Freeing, which gave his verbal expression a depth Valarie had never felt from him before.

"You remembered," Valarie said, trying not to tear up. Feeling a hope rise inside her she was sure had died over the course of her evening spent talking with Lisa.

Lisa thanked Valarie for her hospitality again, looking at her with suspicion but keeping her mouth shut. Wanting to know what Payden had said, but not entirely sure she needed to know or if whatever kind of friendship he shared with Valarie was hers to question. Or if it really mattered, in the long run. Knowing making Valarie the competition was a bad move in more ways than one.

Valarie moved ahead of Lisa and Payden to crack the front door open slowly and check that the block was clear.

Payden and Lisa hurried out the door and to his car after Valarie gave them the nod.

"Be careful," Valarie said. "And remind your guest to change her dressing. I gave her extra bandages and I sanitised her wound with rubbing alcohol. Her cut should heal nicely. I want to see you both again. Or I hope to. You make each other happy. I can tell. And I'm always right about you, Payden."

Payden nodded and winked. He and Lisa drove away moments later.

Valarie closed her front door slowly, watching their car disappear. "Come back soon, Payden. I hope I never have to miss you."

LVII

Payden drove within the speed limit to the bus station in the projects he was almost certain no one he knew would be hanging around at, luckily correct once again. After he parked out of sight, he exited his car and opened the door for Lisa.

As she stood, her hood slipped off.

Payden rubbed the stubble on her head once more, and touched at her bandaged cheek.

She smiled when he did, though the look in her eyes was sad. "Did you want your petroleum jelly back?" she asked, ensuring she faced Payden and away from whomever else might pass by. "I can feel it'll help me scar faster. But, really, you couldn't buy me a fresh, unused container?"

"No time," Payden said, glancing away.

"Just don't tell me—"

"I had to do something to keep my head on straight with you by my side every day. Leaving me every night."

"We've only known each other for—"

"I'm just busting your chops." He paused. "But, no joke, you make an impression fast."

Lisa looked down, smiling. "Like Val?" Her lips trembled as she stared at the ground and her cheeks went loose. "Like Ana?" she asked, pronouncing the name correctly: Awna.

"Yes," Payden said, feeling lost, yet more deeply understood than he had since he'd last seen his Ana, before she'd left his, and everyone's, world. "How do you know about Ana? Was it Valarie? Did she—" He stopped speaking, realising how fast he'd given himself away, how easily, and how it made him feel like a layer of guilt had been cleaned from him. He shook his head. "I'm sorry. Not my business. Anyway, only a few minutes and you're free. Of this place. Of me."

"Of this place, as promised. Not nearly of you." Lisa rubbed the top of her head, moving to pull her hood back on tight. "But thank you for the compliment. Though I feel like... I can't possibly be attractive to you now. Maybe that's the point. Easier for you, right? I know I'm not the one. Not like your first—"

Payden stopped her before she could pull her hood up completely, taking her head into his hands and kissing her full on the mouth, gently, so as not to irritate her healing cut. Returning her responsive, soulful French kiss deeply, with subdued passion. Watching Lisa's closed eyes in between closing his own and feeling a familiar, beautiful sensation that scared him to death.

"Or maybe I'm close," she said as their lips parted. Her eyes glassy, beginning to tear as she covered her head with her hood. "I, honestly, thought I was going to die. In that basement. Possibly by your hand. It took everything I had not to run. But I believed in you. In us."

"I'm glad you trusted me. Or you'd be running still." He paused. "How do you mean, by my—"

"Nothing," she said. "I just... When you came to my house, to talk, I felt a gun in your jacket when I put our keys in it. Not police-issue metal. It was stupid, but I thought, maybe, your throwaway piece was meant for me."

"It was," Payden said, shaking his head when Lisa began to back away, stopping her in place. "It's busy right now, guaranteeing no one ever comes looking for you. I didn't realise you knew I had it. I'm truly sorry I caused you any worry. But that explains a lot of things you've said to me since then. Still, I never meant to—"

"I know. I couldn't make myself believe it was true. I didn't leave."

Payden scanned the area quickly and pulled what appeared to be a bullet and its casing from his front left pants pocket, placing the items in Lisa's right hand and closing her fist around them. "A little present for you. From Verrill's gun. More insurance. Exchanged with the damning evidence from my throwaway. Something else to keep you safe. To ensure you remain that way and no one who matters talks. That throwaway piece, once more, taking care of you. Don't ever let that evidence go. Keep it somewhere secret. By which I mean, don't tell anyone. Not even me."

She kissed him again, crying softly, after placing the bullet and its casing in her front right pants pocket. "Thank you," she whispered into his ear, warm and wet. "Believe it or not, a part of me wishes she could go back to that basement, now." Her eyes went wide a second later as she felt his hands give her ass a slow, firm squeeze. "And how soon you forget my promises."

"I'll never forget your promises," Payden said, looking at his hands. "I never much cared for these mitts, anyway."

"Then trust in me." Lisa smiled, ashamed at how much she'd enjoyed being handled and delighted she'd been handled by the only man she knew loved her damaged flesh when it wasn't hidden away.

"How so?" Payden asked.

"Tell me. You've already unlocked my door."

"What?"

"Tell me. Let me unlock your door for you."

Payden glanced around, ensuring no one was watching or listening. "When? I mean.... What—" His stare fixed on her bandage. "Tell me your cheek's gotten better fast."

"If you kissed it now, you'd be hurting me."

"Never, Lisa."

Lisa looked down, still smiling, but with sadness. "Not intentionally, I know, Payden." She nodded, lost in thought. "One last question?"

Payden nodded and kissed her above her right eye as she closed its lids to experience the warmth of his lips near her scarring flesh.

"Did you really start it? I mean the triple the night before we began working together? I never really had nothing—anything on you, did I? Not even on you and... Verrill's woman."

"I'm going to miss you. And I can't stand the thought of not being able to kiss your cheek and fulfil that promise. If you miss me enough you come back into my life and allow me that privilege, I'll tell you whether you had anything—nothing on me." He paused. "You dumped the tape?"

"Destroyed it, and fair enough," she said looking up into his eyes. "Just one more?"

Payden nodded.

"Did you feel it too? When we first met?" She shook her head. "Don't answer that. I'm sorry I asked. It wasn't fair." The bus's horn sounded and Lisa turned, pulling her hood tighter. "I'll see you, Payden. Sooner than later." She pulled Payden in for a hug, whispering into his ear. "Tell me your middle... It's important now. Trust me. Please give me the chance to unlock your door? If not for me, for Melissa?"

Payden whispered into her ear in reply, shaking lightly.

She pulled away from him, crying involuntarily and not letting go. "It's okay," she said, pulling him closer again and kissing him furiously. Taking her time as her mouth made love to his like she expected to never experience him again. Then she pulled back, letting go of him, just as quickly, her cheeks still wet with tears. "And thank you for trusting me, like you trusted... I'll never be perfect. My childhood... I ain't—I mean, I'm not trying to replace—"

"I wanted to say—I mean, before, in the basement, but—Melissa...." Payden froze, unable to speak.

"I love you, too." Lisa looked at him as she backed away slowly to get in line to board the bus, her eyes soft and doleful. "I always have. In my dreams. Hidden in my heart somewhere for so long. I meant what I said, and what you wouldn't let me say. And I could feel you felt the same." She whispered from her place in line, barely audible, as if she were mouthing the words, "I'll see you again. And I promise I will make you happier than you've ever known. If I can't, I'll bring you so close, you might finally let me become her." She smiled, still unable to speak Ana's name aloud again. Her eyes so full of tearful joy, she hardly resembled the tough, street-smart woman he'd fought so hard not to fall for. A look which—though she couldn't know it—only made him fall harder. "I mean, if you'll pardon the rubber bands, Payden Jeffrey Beck."

Payden's body shook and he wiped away what felt like a tear.

As Lisa got on the bus, she used her hand to ensure he knew she was blowing him a kiss. Not saying goodbye. Promising her return once more, in yet another way. Promising him everything she was.

Within a few minutes, as her bus pulled away, she touched her hands to the bus's window and pressed her forehead against it.

He blew her a kiss in return.

Then she was gone. The woman once known as Detective Lisa Reid now a memory to almost everyone in Payden's precinct.

A whisper in the wind. Yet a noise so loud it had been impossible for him not to hear.

Never to be forgotten.

Epilogue

BAD DOG

Your name is Payden Beck and you're really starting to get under my skin.

Once again, you say farewell to a piece of luggage. An accoutrement. Someone you thought you saw redemption in. Some sense of the self you once were. But the old you is gone. You must accept that, Mr. Beck, or all will be eliminated. Sooner than you think. This may feel as though you've lost it all, but there's so much more can be taken from you. You do not want that to happen. Life is a game. The stakes are higher than you think. Death isn't the worst possible outcome. Don't play not to lose.

You have your moments, Mr. Beck. Moments that worry me now you work alone. Wisely, you keep your distance from your ex-partner and his fiancée in your old precinct and, wisely, you choose not to revisit the city in which you first tasted human emotion to an unacceptable degree. We can only hope you'll, wisely, forget about Lisa and the nauseatingly tender, weak emotions she forced you to experience once more. Unless you wish to ensure she never returns. We'd enjoy that, no?

No?

Too bad if you don't like it, Mr. Beck. I'm running the show.

Your job is to keep me entertained. And I don't mean with sickening displays of love and affection — Remember, I can make Valarie go away if you push us — I mean by doing your duty. Your real one. You forget you're merely a janitor and there will be bigger messes to clean.

You can't fight our nature, so learn to love it like you're wont to love the female trash drawn to you. Chin up. Shoulders straight. This is our life, and you're living it. So, live it the way we're meant to.

Punish. Obey. Never stop. Things are getting worse in every way, and I can't wait to taste the depths of your pain. You will never find happiness, but I expect you to perform as if, you puppet. You monkey. Don't make us put you in your place.

Be a good dog.
Do as you're told.
Stay.

Acknowledgements

A great many thanks to everyone who took the time to read this book, and provide me with their valuable feedback, at the expense of their own time. Thanks, also, to everyone who supported me when I chose to stop being who I wasn't. ~ Mike Golvach

What's Next?

Michael Golvach always has at least one book in the works, including the next book in the exciting "Payden Beck Crime Thriller" series, the plan for which now stands at 12 books, with a new book releasing every November. Please stay tuned to developments and plans by subscribing to our newsletter at the link below.

www.EvolvedPub.com/newsletter/

About the Author

Ever since I was able to read, I've had a book (or a comic book in the early days) in my hands or on my person. I grew up in a non-digital age, in a home with one telephone everyone shared, one television no one watched, and in which movies were a luxury. Aside from radio theatre, books were my best non-human friends.

My love of reading never died. When I was 8 years old, I drew my first series of comic books. They were terrible, but I still love them. To me, they represent the moment the wise-old-man inside my little boy's head finally made me aware I loved to create.

As it turned out, I enjoyed writing much more than I enjoyed drawing, but I've spent most of my life doing some form of creative work. And when not, I've worked some boring jobs in very creative ways.

To this day, I love to write and to share my creations with others. I'm the guy who will watch a good movie twenty more times, if it means I get to introduce it to someone else and participate in their joy of discovering something entertaining or valuable. I can't be quite so intimately participatory with my own writing, but I do love to know I've brightened someone's day, made them think, feel or—at the very least—provided them with a welcome distraction for a while.

For more, please visit Michael Golvach online at:
Personal Website: www. MikeGolvach.net
Publisher Website: www.EvolvedPub.com
Goodreads: Michael Golvach
Twitter: @MikeGolvach
Facebook: /MichaelGolvach

More from Evolved Publishing

We offer great books across multiple genres, featuring high-quality editing (which we believe is second-to-none) and fantastic covers.

As a hybrid small press, your support as loyal readers is so important to us, and we have strived, with tireless dedication and sheer determination, to deliver on the promise of our motto:
QUALITY IS PRIORITY #1!

Please check out all of our great books, which you can find at this link:

www.EvolvedPub.com/Catalog/

Thank you!

CPSIA information can be obtained
at www.ICGtesting.com
Printed in the USA
BVHW080215170323
660601BV00007B/564